IMAGES
of America

SHOREHAM

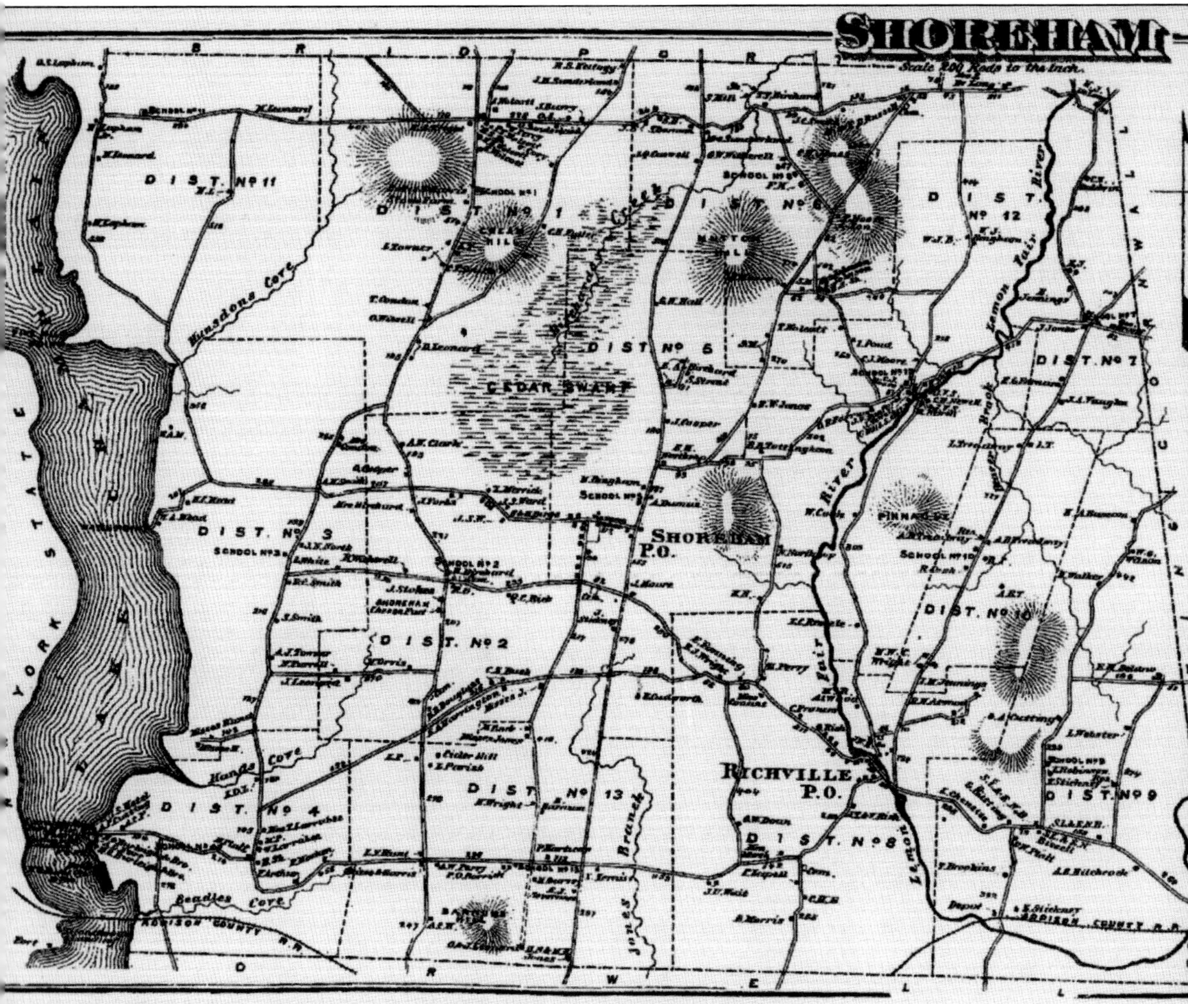

Map from 1871 Addison County Beers Atlas

This map of Shoreham comes from the 1871 Beers Atlas of Addison County. (Courtesy of the author.)

On the Cover: Virginia (Stewart) Larrabee, who co-owned Larrabee's Point Orchard with her husband, Wesley Larrabee, takes a break from picking in September 1946. (Courtesy of Linda Larrabee.)

IMAGES
of America

SHOREHAM

Susan Holt MacIntire

ARCADIA
PUBLISHING

ISBN 978-1-4671-2016-6

Published by Arcadia Publishing
Charleston, South Carolina

Printed in the United States of America

Library of Congress Control Number: 2013931869

For all general information, please contact Arcadia Publishing:
Telephone 843-853-2070
Fax 843-853-0044
E-mail sales@arcadiapublishing.com
For customer service and orders:
Toll-Free 1-888-313-2665

Visit us on the Internet at www.arcadiapublishing.com

This book is dedicated to the memory of two very special men. Wilson Gilmore MacIntire, my husband of 48 years, always encouraged and supported me in all my endeavors. Sanford Stowell Witherell, my mentor and friend, taught me about Shoreham history and shared his love for this town.

Contents

ACKNOWLEDGMENTS

For helping me identify people in photographs from before my time in Shoreham, I would like to thank Arlene Stanley, Eleanor Brisson, Harris Brisson, and Betty and Bob Douglas. For generously sharing their photographs to use in this book, I would like to thank Kirk LaDuke, Cora Waag, Sandy Witherell, Mary Esther McFarlane, Phil Kivlin, H. Kent Wright III, John Sullivan, Edwin James, Linda Larrabee, and May Small.

Unless otherwise noted, all images appear courtesy of the Shoreham Historical Society.

Introduction

In 1759, Capt. Ephraim Doolittle and his detachment were ordered to cut a road from Fort No. 4 in Charlestown, New Hampshire, to Crown Point, New York. As they neared Lake Champlain on the western border of Vermont, they were struck by the beauty and fertility of the rolling hills in the Champlain Valley. Upon returning home to Worcester, Massachusetts, Doolittle enthusiastically sought investors to sponsor the purchase of a charter for a town in this area from Benning Wentworth, King George III's governor of the New Hampshire grants. He obtained enough money to purchase two towns, and Shoreham and Bridport were both chartered on October 8, 1761.

The first group of settlers, which included Doolittle and 13 of his men, came in 1766. They built a log cabin near a spring at the base of Mutton Hill and cleared 25 acres that first summer. They returned the next year, some of the men bringing their families. As the political situation grew worse and war with England seemed imminent, most of the families went south to safety.

The first victory of the Revolutionary War was launched from Shoreham in the early morning hours of May 10, 1775. Ethan Allen, Benedict Arnold, and 83 of the 270 men assembled in a ravine at Hand's Cove rowed over to capture Fort Ticonderoga from the British. They were led to a covered side passage by the teenage Nathan Beman, whose family farmed by the lake and often went to the fort to sell vegetables to the soldiers.

After the Revolution ended, the settlement of Shoreham began in earnest. The town was surveyed into five divisions. The first, third, and fourth divisions were divided into 100-acre lots. The second division, along the lakeshore, was divided into 26-acre lots, and lot 37 of the first division, in the geographical center of town, was divided into one-acre lots for the village. Each of the original 67 investors received one lot in every division, which they could then sell to recoup their money. Four lots in each division were also set aside for a school right, a glebe right, propagation of the gospel, and a ministerial right.

The town grew by leaps and bounds in the early 1800s. All of the land was cleared, and, in addition to farms, supporting business such as mills, blacksmiths, cobblers, and shopkeepers became established. Large families were the norm, and, since farms could only be divided so many times to support sons and their families, many young people went west to seek their fortunes when the Erie Canal opened in 1823. Many of those that remained became wealthy farmers, breeding top-quality Spanish merino sheep. In the mid-1800s, Shoreham also became known for breeding Hamiltonian and Morgan horses for the racing circuits in Vermont and New York.

Hotels soon arose along the beautiful shore of Lake Champlain. Vacationers came by boat from hot cities to enjoy cool summers by the lake. Menus from the gourmet meals once served on a daily basis have been kept through the years and can still be seen today.

Farmers also discovered that the soil and climate were very suitable to producing apples with superior taste. Many orchards were planted, and remain in production today. As the 1800s drew to a close, the price of wool plummeted, and the population of sheep started to decline. Farmers sold their prized merino sheep out west, and some, like the Witherell family, took sheep by boat to auctions in South Africa. Shoreham remained a rural area, with dairy farming and apple orchards, while larger cities drew young people to work in new factories.

The dairy business also grew from solely supporting the local people into large businesses shipping milk, butter, and cheese to Boston and markets beyond via train. The Addison Branch train went to Ticonderoga, New York, over a floating bridge on Lake Champlain, and traversed the Lemon Fair River from Shoreham to Whiting over the still-standing covered railroad bridge. The Shoreham unit of New England Dairies, Inc., was the largest cheese-making plant in the state and one of the largest east of the Mississippi River.

By the 1950s, Shoreham's population was down to 500. However, today, Shoreham is once again gaining population. There are fewer farms, but they are now larger. Professors from Middlebury College, software developers, and an assortment of other professionals now call Shoreham home. This small town of friendly people is a great place to raise a family and a safe place to call home.

One

Shoreham Village

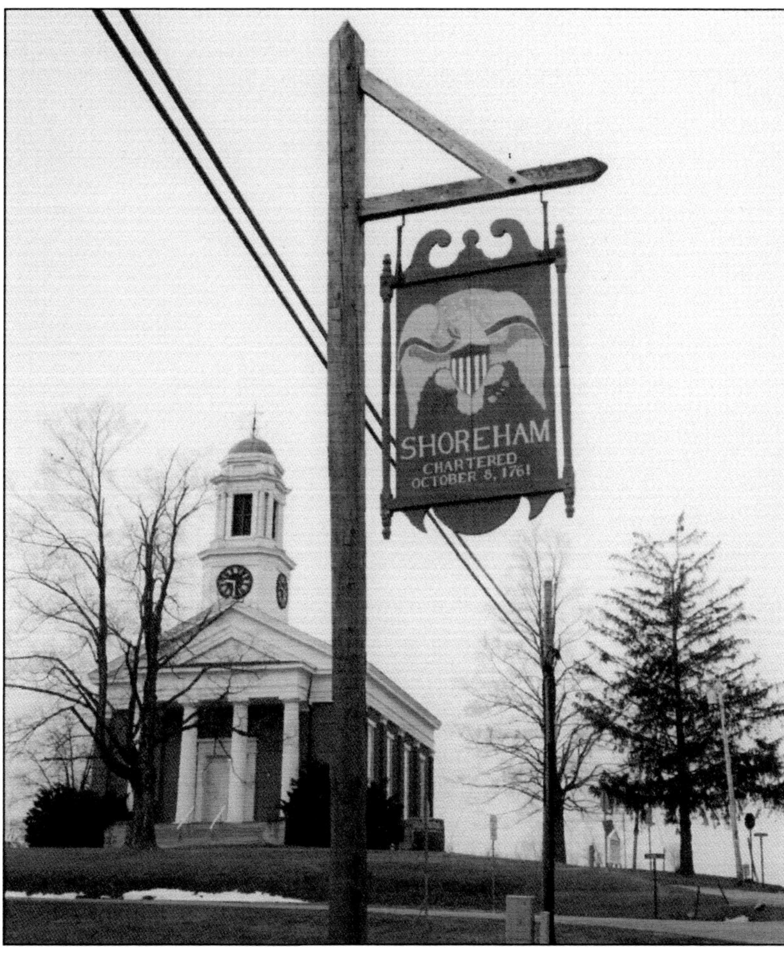

This sign used to hang on the Shoreham Common to welcome all to the town. It is a replica of the Chipman Tavern sign, which hung for many years in front of the tavern on Cream Hill Road. The tavern was taken down and moved to Connecticut, and the original sign is now in the Vermont Historical Society Museum in Montpelier.

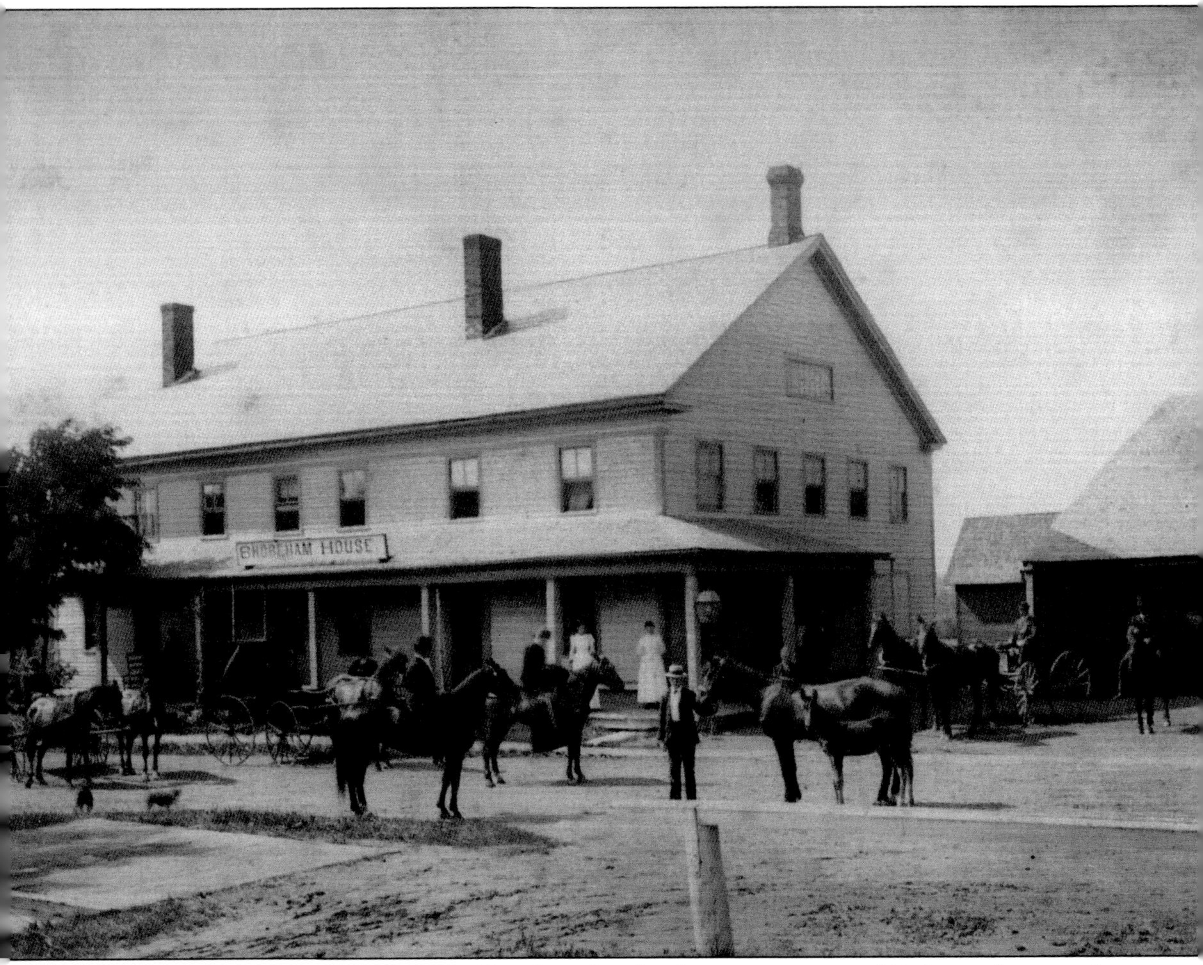

Built in 1799 by Joseph Miller, the Shoreham Inn has been in use as a public house for more than 200 years. The name has changed over the years, from the Hunsdon Hotel to the Bissell House to the Shoreham Hotel. Today, the Shoreham Inn takes guests and has a pub and fine dining open to the general public five days a week.

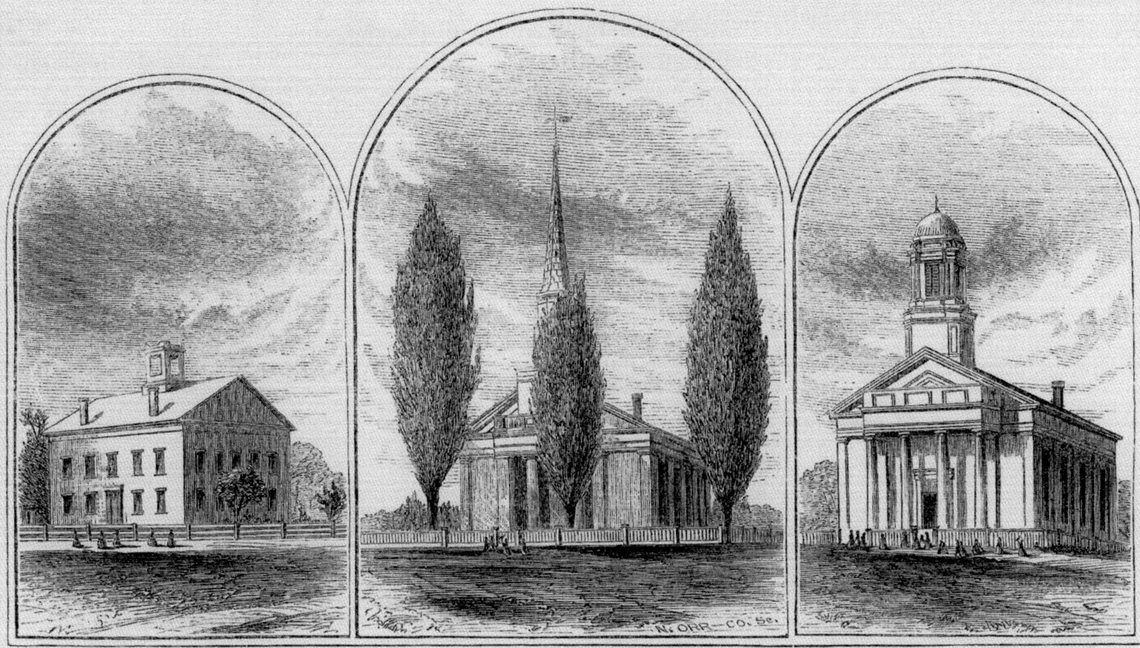

NEWTON ACADEMY. UNIVERSALIST CHURCH. CONGREGATIONAL CHURCH.

When the original proprietors of the town had it surveyed, they kept a 100-acre parcel in the geographical center of town for the village. Of that 100 acres, 23 acres were put aside as a "common" for the common good of all citizens. Public buildings were placed on the western side of the common, which was on higher ground. This engraving from Josiah F. Goodhue's 1861 *History of the Town of Shoreham, Vermont* shows the public buildings that were there at that time.

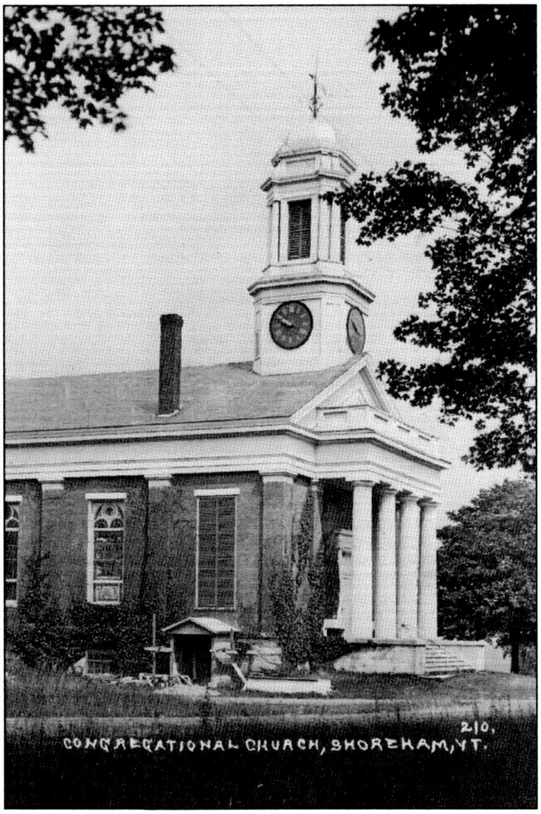

Members of the United Church of Christ (Congregational church) formed a church in town in 1794. By 1800, they had built a large Federal-style church on the west side of the common. It had an outside staircase called a "porch" that led upstairs to the Negro pew. By the 1840s, church attendance had fallen off enough that they decided to build a smaller building. This current Congregational church was built in 1846; in 1847, the original church was taken to Larrabee's Point to be used as a wool warehouse.

Newton Academy (below) was built in 1810 as an institution of higher learning by members of the Universalist church. They also used the chapel upstairs for their worship services until they could afford to build a separate church in 1852. The school was incorporated in 1811. Mathematics, languages, and the classics were taught. In 1854, a wing was added to accommodate boarding students, since its excellent reputation brought students from all over New England.

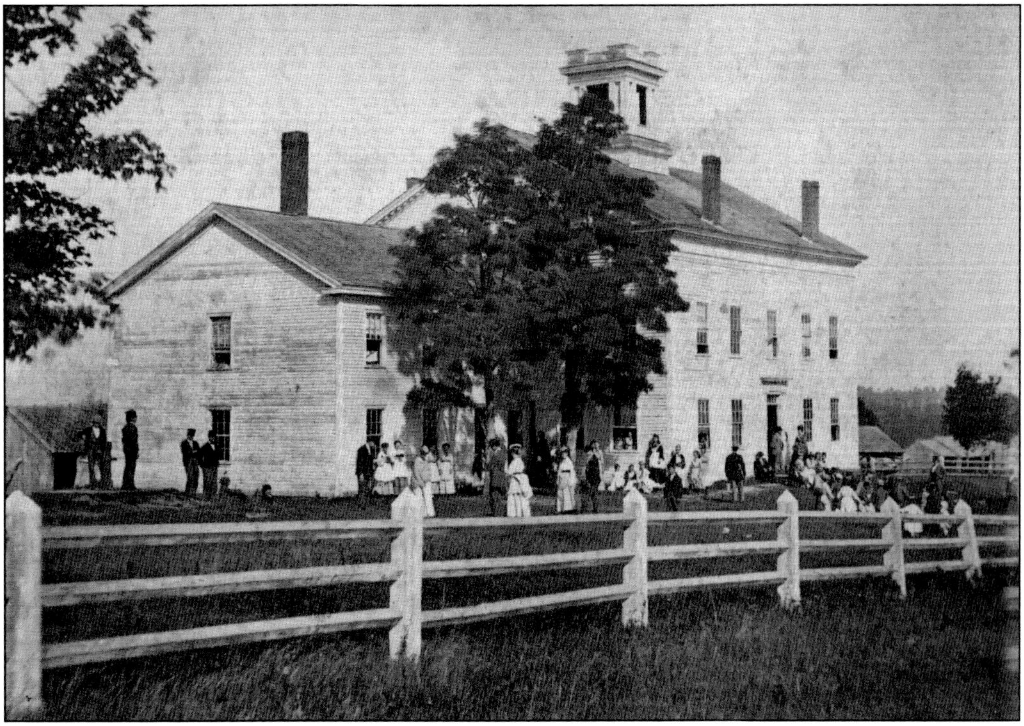

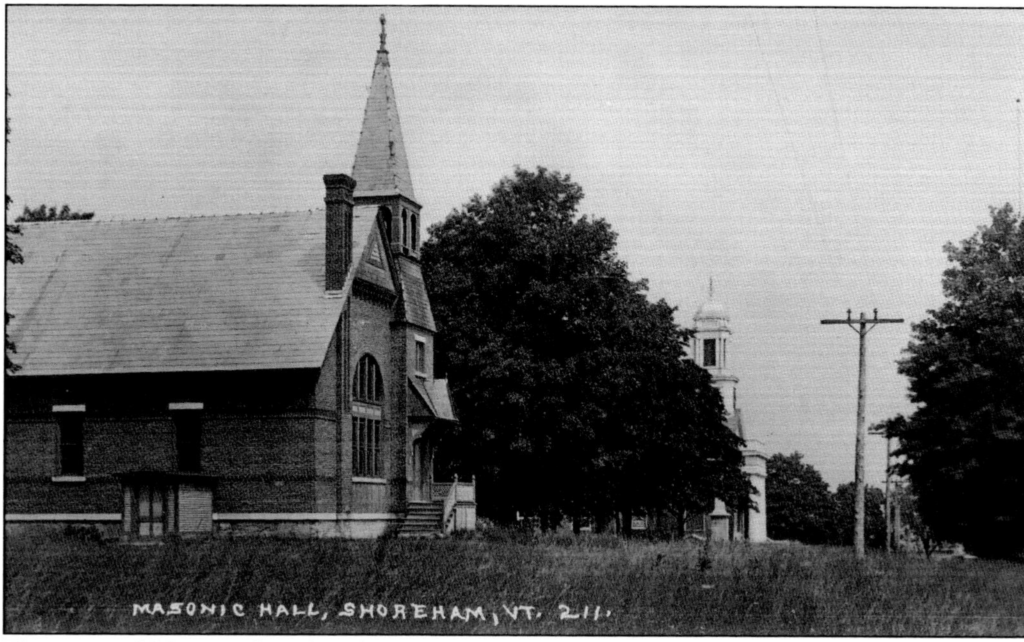

The original Universalist church, seen in the town engraving on page 11, burned one cold Christmas night when the fire in the cellar escaped the furnace. Everyone got out safely, and this smaller Universalist church was built in 1885. As the religious society dwindled, they sold the building to the Simonds Lodge Masons in 1906. It functioned as their meeting place for 80 years until that group also dwindled. In 1987, the Simonds Lodge voted to disband and have their membership transferred to Morning Sun Lodge No. 5 in Bridport. The building is now home to the Vermont Music Conservatory.

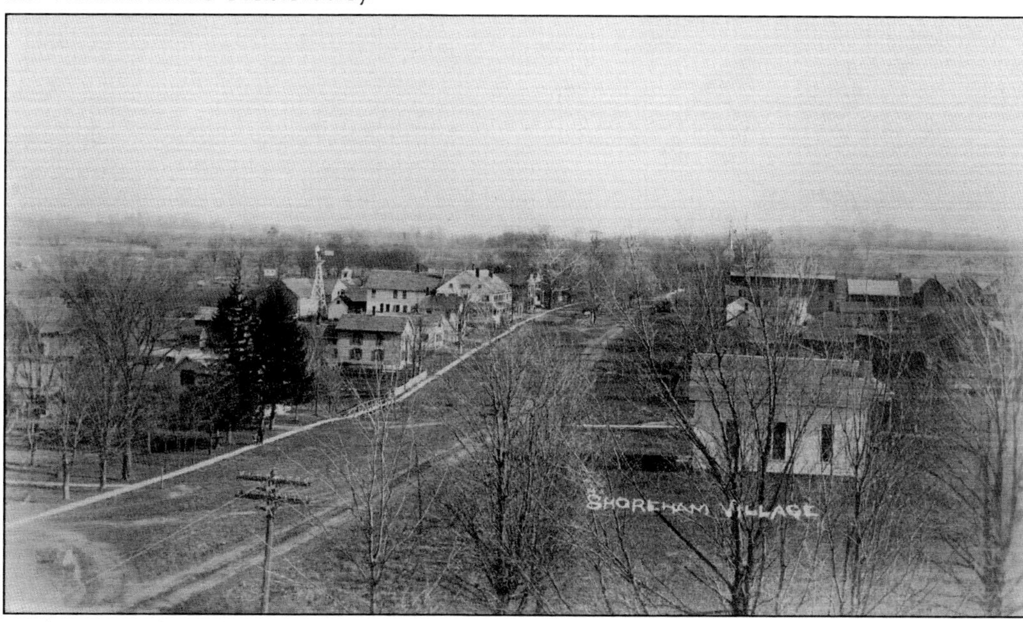

Looking east from the Congregational church on Main Street, the first building on the right is the Federation building, which was used as men's club rooms. The 1871 Beers Atlas map of Shoreham village labeled it as the YMCA.

The Shoreham Union Library Society was formed in 1821. Books were housed in a library room at Newton Academy. Dr. Mary Platt had this library built in 1906 to honor her late husband, Dr. William Platt. She then sold it to the town for $1. With a new addition, it still serves the people of Shoreham.

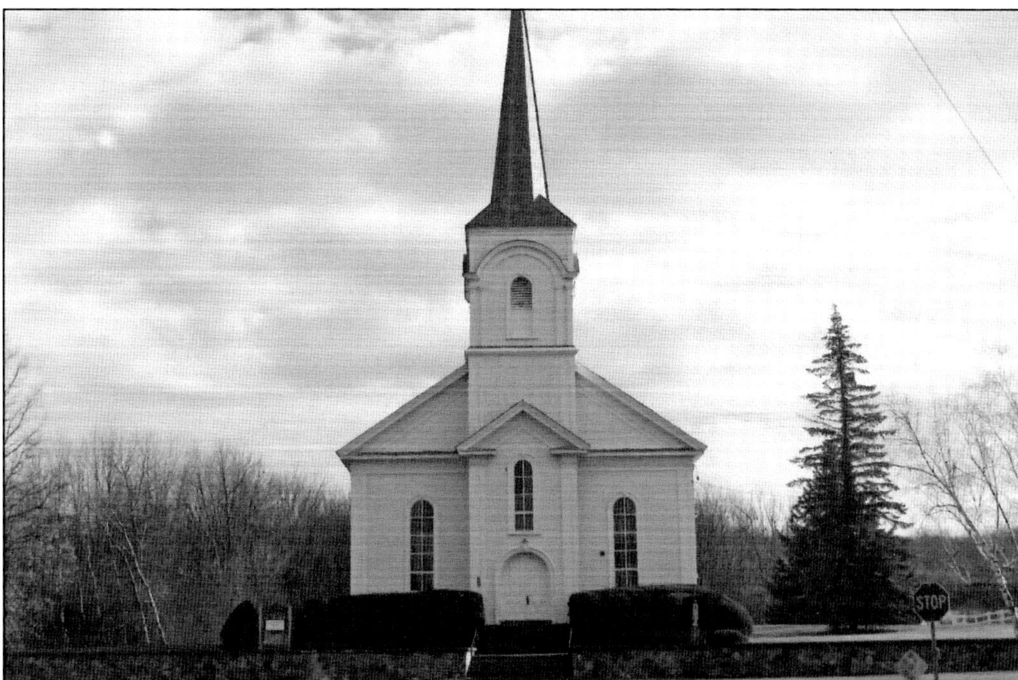

Catholics in Shoreham first organized for worship in 1856, and they bought the old Turrill tavern called Hill House. As it deteriorated with age, St. Genevieve's Church was built in 1873 by the significant number of French Canadian and Irish immigrants who moved to town in the mid-1800s. For a time, they shared a priest with Orwell, and then Middlebury; today, they share a priest with neighboring Bridport. (Courtesy of Mary Esther Macfarlane.)

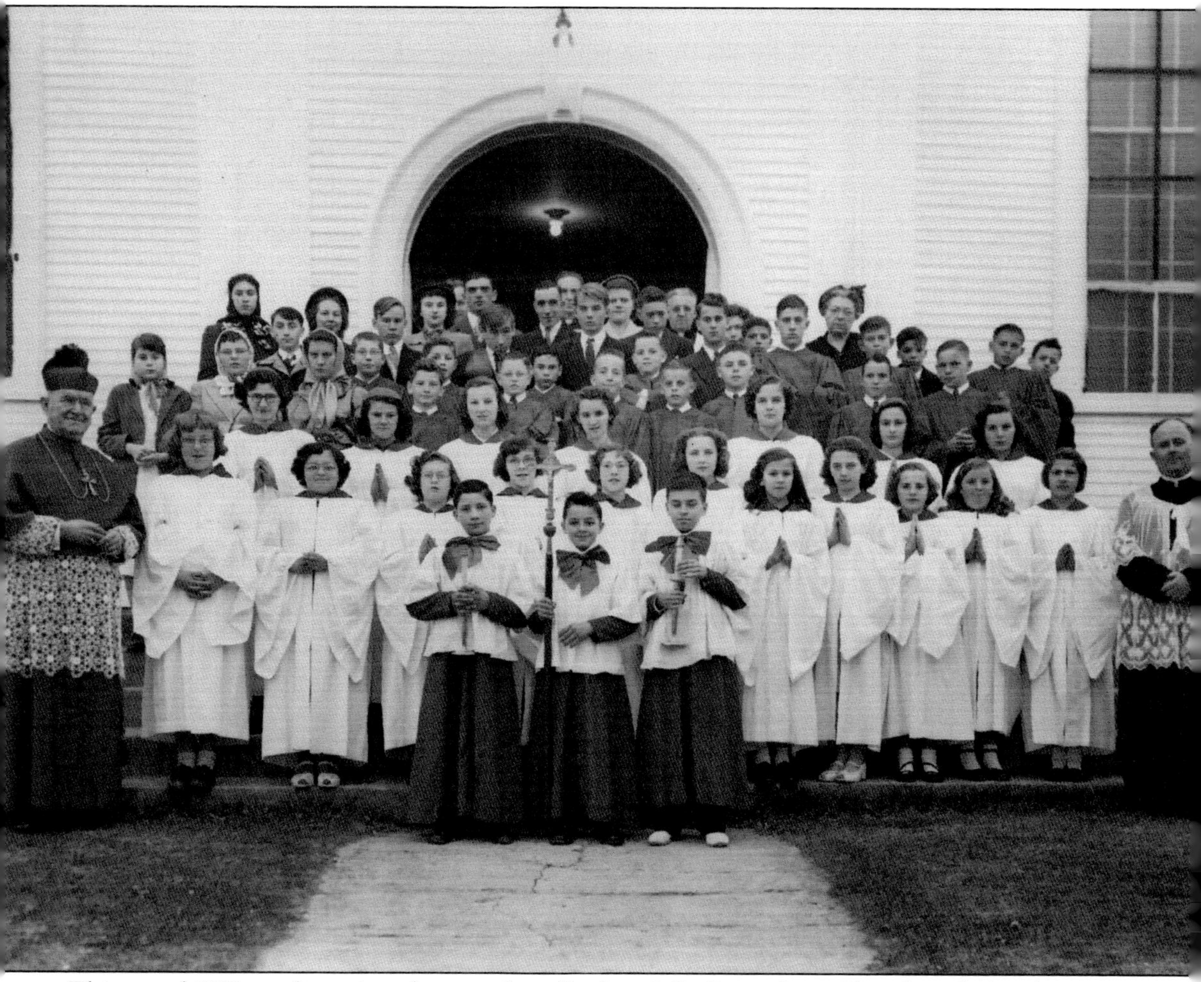

This proud 1951 confirmation class was from Bridport's St. Bernadette Church and Shoreham's St. Genevieve's Church. They are, from left to right, (first row) Eugene Gaboriault, Tom Blair, and Dwight Menard; (second row) Bishop Edward Francis Ryan, unidentified, Maureen Sullivan, Shirley Rule, Brenda Shackett, Arlene Stanley, Kathy Donovan, unidentified, Betty Cook, Martha Doane, unidentified, Yvette LaRoche, and Fr. Joseph P. Sawyer; (third row) unidentified, Jean Ann Cole, Janet Barnes, unidentified, Mary Esther Brisson, Patricia Barnes, and Marguerite Lavoie; (fourth row) unidentified, Shirley Giard, three unidentified children, Hector Rochon, and the rest of the row is unidentified, from Bridport; (fifth row) Olive Barnes, Willard Barnes, two unidentified, Norma Barnes, four unidentified children, Wanita Stevers, six unidentified children, Lucia Shackett, and Bob Russ. (Courtesy of Kirk LaDuke.)

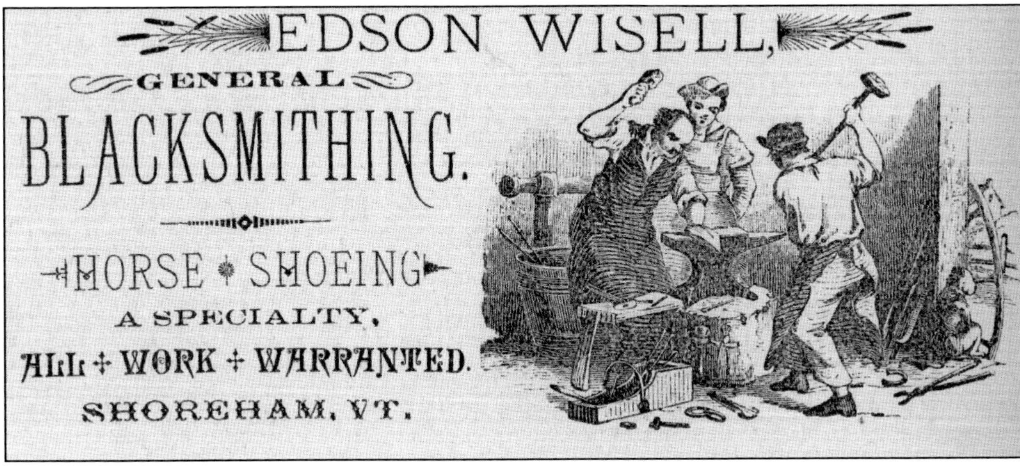

This advertisement for Edson Wisell's village blacksmith shop was taken from the 1881–1882 *Gazetteer and Business Directory of Addison County*. This business was later taken over and run in the same location by Wisell's son Wilbur.

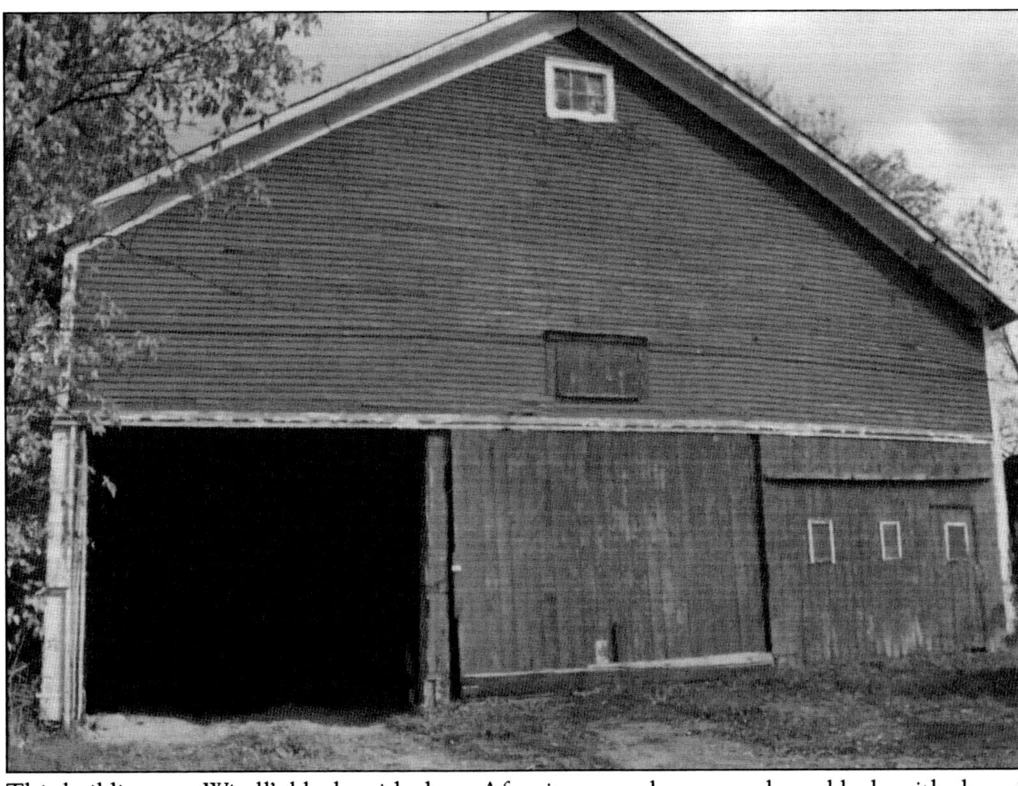
This building was Wisell's blacksmith shop. After it was no longer used as a blacksmith shop, it was acquired by the town and used for storage by the highway department. It currently houses the recycle truck.

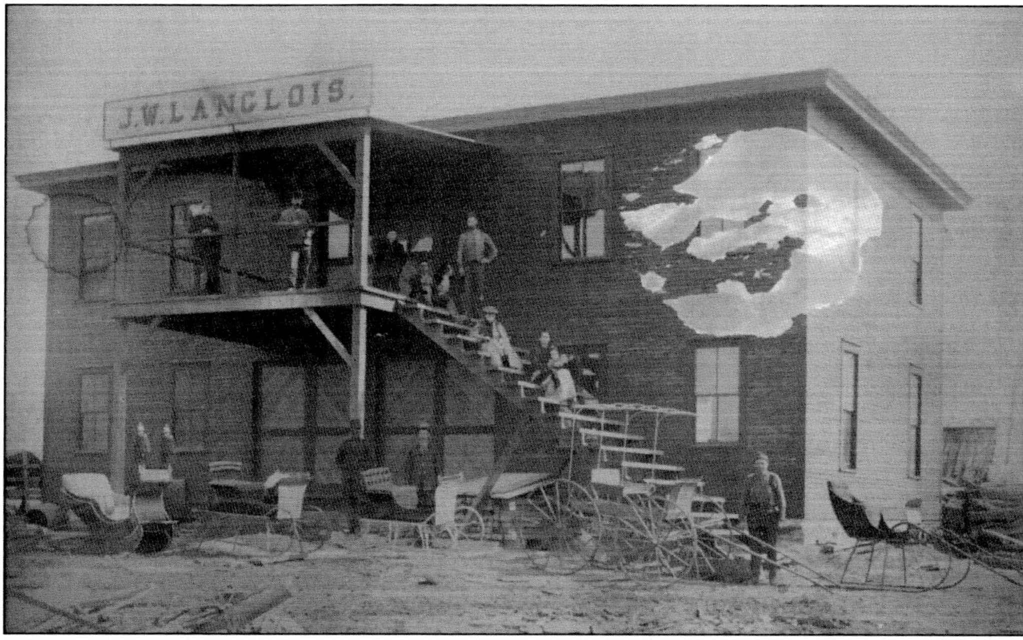

William Langlois, born in Canada in 1834, came to Shoreham with his wife and four children in the late 1860s. He built a business manufacturing carriages and sleighs in this building, which he erected on the east side of the common. In the 1900s, it housed the fire trucks and rescue squad equipment until the new town garage was built.

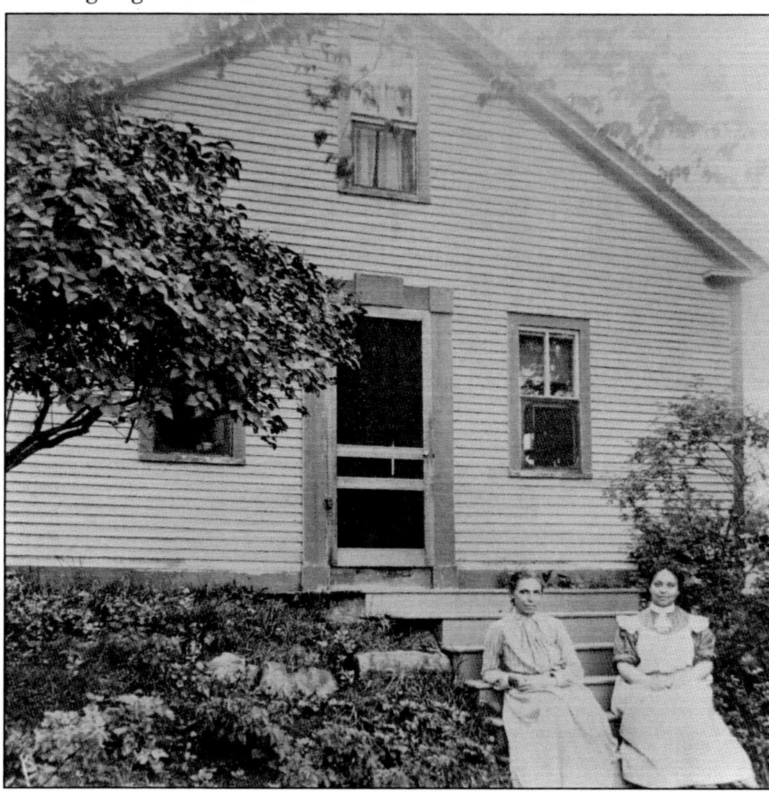

Philomen Anderson, the daughter of William and Therese Langlois, and her daughter Marian Annette Anderson sit on the front step of their house on Main Street. In 1873, Philomen married William John Anderson, who was born into slavery in Virginia and came to Vermont after befriending some Shoreham soldiers during the Civil War.

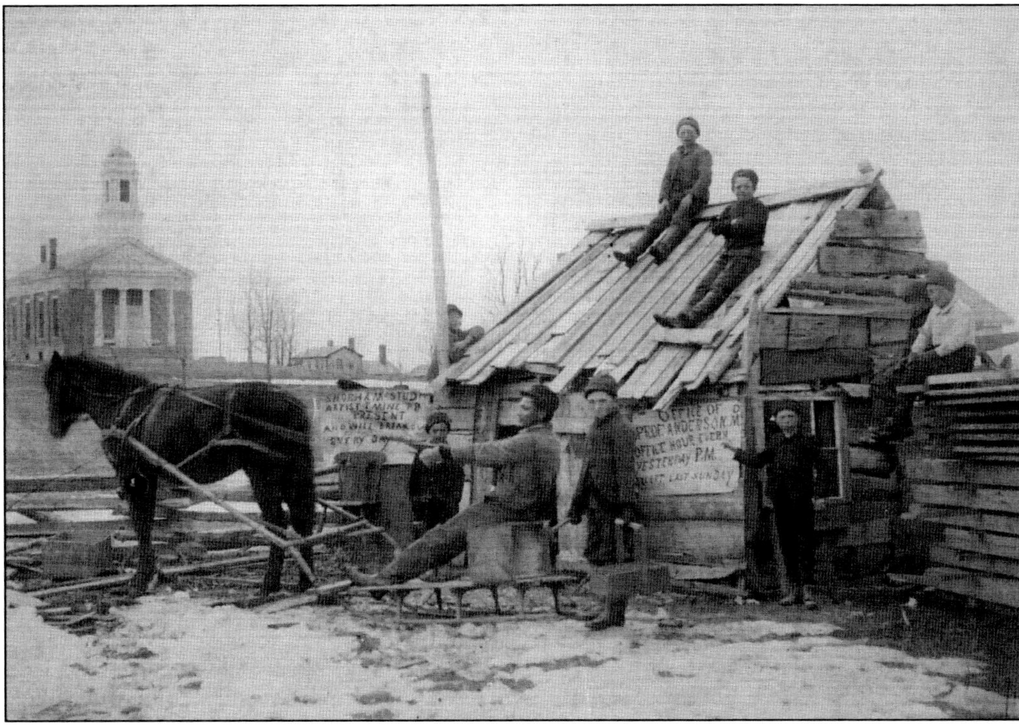

A group of local boys led by William John Anderson Jr. built this clubhouse on the common. The signs on the building read, "Office of Prof. Anderson. Office hours every yesterday p.m. except last Sunday."

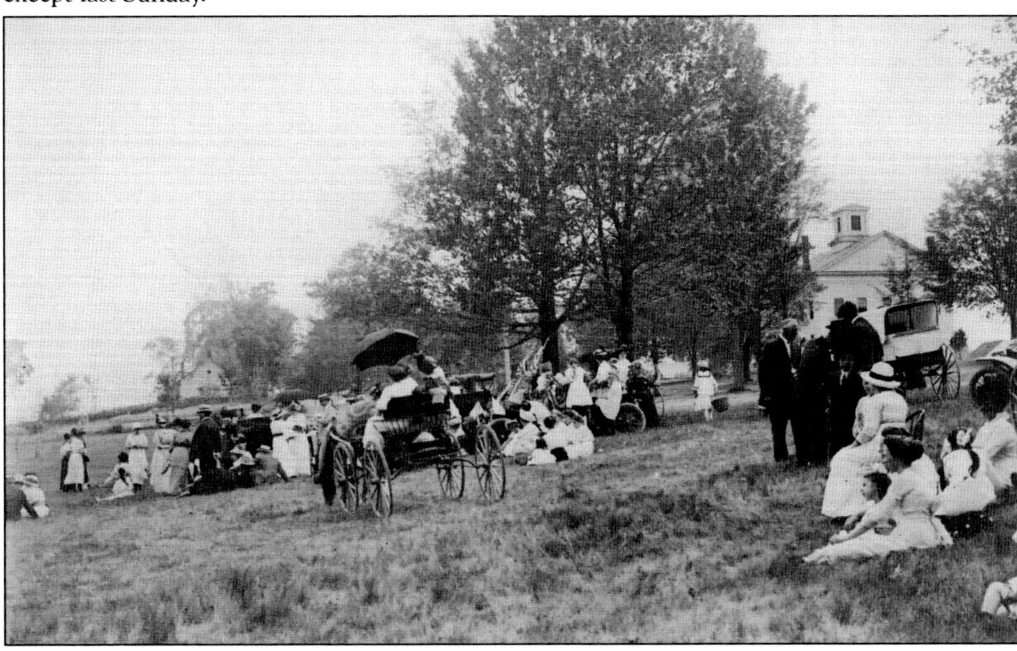

Field Days in Shoreham were held for a couple of days to celebrate the Fourth of July. There were games, music, and patriotic speeches on the common. There is an automobile fender on the far right of this photograph, which gives a clue about the era when this undated photograph was taken.

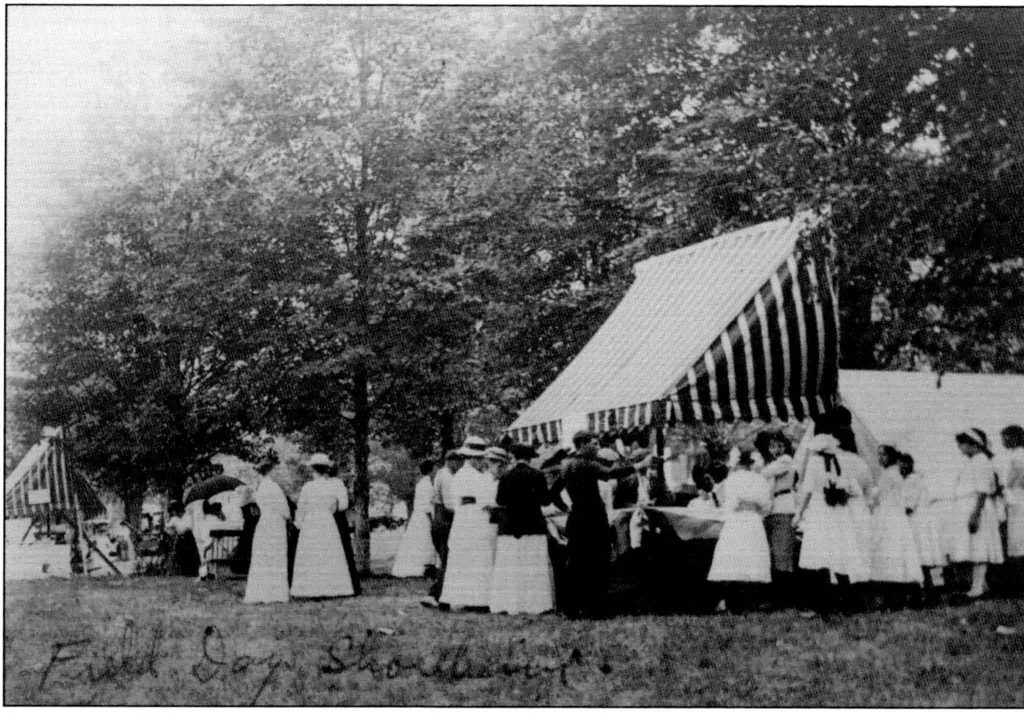

Another Field Days celebration is seen here with booths set up under awnings, offering baked goods and interesting displays for people to enjoy.

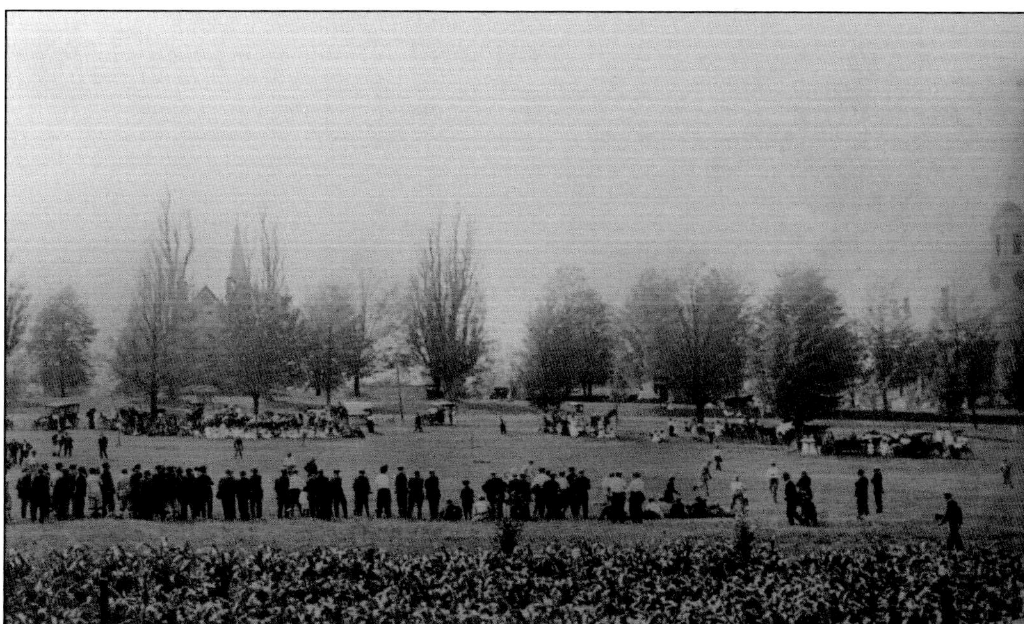

This baseball game on the common in the early 1900s drew a large, cheering crowd. This tradition still occurs every summer.

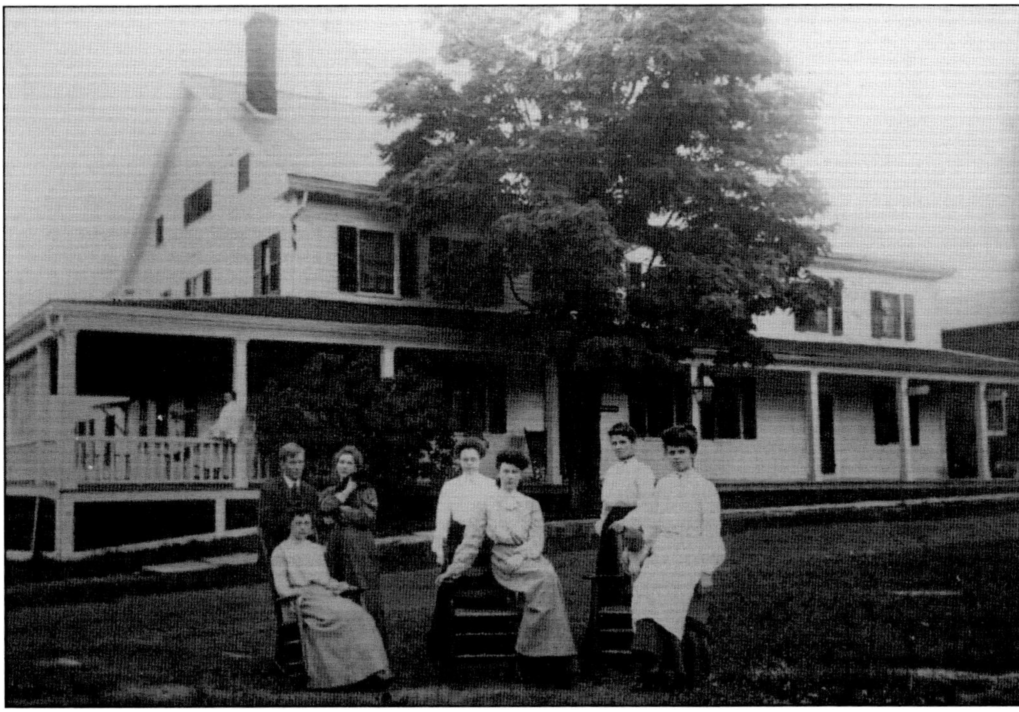

Guests and staff relax on the lawn in front of the Shoreham Inn around 1900. Even the inn's black cat made her way into the photograph.

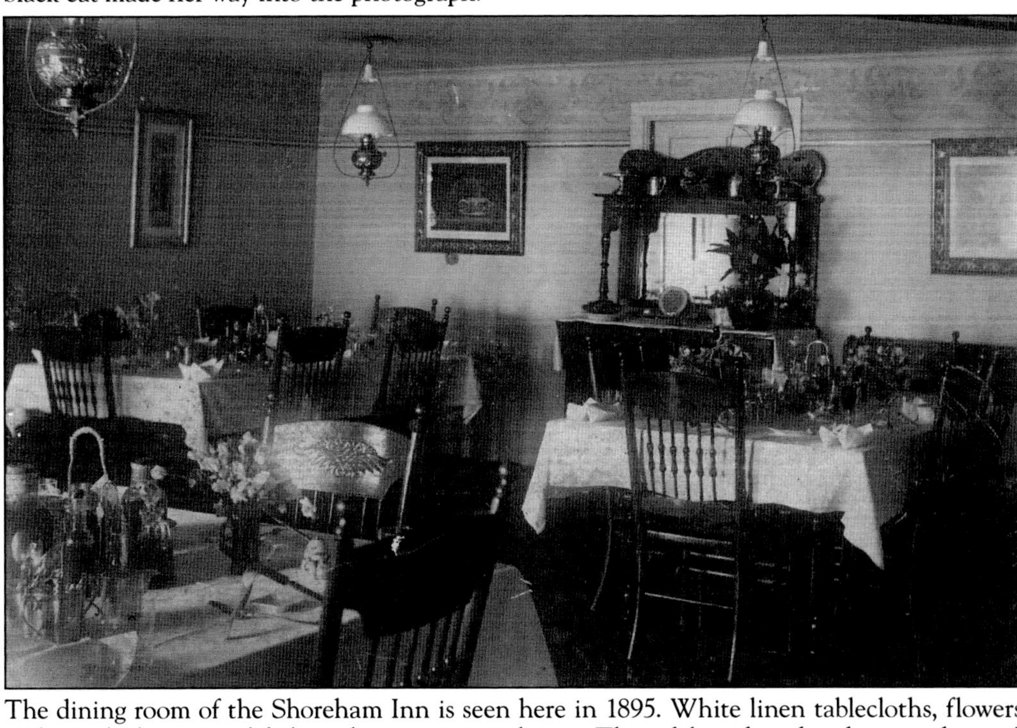

The dining room of the Shoreham Inn is seen here in 1895. White linen tablecloths, flowers, and upright knives and forks indicate gracious dining. The sideboard in the photograph is still in the dining room.

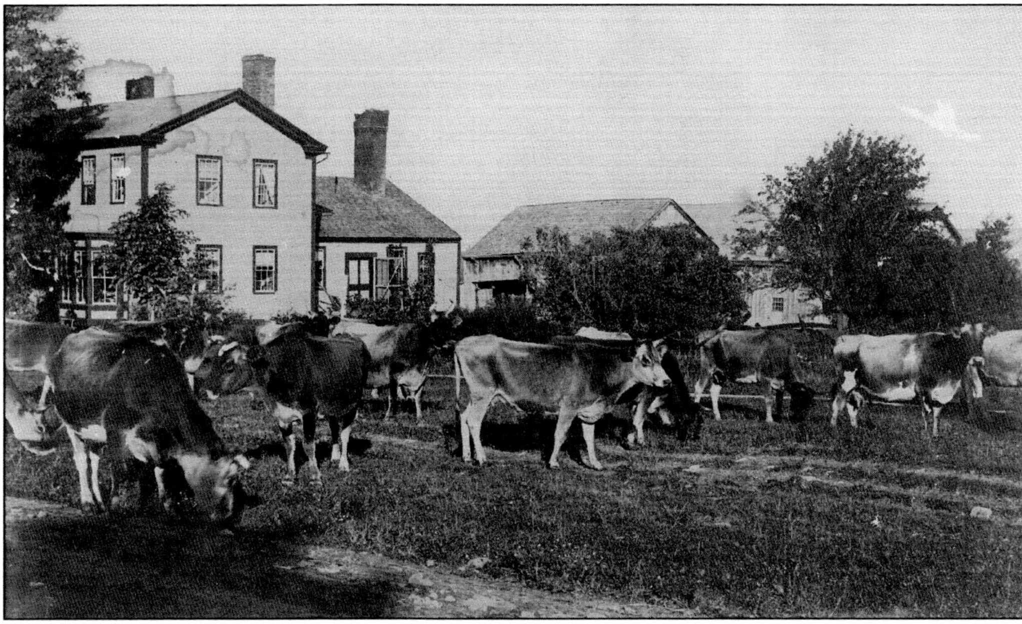

Cows and sheep roamed freely everywhere in the early days. These Jersey cows on Main Street belonged to the Burge family, who lived in the house behind them. The house is still there and is now owned by an art dealer.

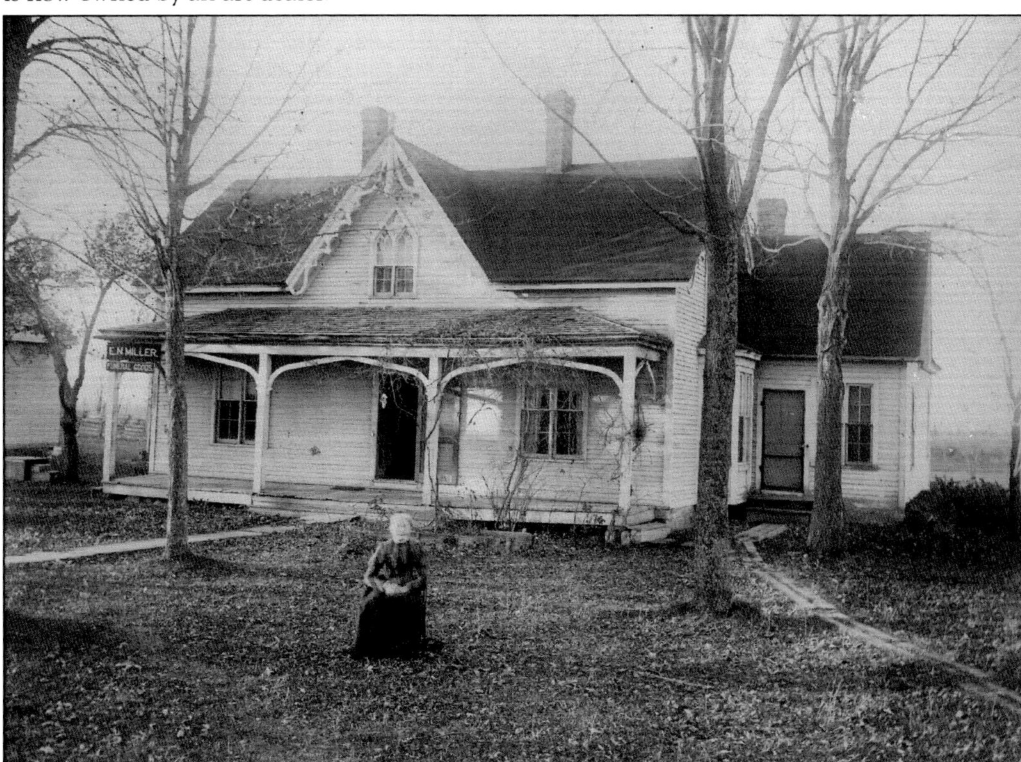

Mrs. Miller poses in her front yard as she watches activity on the common across the street. She and her husband had a small shop selling funeral goods inside the house.

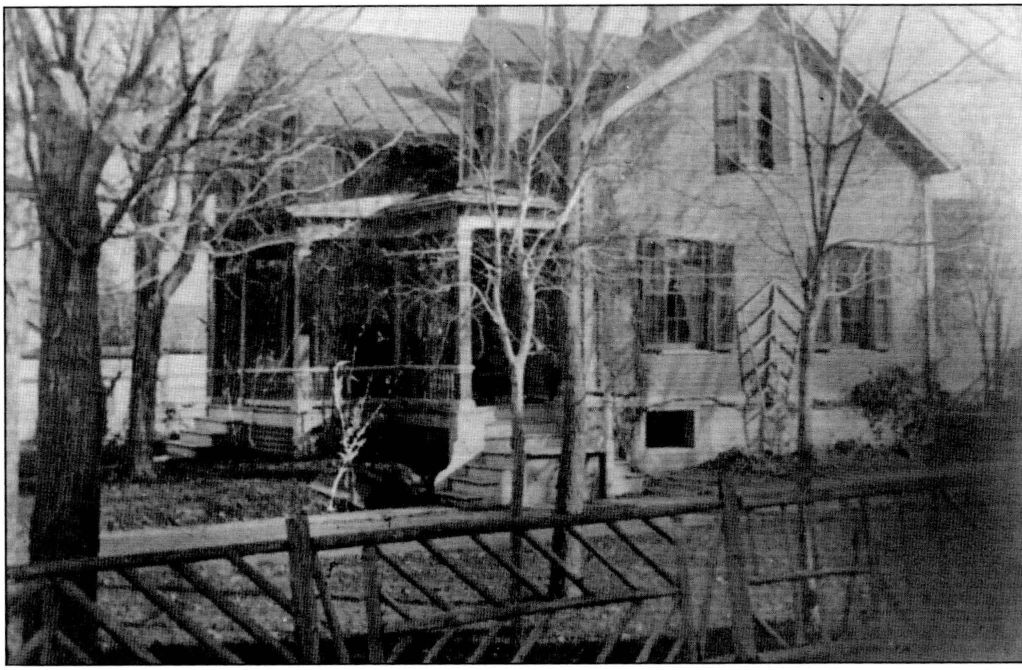

This house was owned by Clayton Nelson North when this photograph was taken. He owned the general store across the street from his house. Note the fancy log fence to the west of his house.

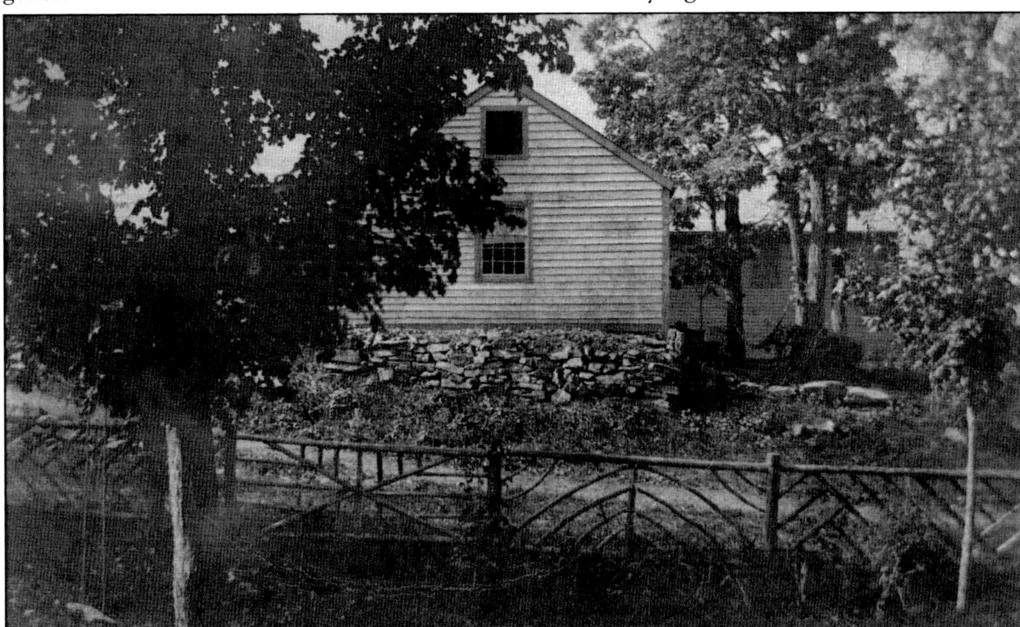

This house is just west of the residence above. Another section of the fence is also visible in this photograph. Rev. Daniel Oliver Morton lived here when he served as a pastor at the Shoreham Congregational Church. His son Levi Parsons Morton, who went on to become the vice president of the United States under Pres. Benjamin Harrison, was born in a house north of the village, but he moved to this house when he was two years old and grew up in the village. (Courtesy of Kirk LaDuke.)

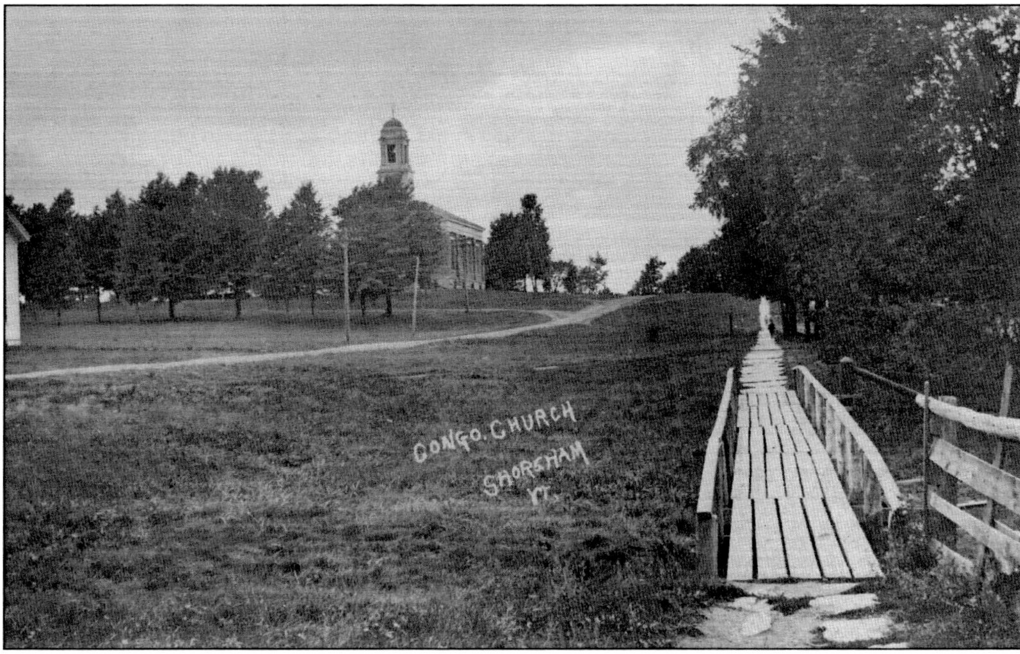

A sidewalk ran on both sides of Main Street in the 1800s. Parts of it were slate, parts of it were brick, and a small wooden bridge went over the stream that trickled down to Great Cedar Swamp, north of the village.

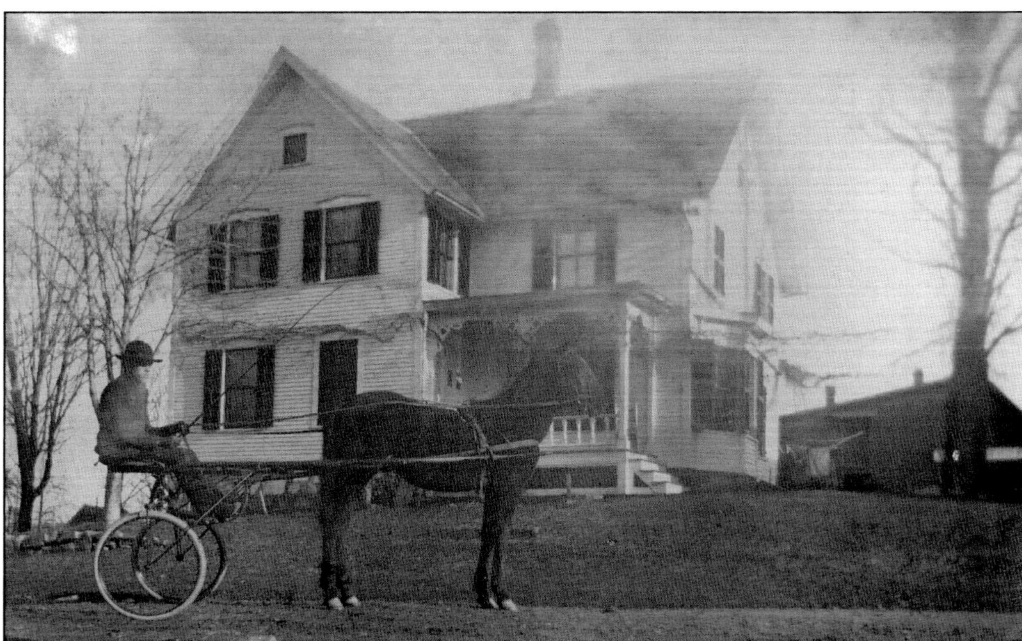

After Dr. William Platt purchased the house where Levi Morton grew up, he added a second floor and a bay window and updated it with Victorian-style trim. He is seen here in front of the house in his racing sulky with his Hamiltonian horse. (Courtesy of Kirk LaDuke.)

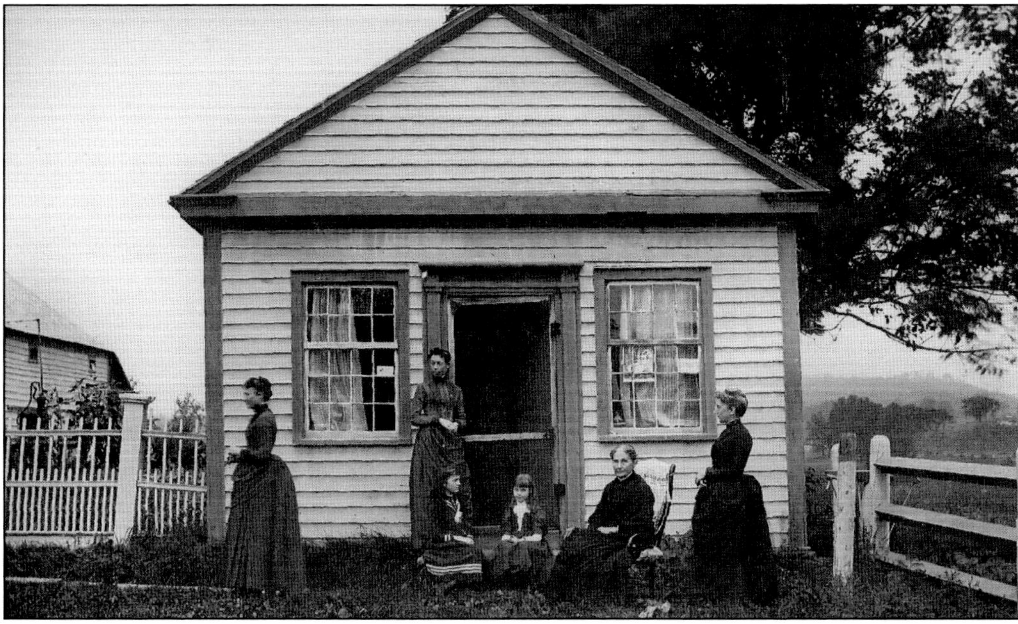

This small building began as Ashbel Catlin's cobbler shop. Later, it became Udney Everest's law office. When this photograph was taken, it was home to Marcia Royce's millinery shop. From left to right are Charlotte (Douglas) Howard, Marcia (Douglas) Royce, Florence (Howard) Witherell, Bernice (Douglas) Reed, Naomi (Tupper) Douglas, and Helen (Burge) Douglas.

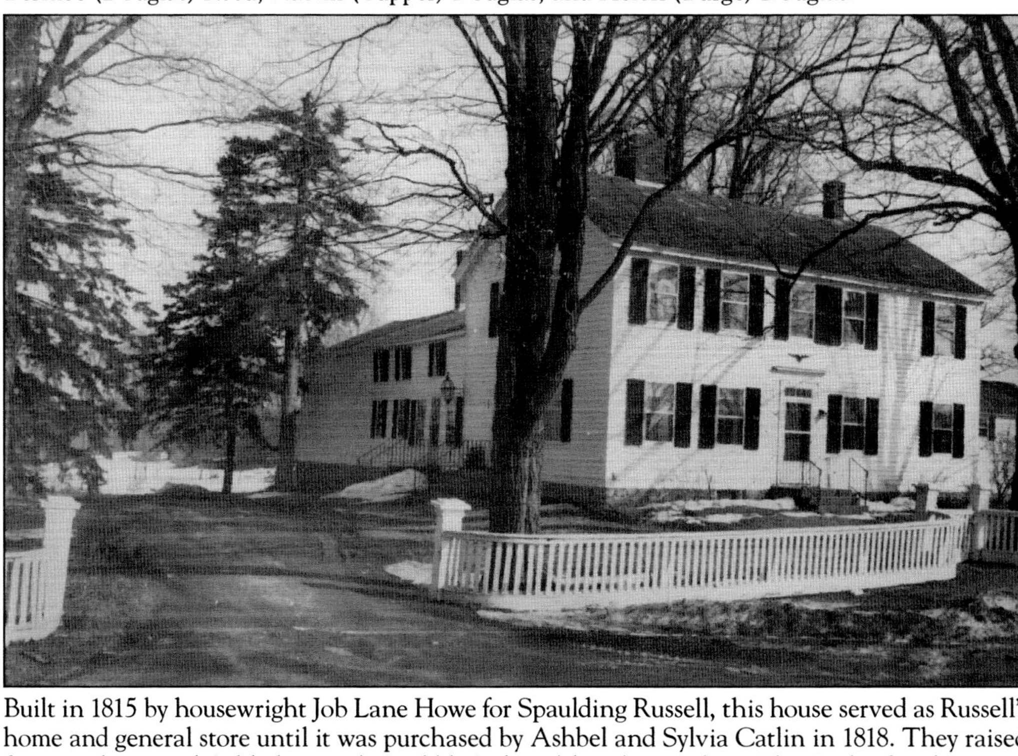

Built in 1815 by housewright Job Lane Howe for Spaulding Russell, this house served as Russell's home and general store until it was purchased by Ashbel and Sylvia Catlin in 1818. They raised five sons here, and Ashbel set up his cobbler's shop (above) next door. The Catlin family owned the house for the next 136 years. (Courtesy of the author.)

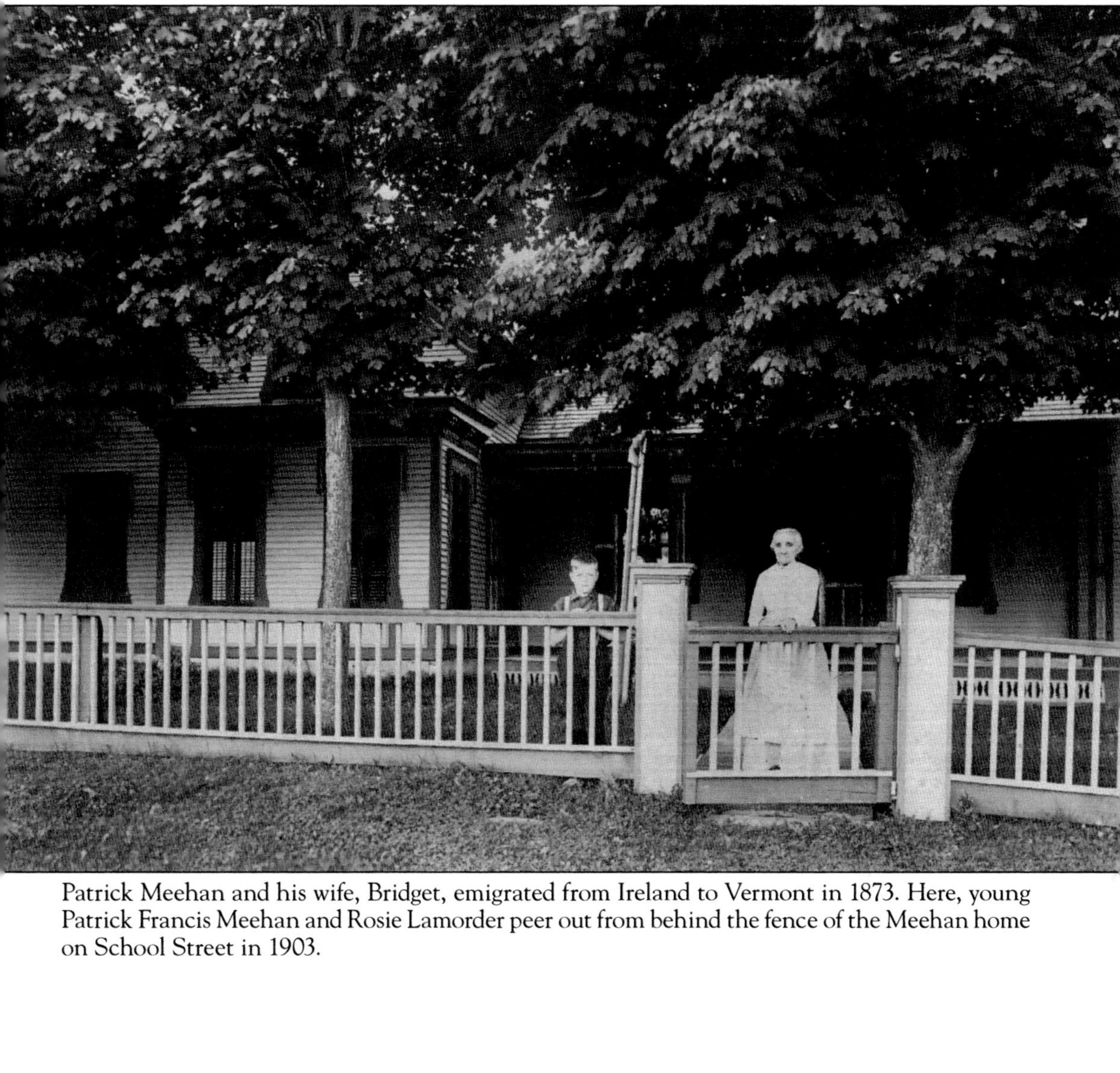

Patrick Meehan and his wife, Bridget, emigrated from Ireland to Vermont in 1873. Here, young Patrick Francis Meehan and Rosie Lamorder peer out from behind the fence of the Meehan home on School Street in 1903.

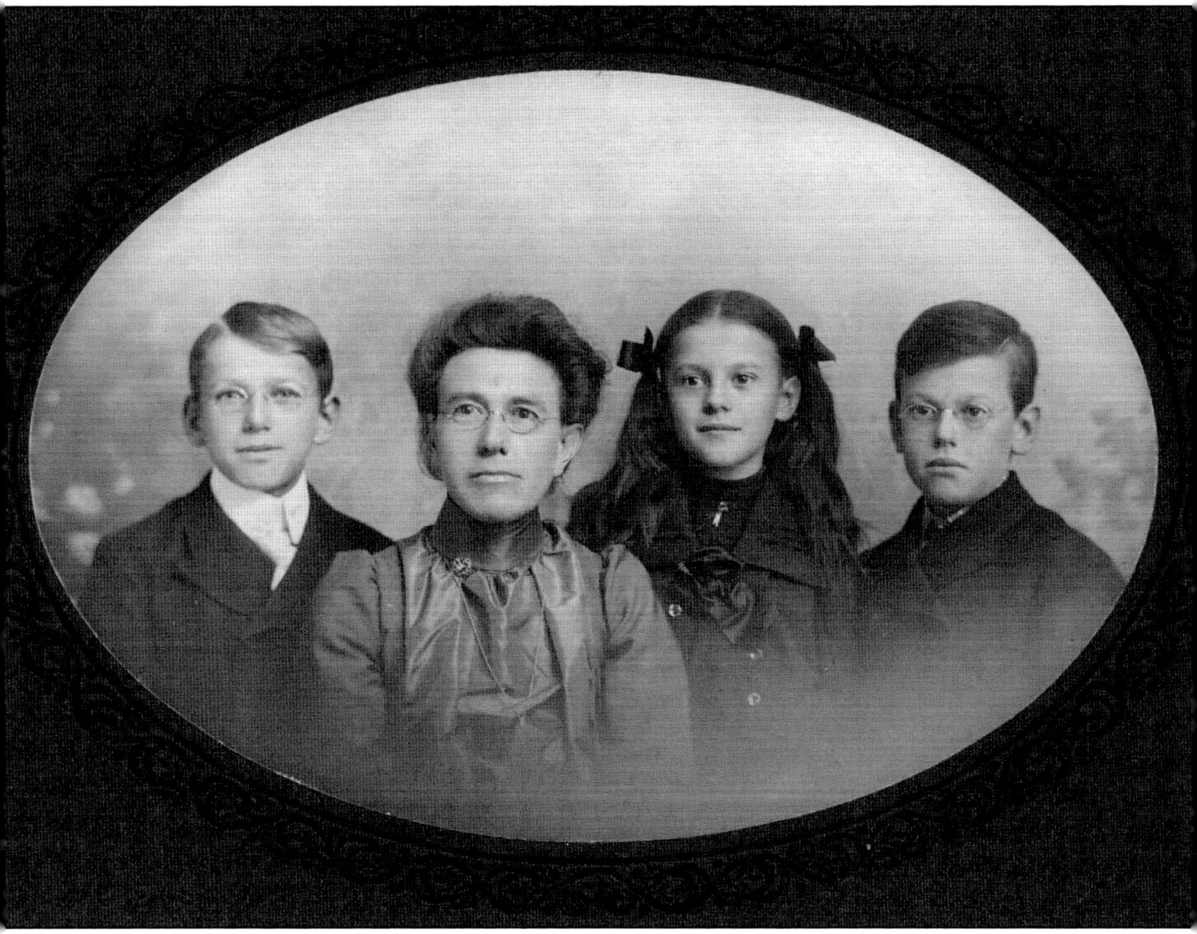

Patrick P. Meehan (1861–1938) married Effie (Griffin) Darrah, a widow with three children, whom he raised as his own. This photograph was taken shortly after the wedding, on December 16, 1910, in Shoreham. From left to right are Frank Darrah, Effie Meehan, Charlotte Darrah, and Jesse Darrah.

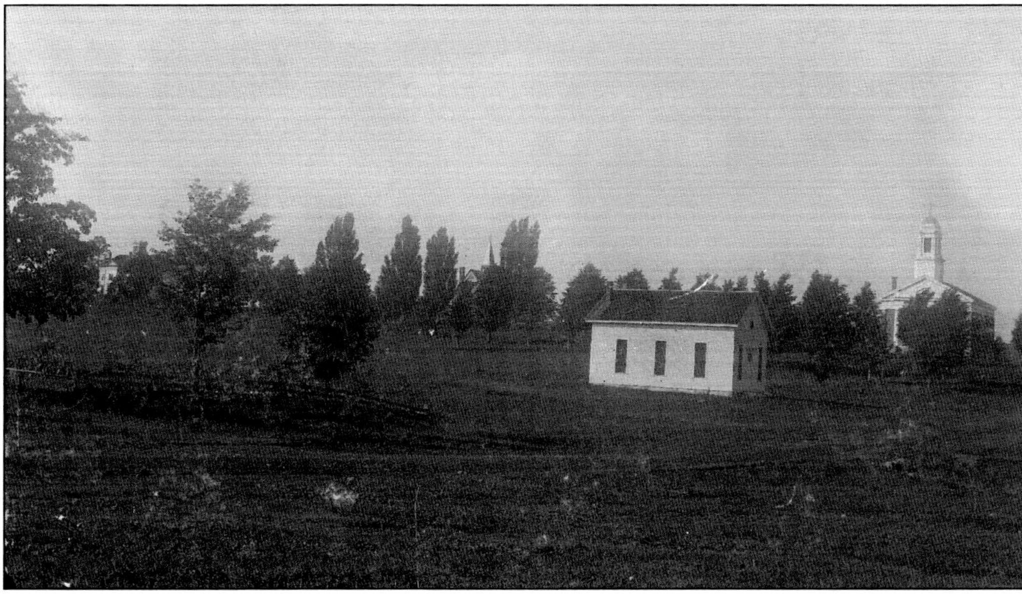

The Federation building, on the north end of the common, served as men's club rooms and a WMCA in the 1800s. It burned in 1917.

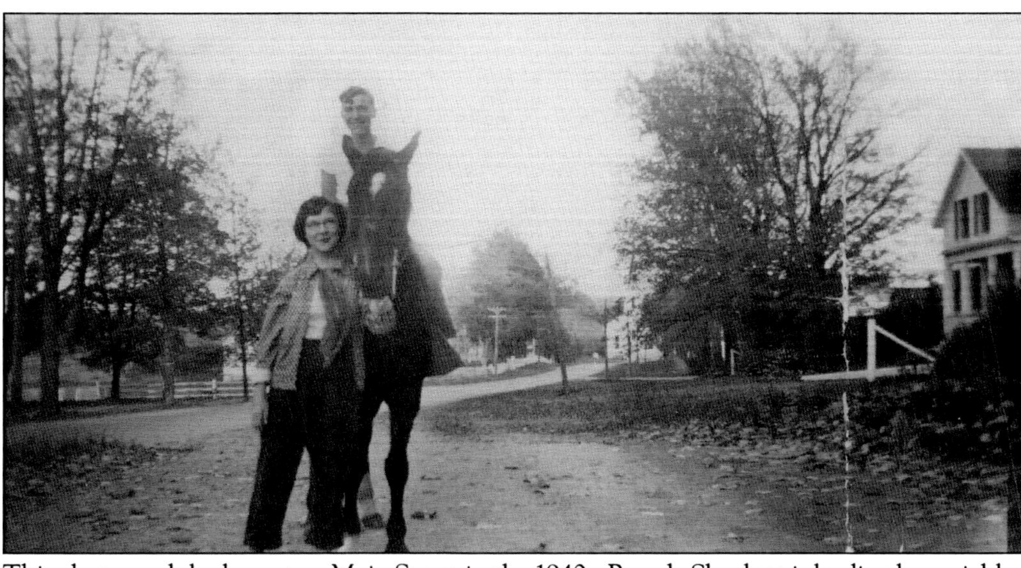

This photograph looks east on Main Street in the 1940s. Brenda Shackett is leading her neighbor David Farr on Captain, a family pet. (Courtesy of Kirk LaDuke.)

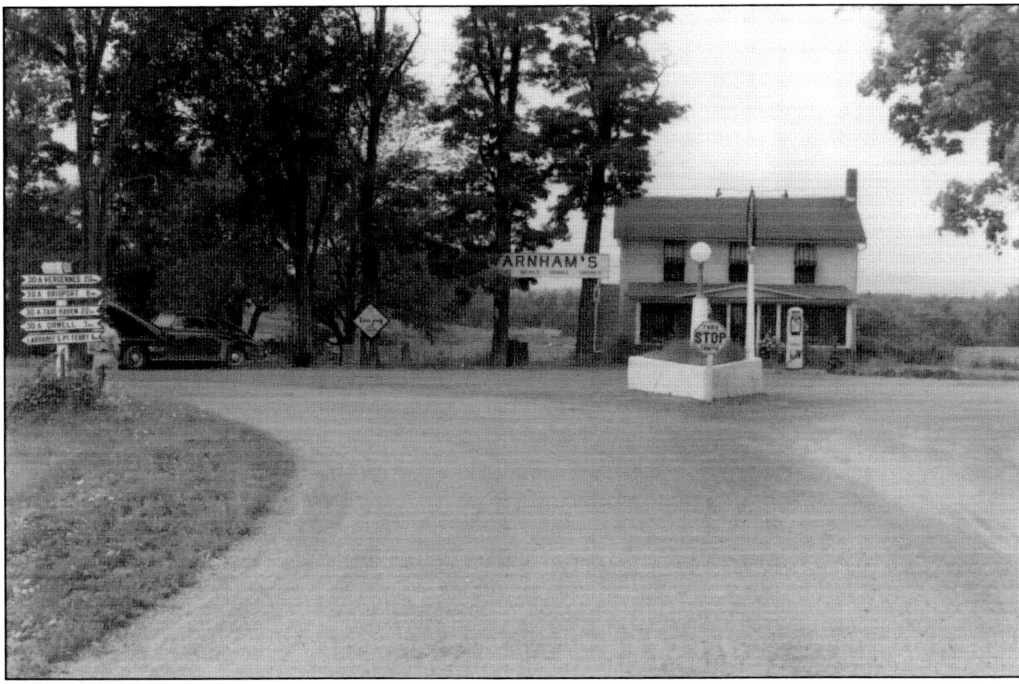

Farnham's Tea Room served meals and had comfortable rooms for weary travelers. It was located on the corner of Routes 22A and 74 East. Interestingly, the signs here call the road Route 30A.

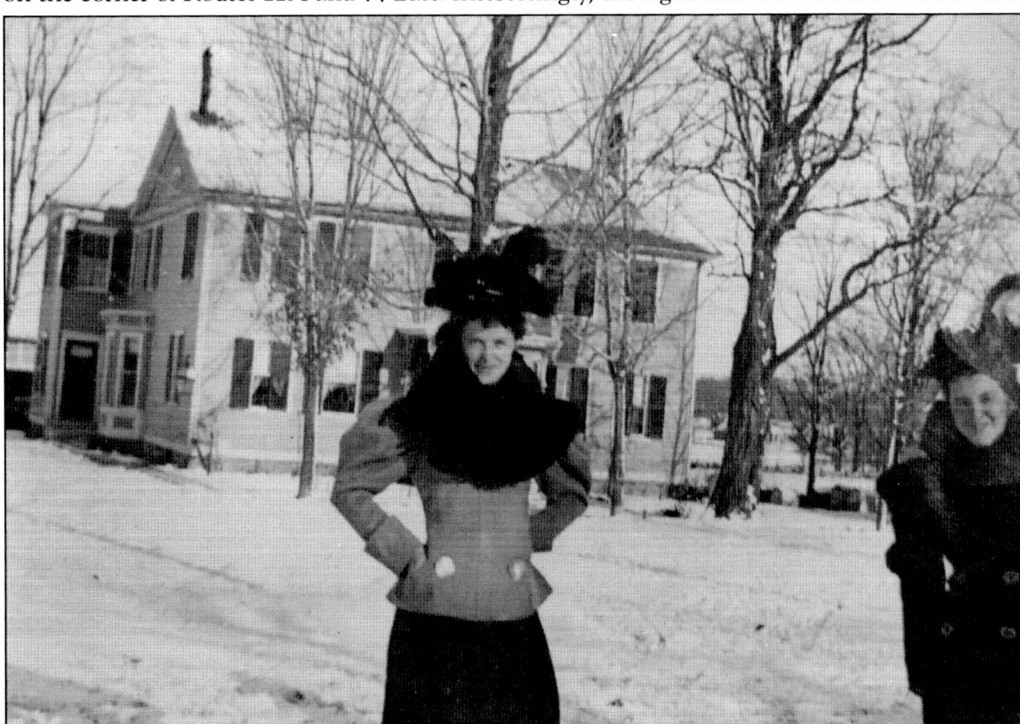

Elizabeth North (left) and Clara Moore stand in front of Dr. Charles Howard's home on Main Street. Elizabeth went on to marry the next town physician, Isaac Sharon.

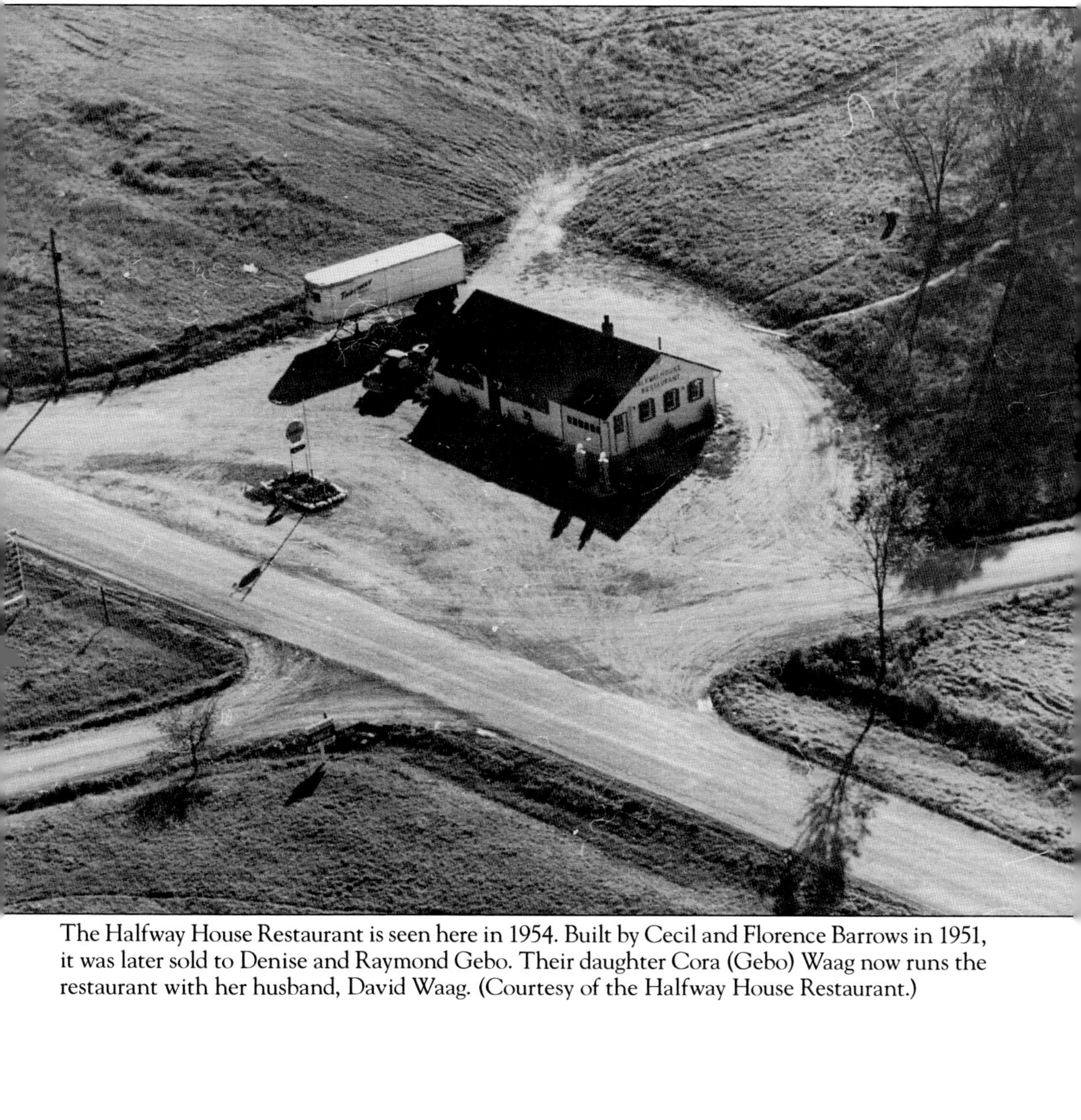

The Halfway House Restaurant is seen here in 1954. Built by Cecil and Florence Barrows in 1951, it was later sold to Denise and Raymond Gebo. Their daughter Cora (Gebo) Waag now runs the restaurant with her husband, David Waag. (Courtesy of the Halfway House Restaurant.)

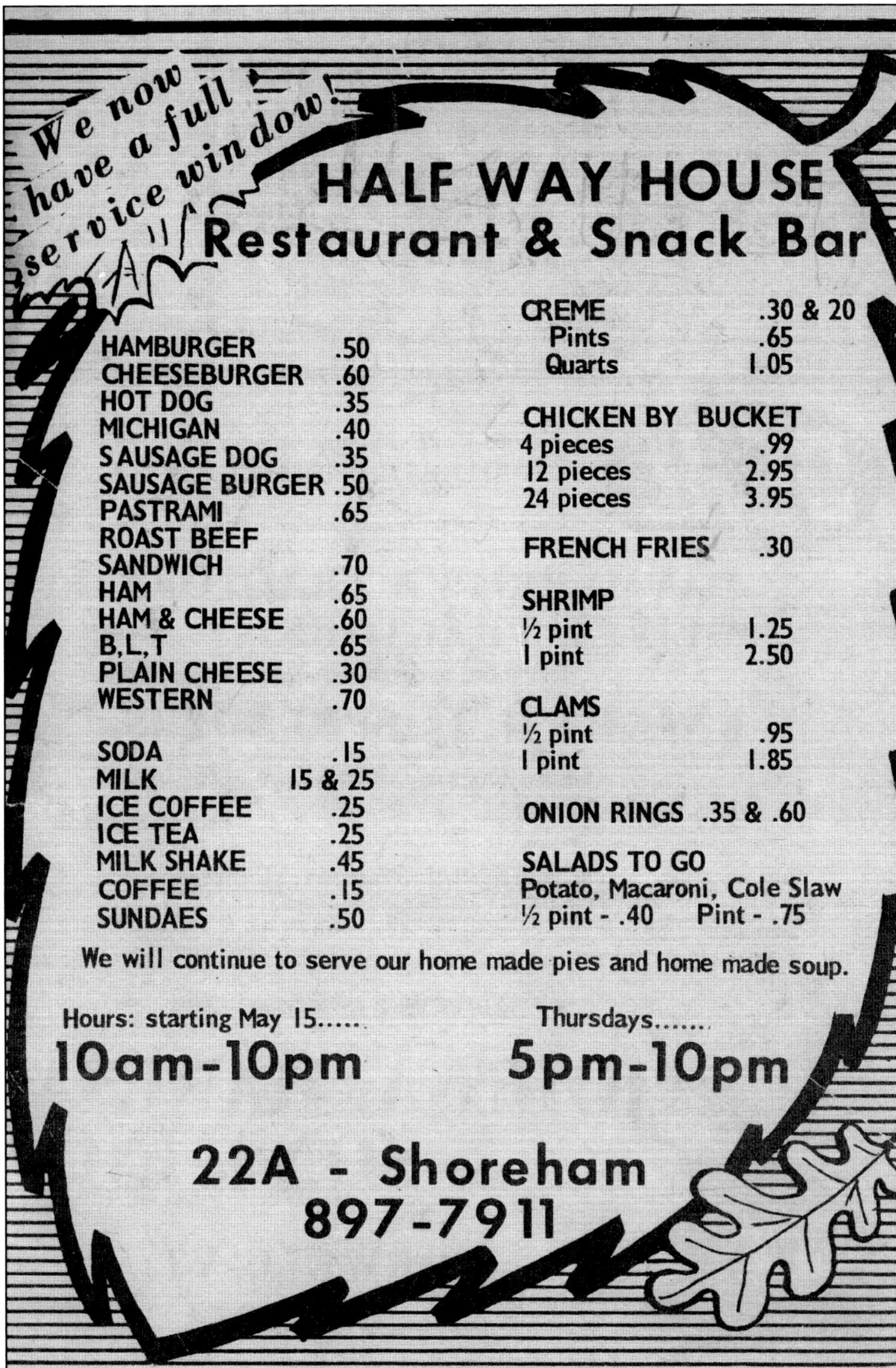

We now have a full service window!

HALF WAY HOUSE
Restaurant & Snack Bar

HAMBURGER	.50
CHEESEBURGER	.60
HOT DOG	.35
MICHIGAN	.40
SAUSAGE DOG	.35
SAUSAGE BURGER	.50
PASTRAMI	.65
ROAST BEEF SANDWICH	.70
HAM	.65
HAM & CHEESE	.60
B,L,T	.65
PLAIN CHEESE	.30
WESTERN	.70
SODA	.15
MILK	15 & 25
ICE COFFEE	.25
ICE TEA	.25
MILK SHAKE	.45
COFFEE	.15
SUNDAES	.50

CREME	.30 & 20
Pints	.65
Quarts	1.05
CHICKEN BY BUCKET	
4 pieces	.99
12 pieces	2.95
24 pieces	3.95
FRENCH FRIES	.30
SHRIMP	
½ pint	1.25
1 pint	2.50
CLAMS	
½ pint	.95
1 pint	1.85
ONION RINGS	.35 & .60

SALADS TO GO
Potato, Macaroni, Cole Slaw
½ pint - .40 Pint - .75

We will continue to serve our home made pies and home made soup.

Hours: starting May 15..... 10am-10pm

Thursdays...... 5pm-10pm

22A - Shoreham
897-7911

This is the first menu at the Halfway House. Many of the same dishes are still being served there but no longer at those prices. (Courtesy of the Halfway House Restaurant.)

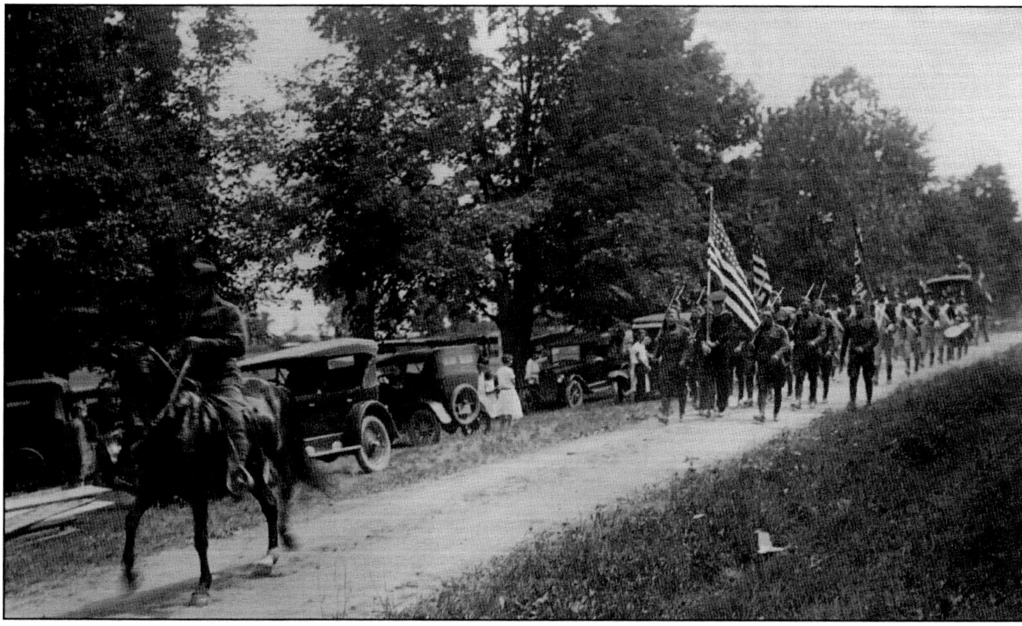

There have been many parades in Shoreham over the years. This one occurred on the Fourth of July in 1912. People lined both sides of the street to welcome soldiers, view the floats, and see the town's latest equipment.

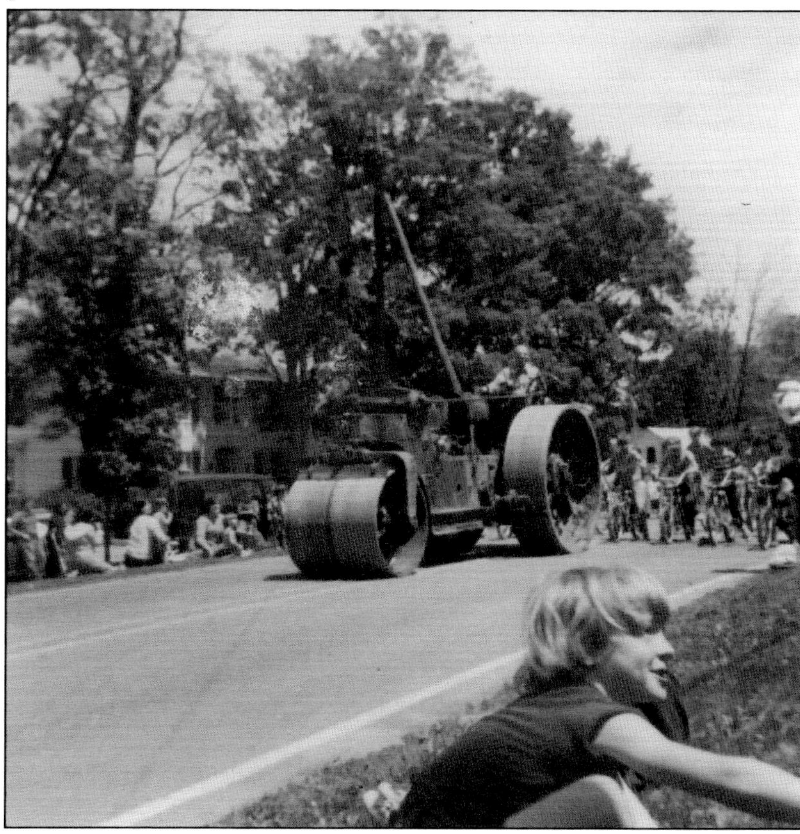

Road foreman Quentin Shackett drives the new town roller in a later Fourth of July parade. (Courtesy of Kirk LaDuke.)

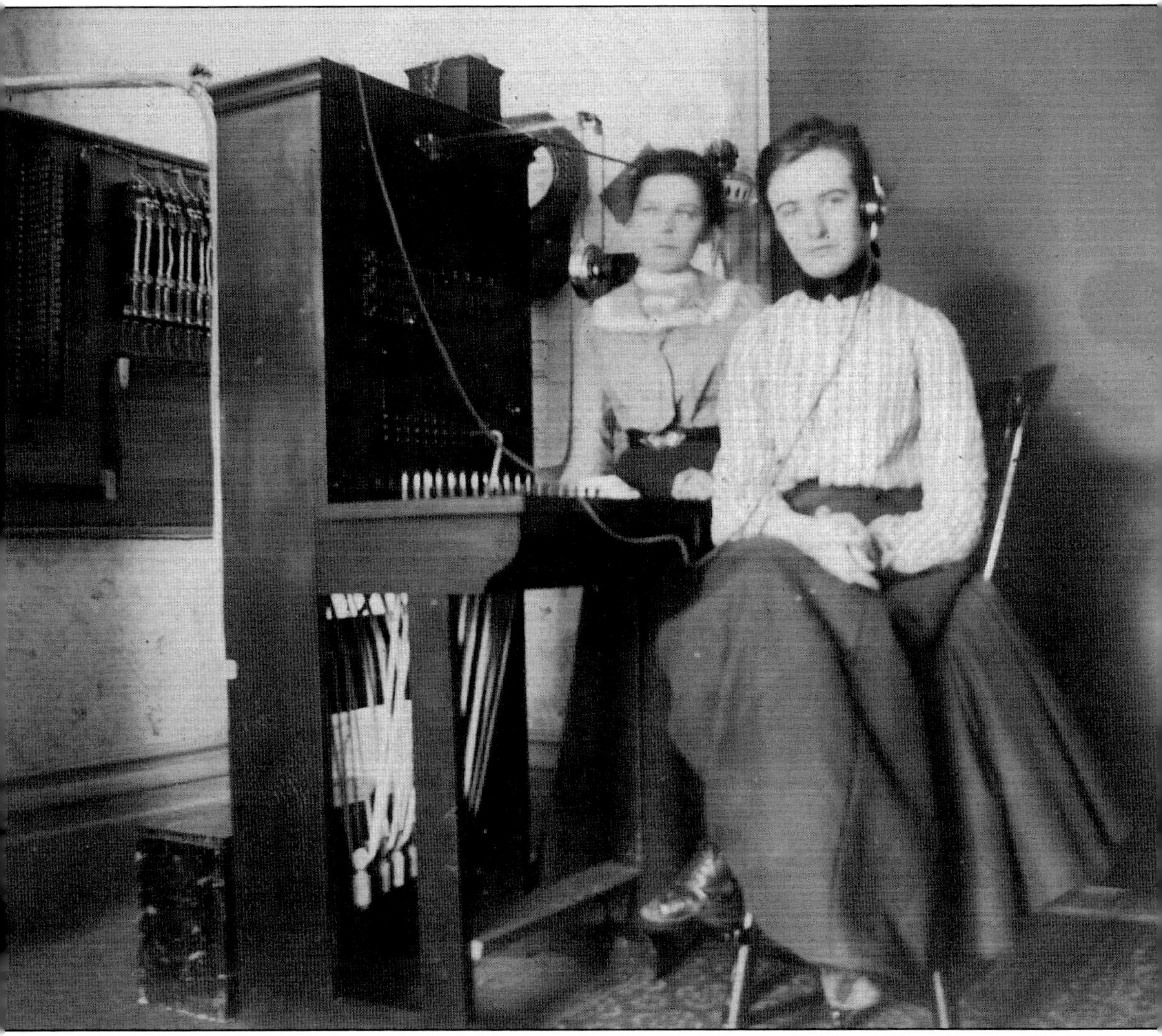

The Shoreham Telephone & Telegraph Company was incorporated in 1894. Standing on the left by the first telephone switchboard of the Shoreham Telephone Company is Mabel (Towner) Wisell, with Elizabeth (Tottingham) Belden sitting next to her. Switchboards like this one were used until 1959, when dial phones came into use. As technology advanced, the Shoreham Telephone Company later added computer DSL lines. In 2012, it was sold to OTT Communications.

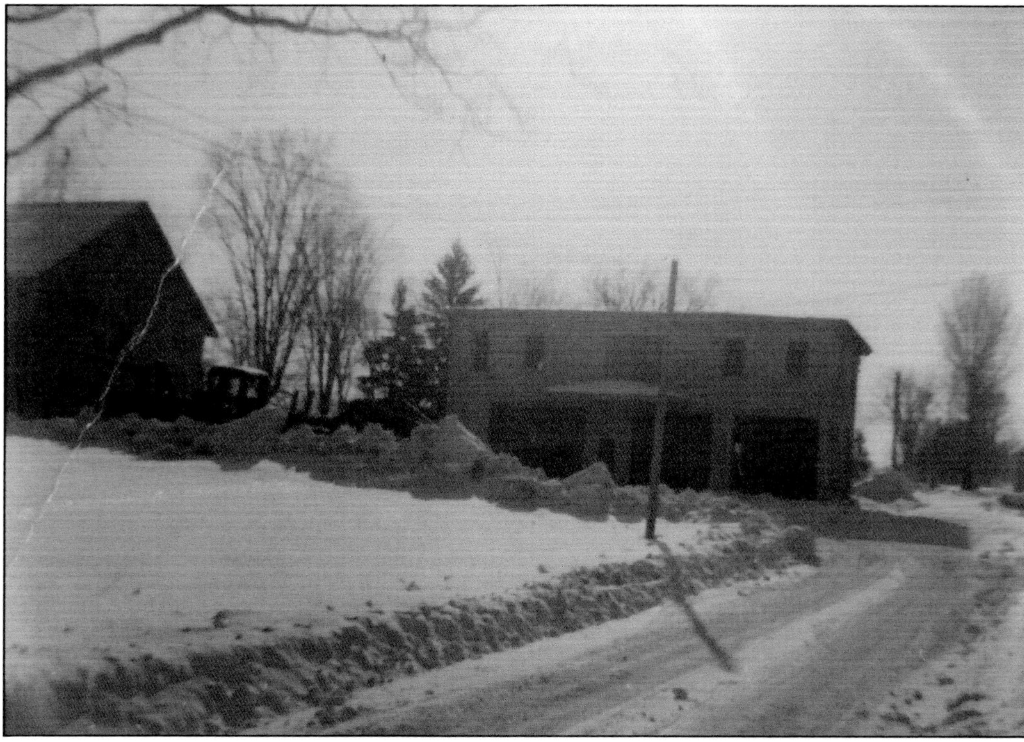

Built for William Langlois's wheelwright shop in the 1800s, this building became the home of the fire and rescue squad in the 1900s. Several fire trucks and the rescue squad rig were housed downstairs in the bays. The upstairs was one large meeting room that held meetings and practice sessions. (Courtesy of Kirk LaDuke.)

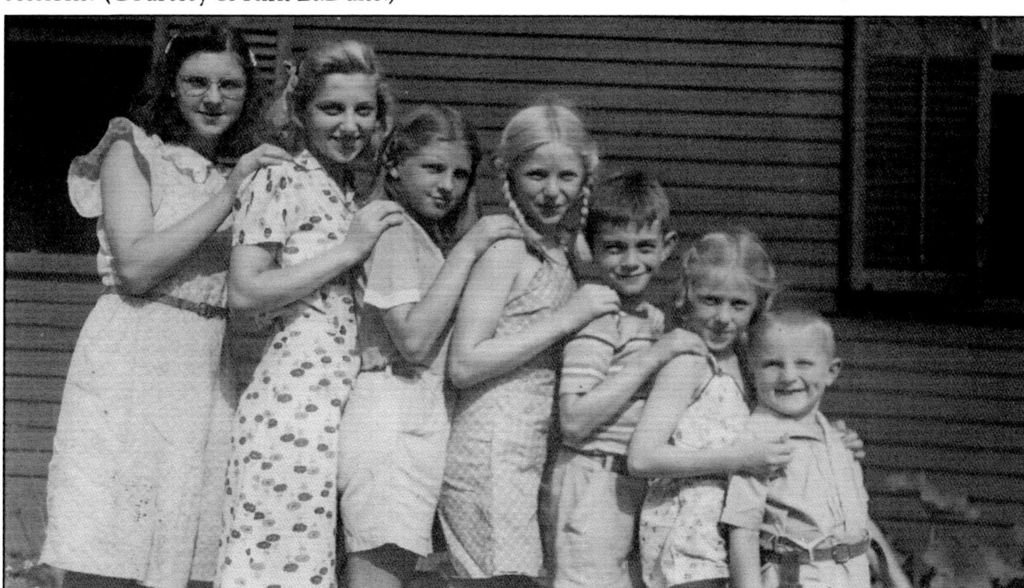

Children in the small village all played together and looked after one another. This group photograph from 1941 shows, from left to right, Beverly Hayden, Jean Dudley, Joyce Hayden, Barbara Dudley, Theodore Sanders, Joanne Dudley, and John Birchard. (Courtesy of Kirk LaDuke.)

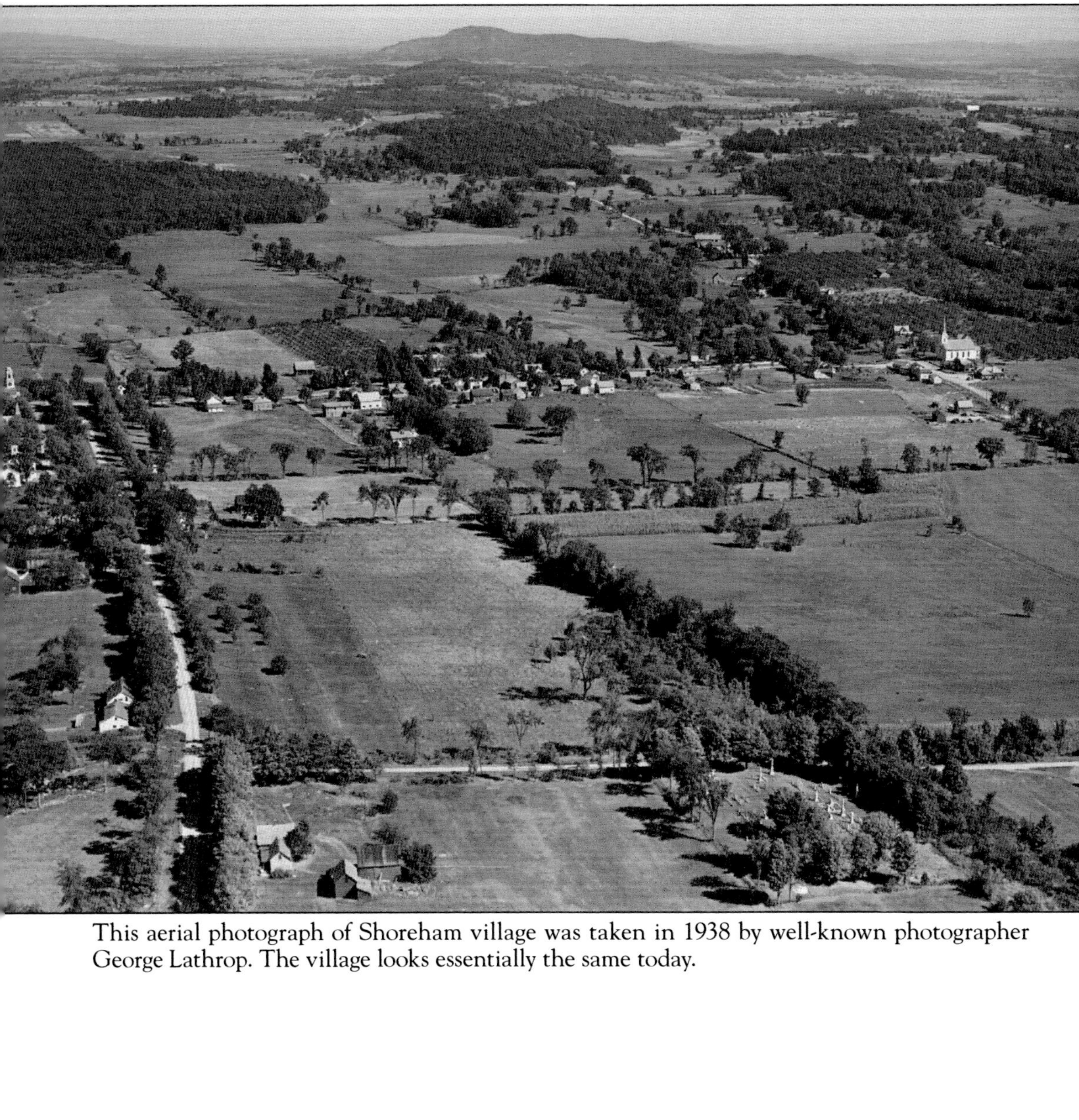

This aerial photograph of Shoreham village was taken in 1938 by well-known photographer George Lathrop. The village looks essentially the same today.

Two

Larrabee's Point

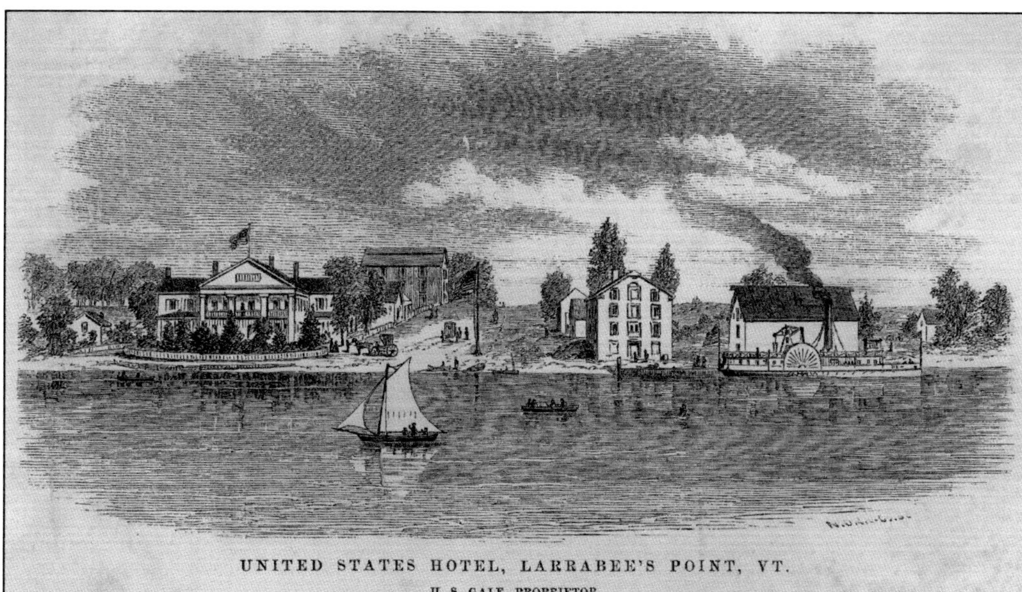

Larrabee's Point provided water transportation access in and out of Shoreham in the 1800s. Guests from urban areas traveled north via the Hudson River to the canal, then to Lake George and Lake Champlain to spend the summer at the elegant United States Hotel. The black marble quarry just south of Larrabee's Point shipped its pure black marble out on barges. The oldest continuously running ferry in the United States goes between Larrabee's Point in Shoreham and Ticonderoga, across the lake in New York.

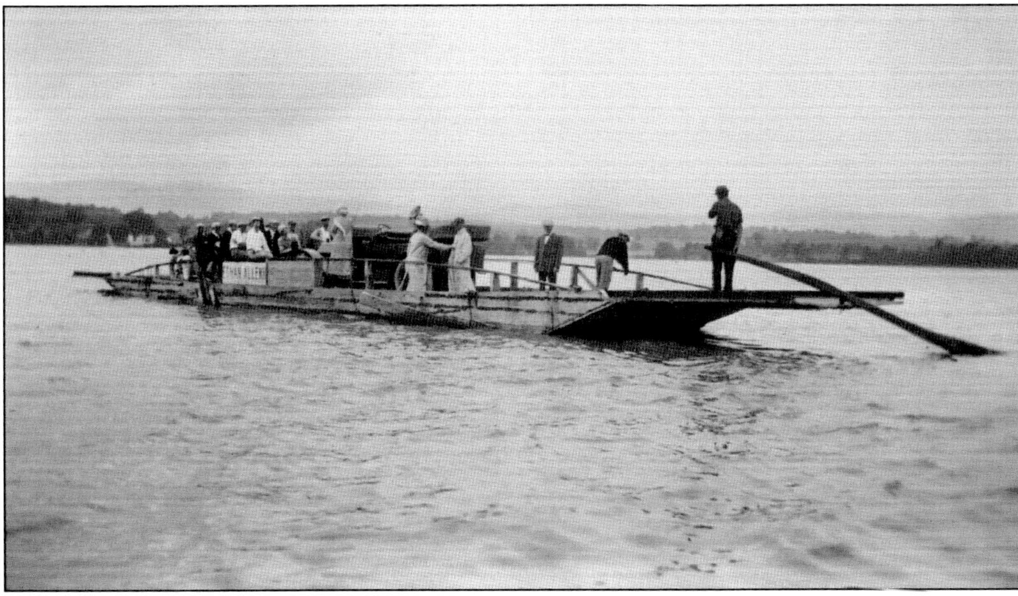

Sail ferries ran between Larrabee's Point and Ticonderoga as early as 1759. This man-powered ferry is seen here in 1912.

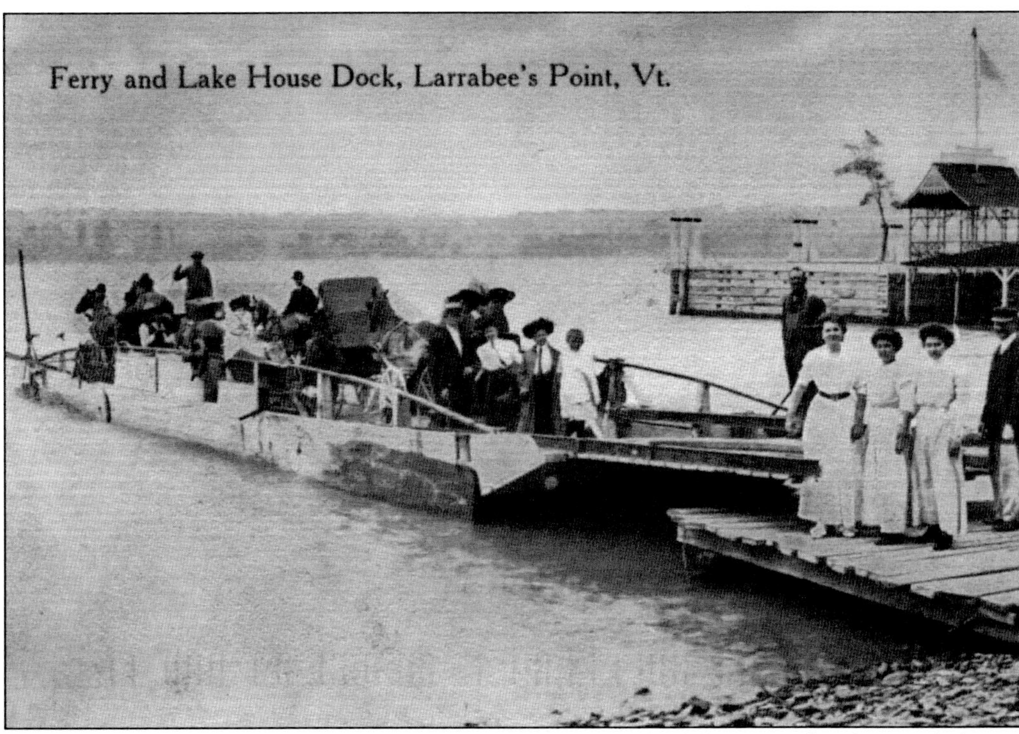

This ferry takes guests from the United States Hotel across the lake. Note the elegant shelter on the dock, which was built by the hotel to shade waiting passengers.

When coal-powered steam engines became more widespread, the ferry adapted to this new technology for a faster trip across the lake.

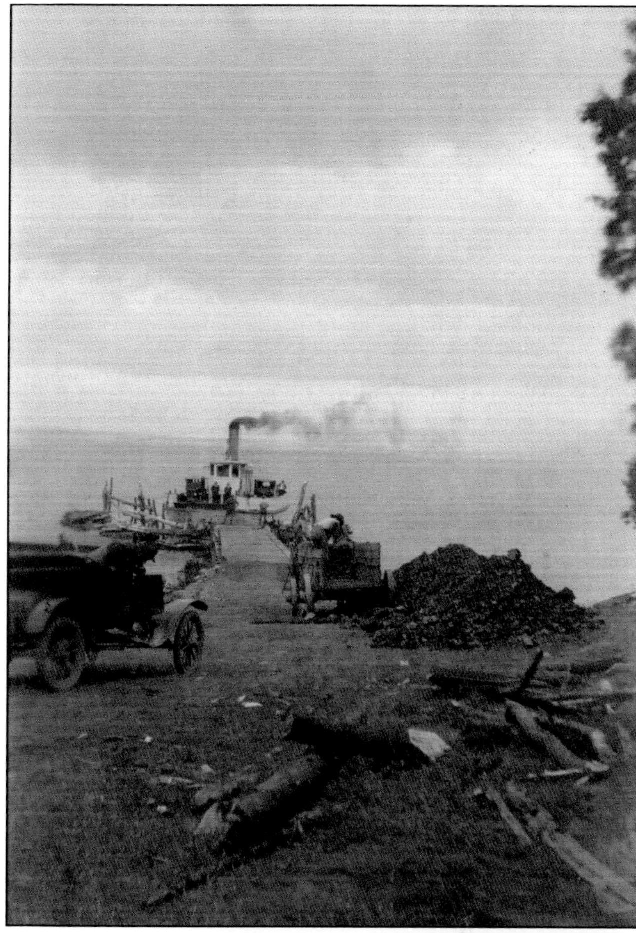

In 1952, when this photograph was taken, the ferry was powered by a tugboat fastened to the south side of the barge. This made for more reliable crossings.

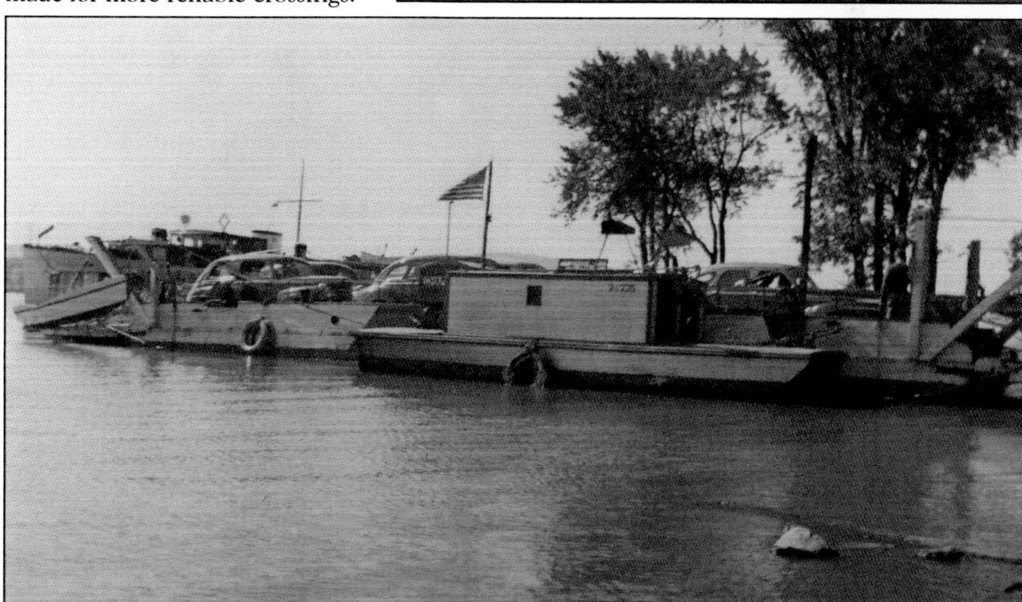

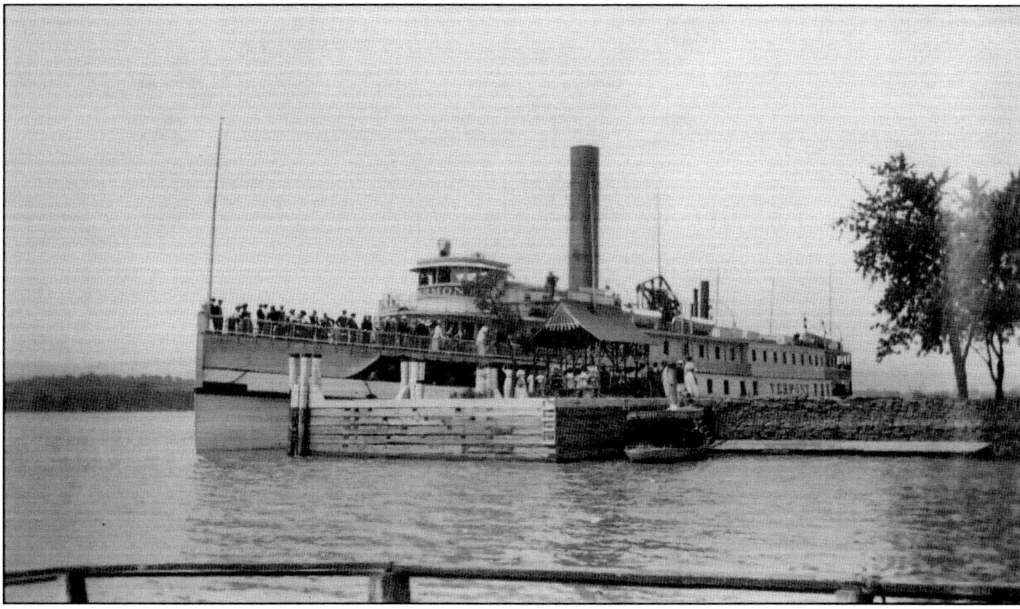

The larger steamships that traveled Lake Champlain stopped at Larrabee's Point, bringing folks from Burlington, Plattsburgh, and as far north as Montreal. This photograph of the *Vermont* was taken in August 1914.

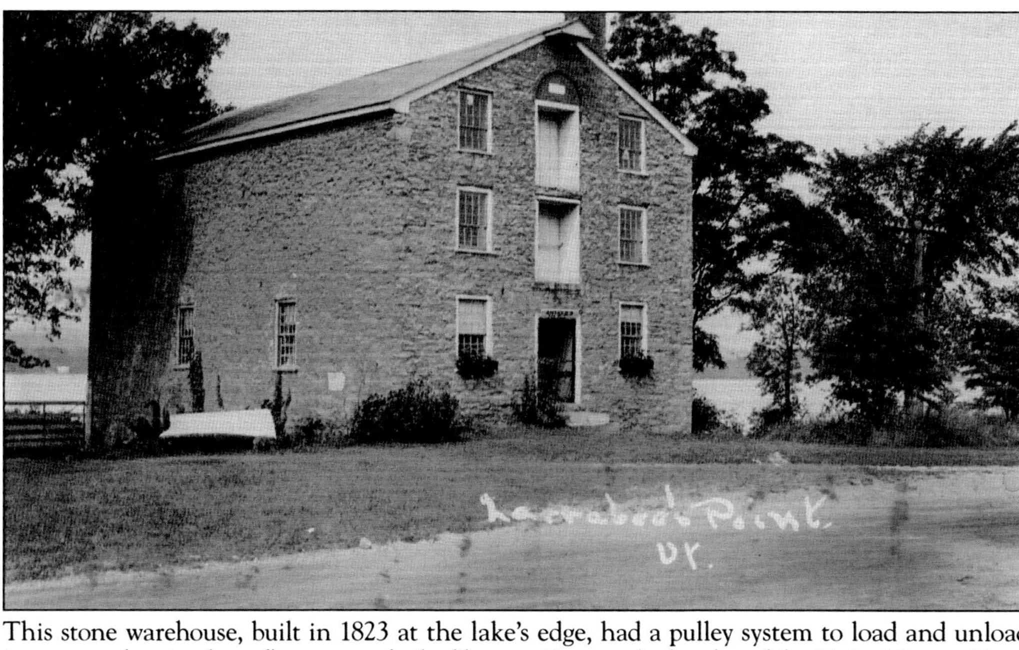

This stone warehouse, built in 1823 at the lake's edge, had a pulley system to load and unload items stored on its three floors onto docked barges. During the heyday of the United States Hotel at Larrabee's Point, there was a casino on the ground floor run by the hotel. Later, the stone building was home to an antique shop.

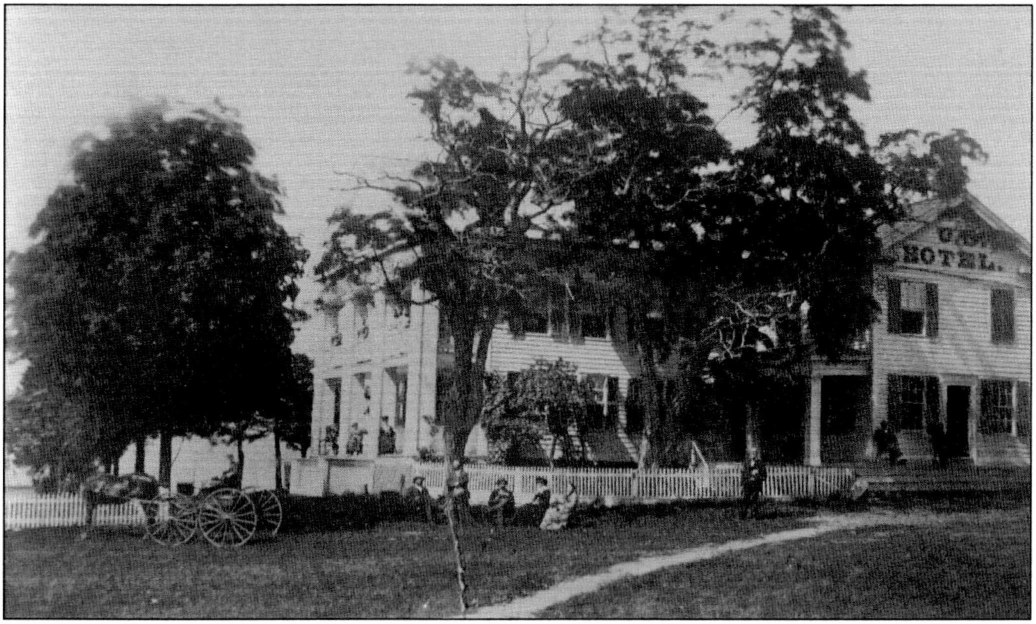

There had been a series of taverns at Larrabee's Point since before the American Revolution. The elegant United States Hotel was built on the old tavern site by Samuel H. Holley and Benjamin Bowen Brown in 1840.

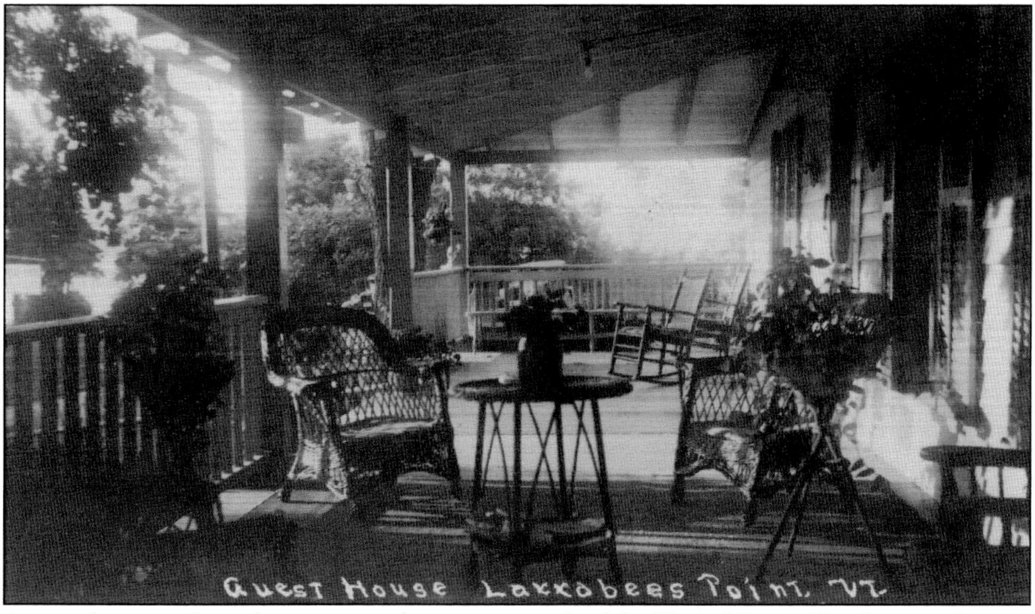

Across the street from the stone warehouse, just south of the United States Hotel, was a pleasant guesthouse for overflow guests from the hotel.

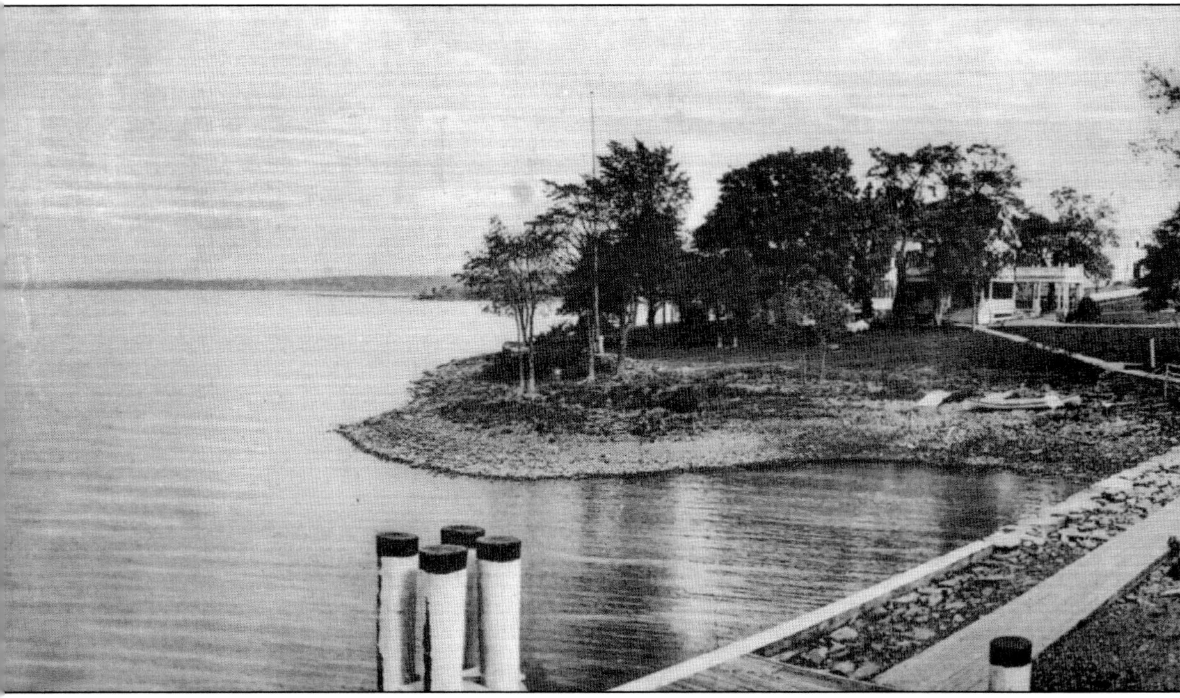

This double postcard taken from a boat just off Larrabee's Point gives a clear picture of how the point

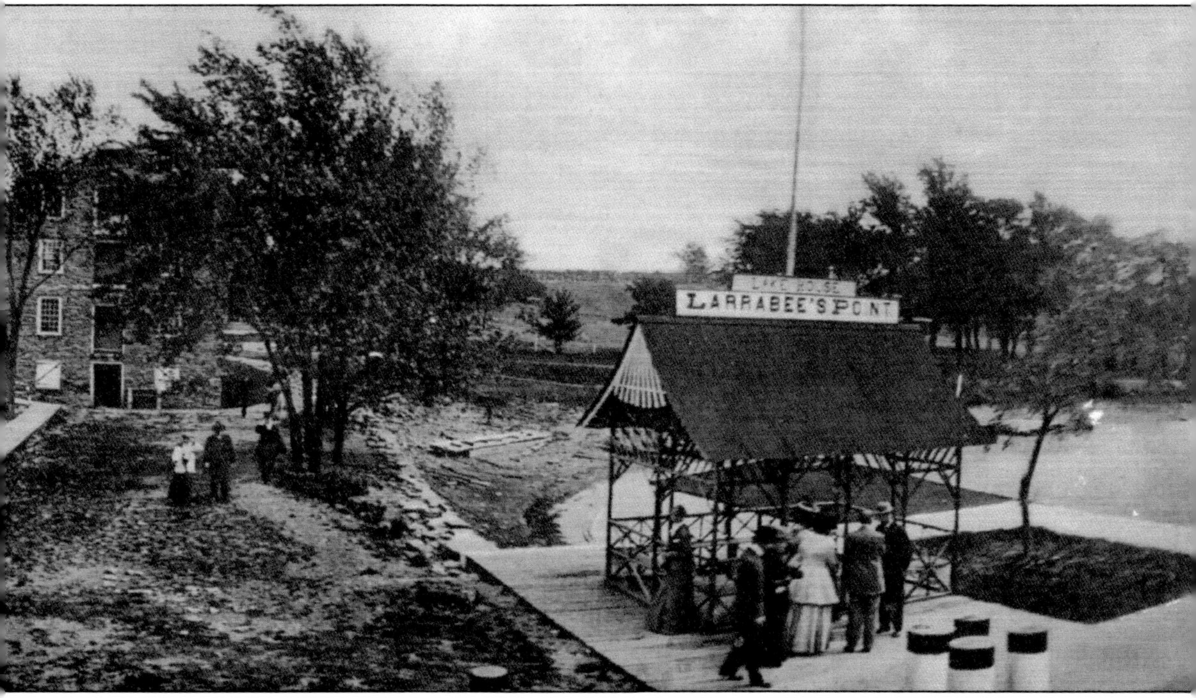

of land juts out into Lake Champlain, as well as the amenities available for summer guests.

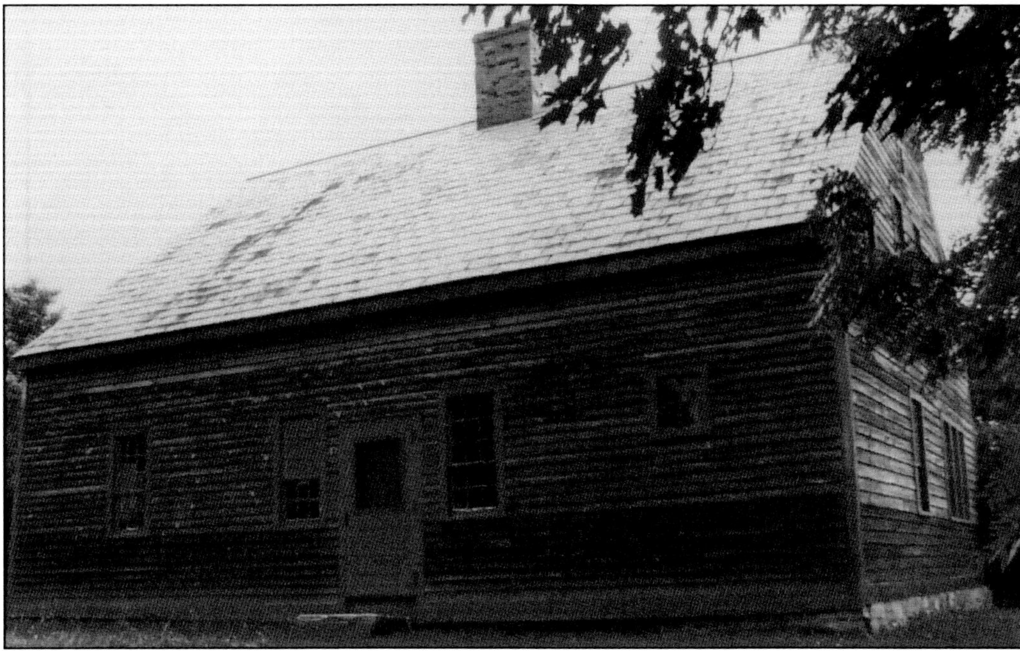

The block house at Hand's Cove, just north of Larrabee's Point, is believed to be the oldest house in Shoreham. It was the rendezvous point for Ethan Allen and his officers in the Revolutionary War, who rowed across the lake before dawn on the morning of May 10, 1775, to take Fort Ticonderoga from the British. It is called the block house because the west wall, facing the lake, is constructed of 10-inch-square blocks of wood to deflect arrows and bullets that might attack it from the lake.

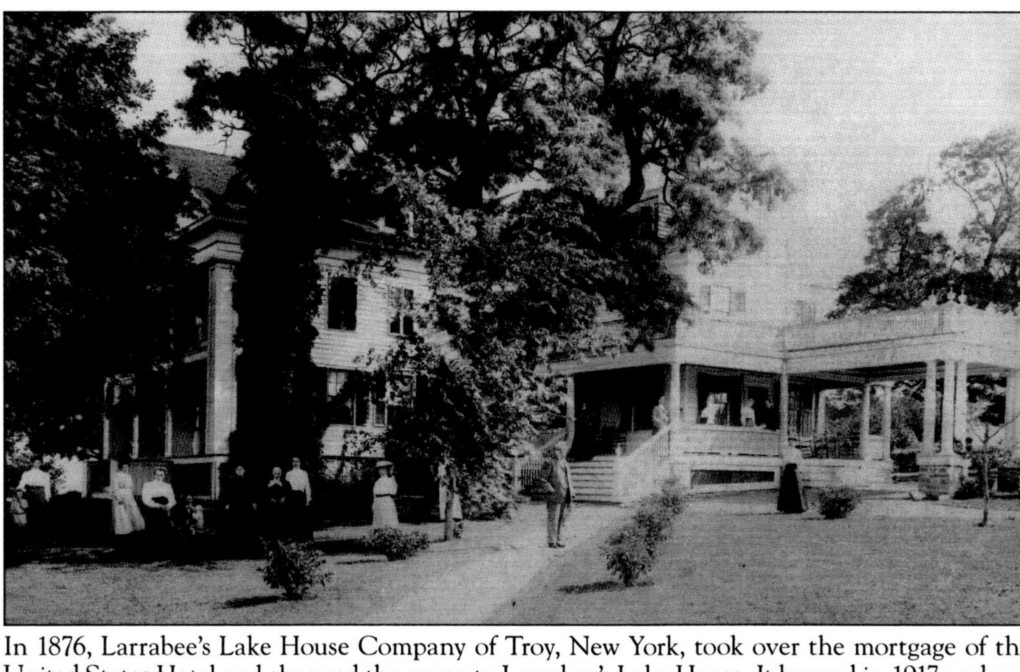

In 1876, Larrabee's Lake House Company of Troy, New York, took over the mortgage of the United States Hotel and changed the name to Larrabee's Lake House. It burned in 1917 and was never rebuilt.

Three

Richville

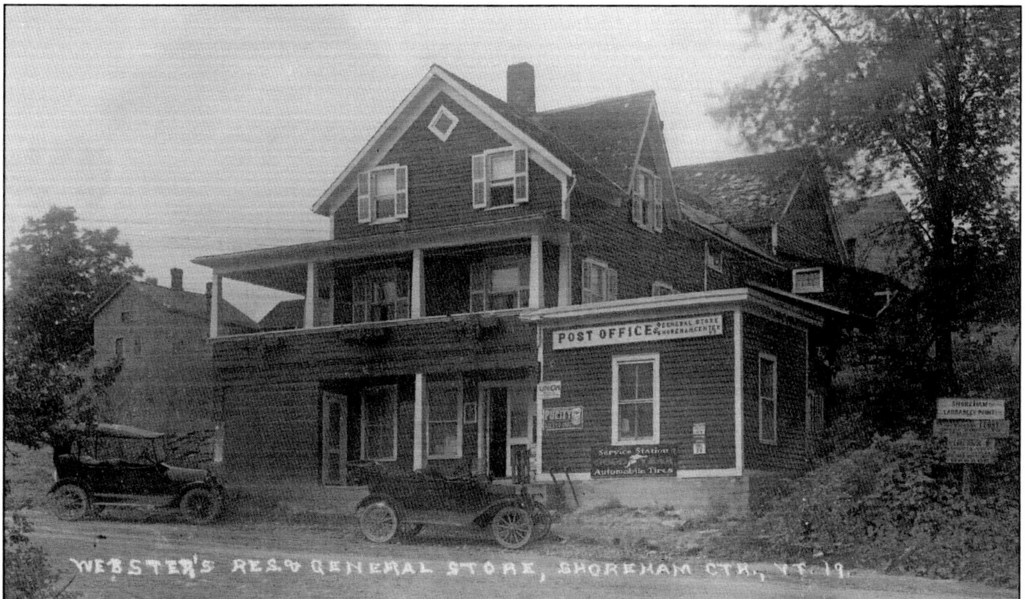

Richville was a small hamlet in Shoreham first settled by the Rich family. There was a period of 20 years in the early 1900s when mail delivery was sent to Richville, New York, so, to prevent confusion, the post office name was changed to Shoreham Center. In the early 1930s, it reverted to Richville. This general store was run by Charles Rich, later by Henry Ward, and then by the Websters, whose name is seen here.

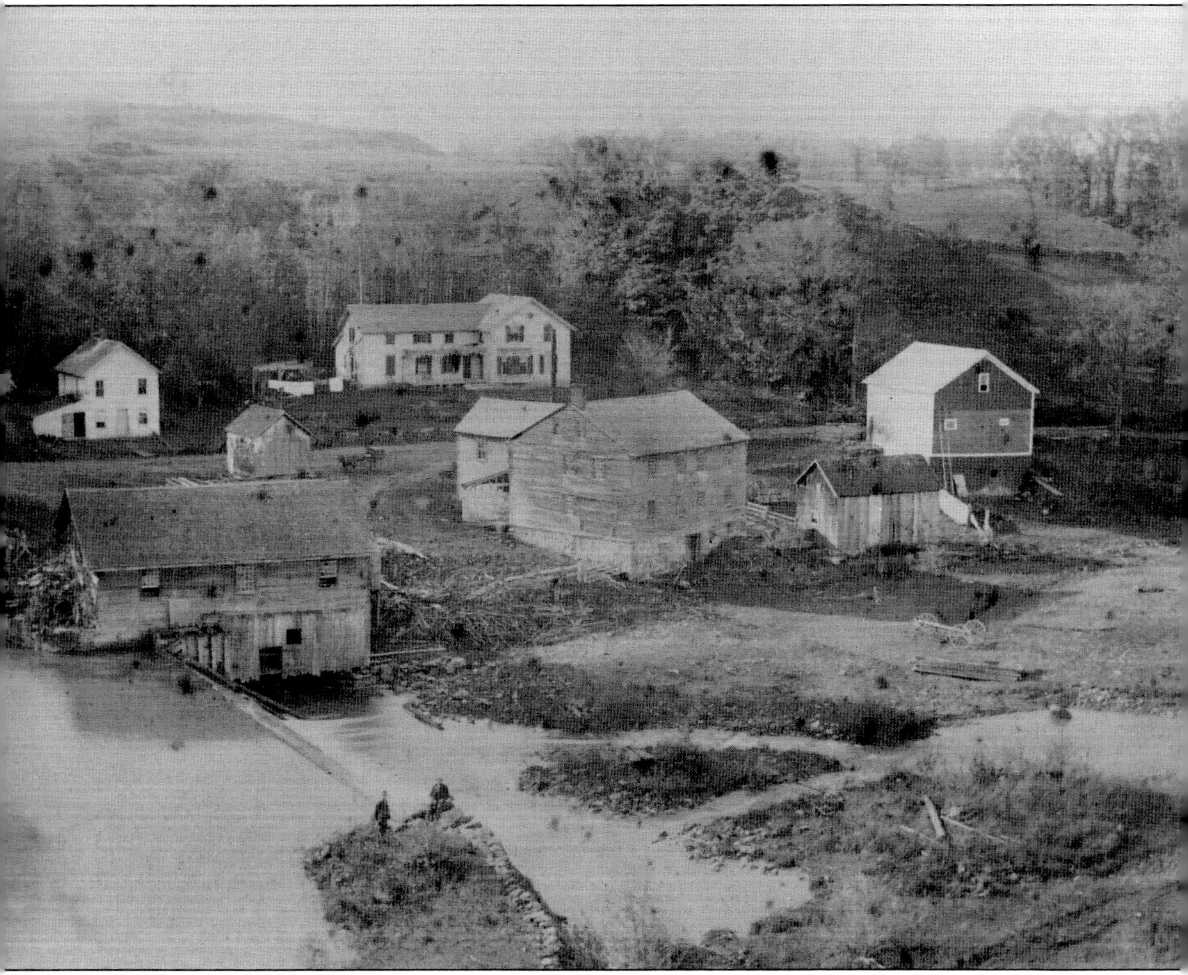

Edgar Newell (1844–1917) ran a sawmill on the Lemon Fair River. His father, Edmund, a cooper, lived next door and ran the butter tub factory in conjunction with the sawmill.

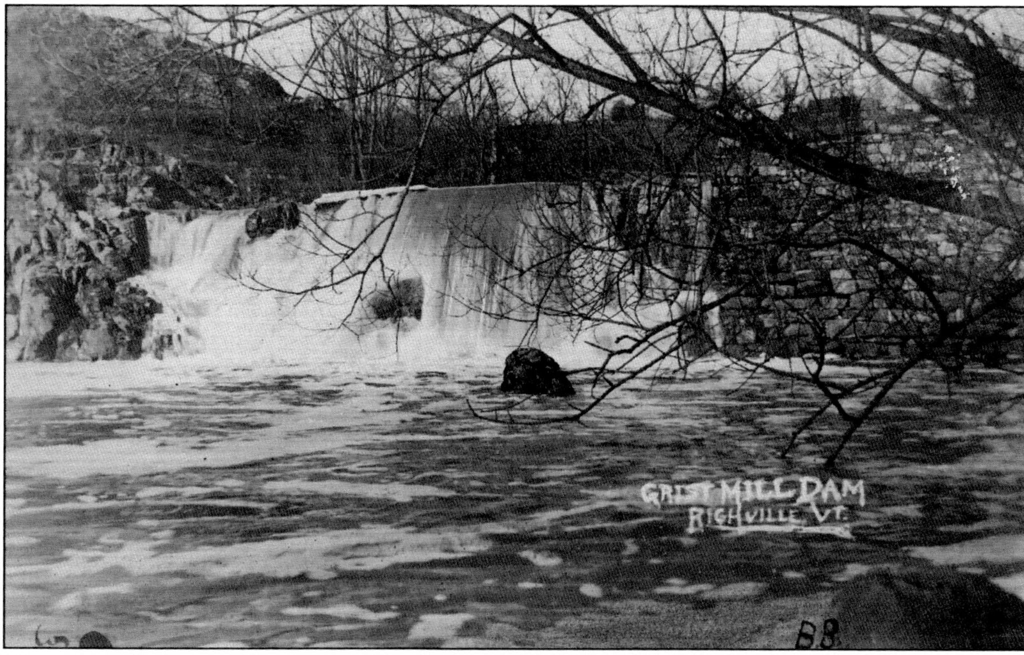

The gristmill dam on the Lemon Fair River in Richville controlled waters for the gristmill and butter tub factory below on the river.

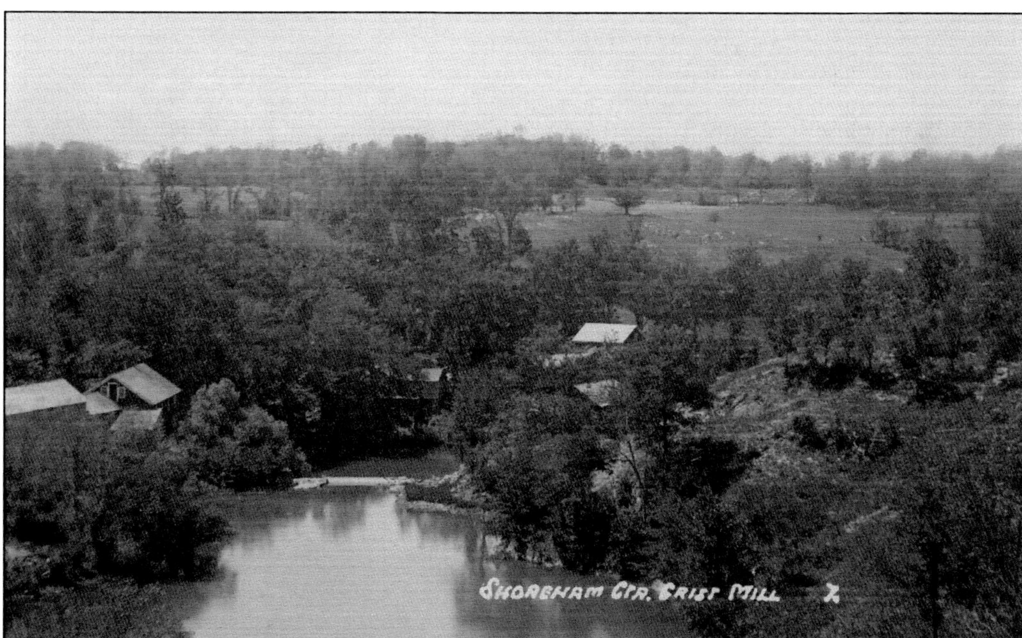

The gristmill on the Lemon Fair River is seen here. From 1798 to 1818, the site was an iron foundry run by Charles Rich. In 1818, Rich changed the machinery in his foundry to make a carding mill, satisfying the needs of a growing number of sheep farmers.

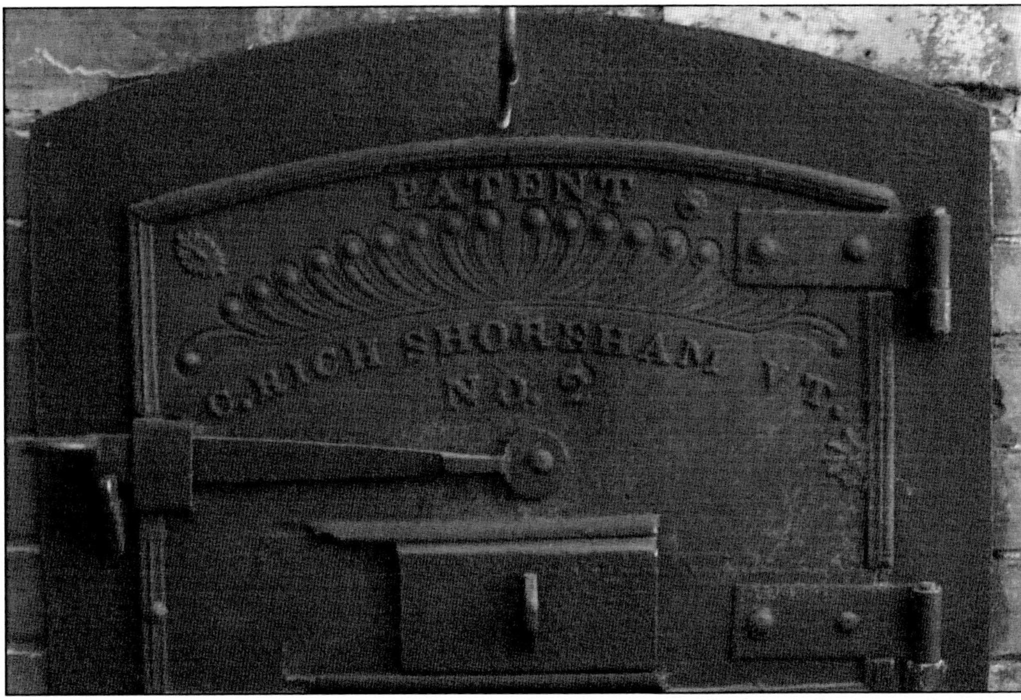

In his iron foundry, Charles Rich made doors for beehive ovens, which were built into fireplaces, as replacements for the scorched wooden doors in use at the time. (Courtesy of the author.)

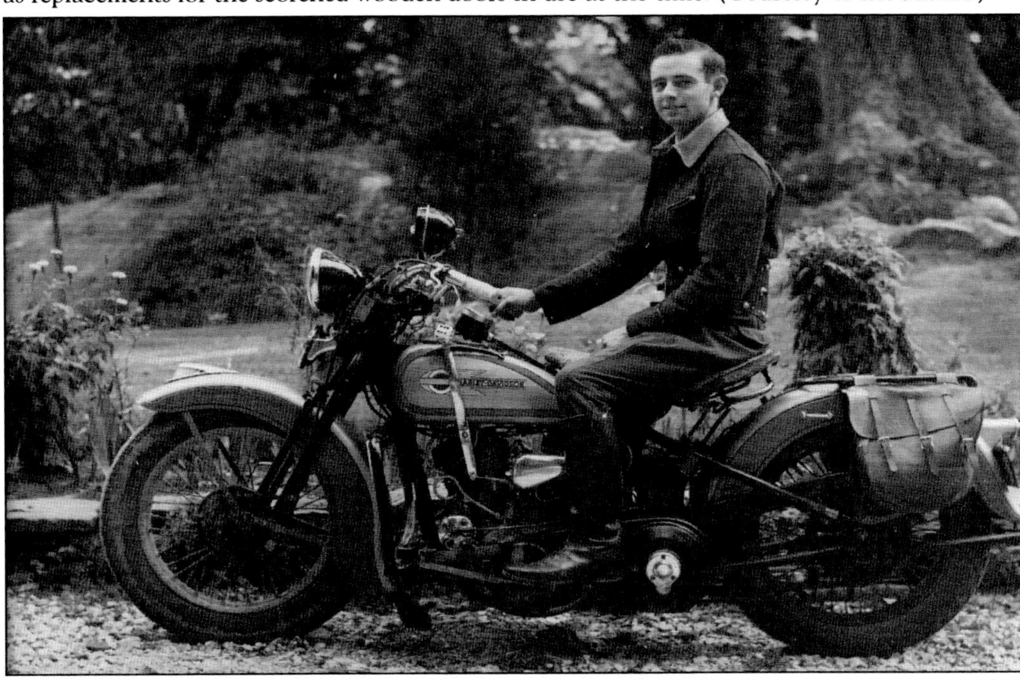

Thomas Rich Buttolph is seen here on his 1936 motorcycle. Buttolph was a direct descendant of Charles Rich (1771–1824), who was a member of the Vermont House of Representatives from 1800 to 1811 and a US congressman from 1813 to 1815 and 1817 to 1824. (Courtesy of Halfway House Restaurant.)

Henry C. Ward (1872–1943) was a merchant in Richville and had a post office in his store. He was responsible for changing the name of Richville to Shoreham Center to avoid confusion with mail delivery. It reverted back to Richville in 1932. He also built the Richville Creamery, across the road from the store.

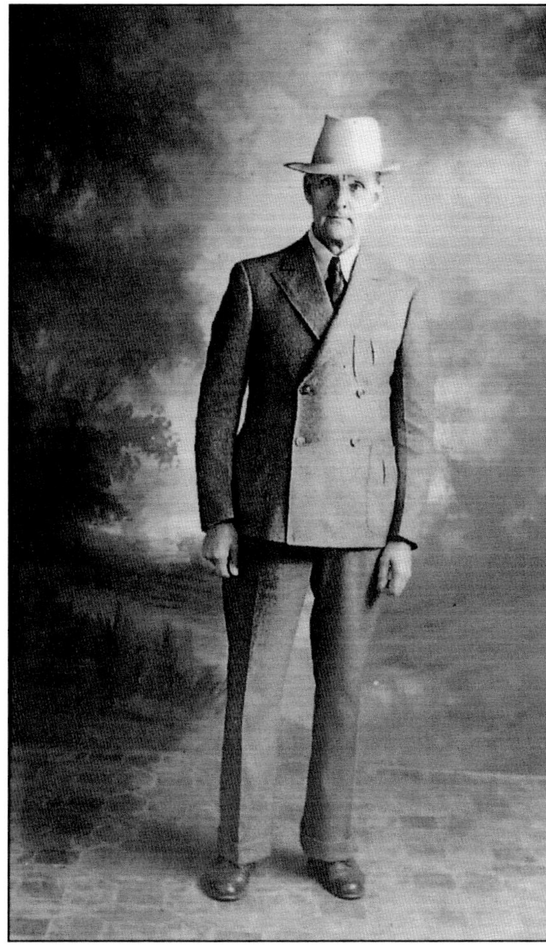

The Richville Creamery (below) had a huge boiler in the basement for sterilizing equipment. The first floor held equipment for making butter, and the upper floor was a community hall reached by an outside staircase. A kitchen and dining room were at one end, a stage was in the center, and it featured separate coatrooms for men and women. The rest was a large room with a dance floor. Dinner dances with live orchestras were held every Saturday night.

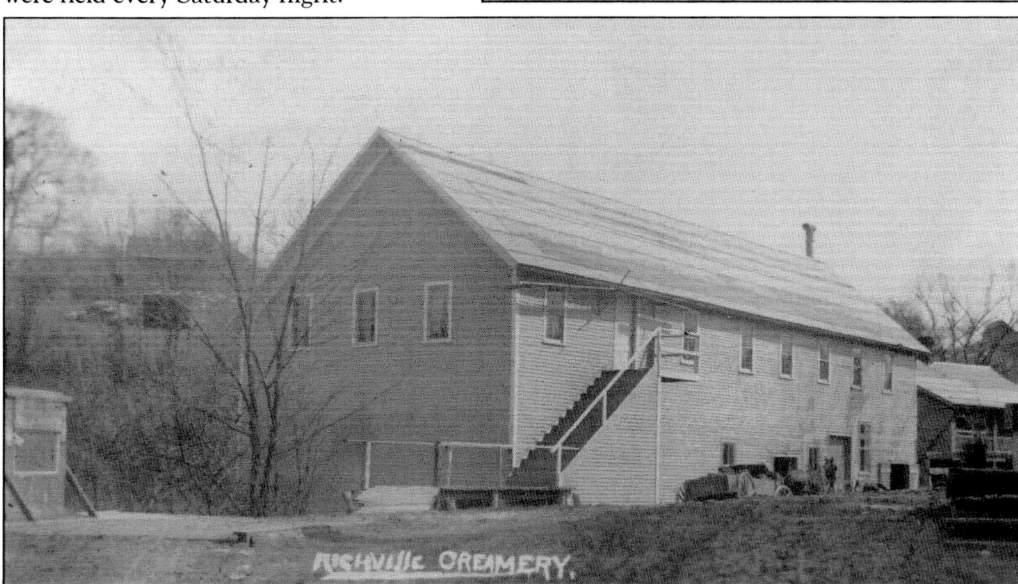

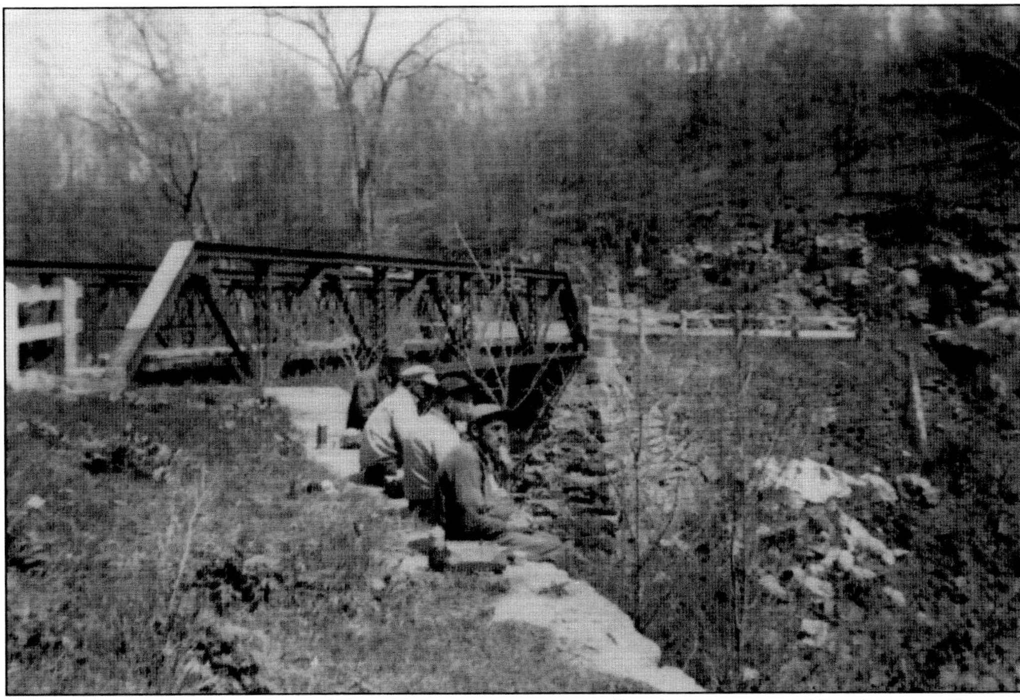

The old Richville Bridge over the Lemon Fair River needed replacement, and funds were allocated in 1962. Seen here contemplating removing the existing bridge as they eat their lunches are, from left to right, Buster Edwards, John Elithorpe, Paul Blair, and Harry Duffany.

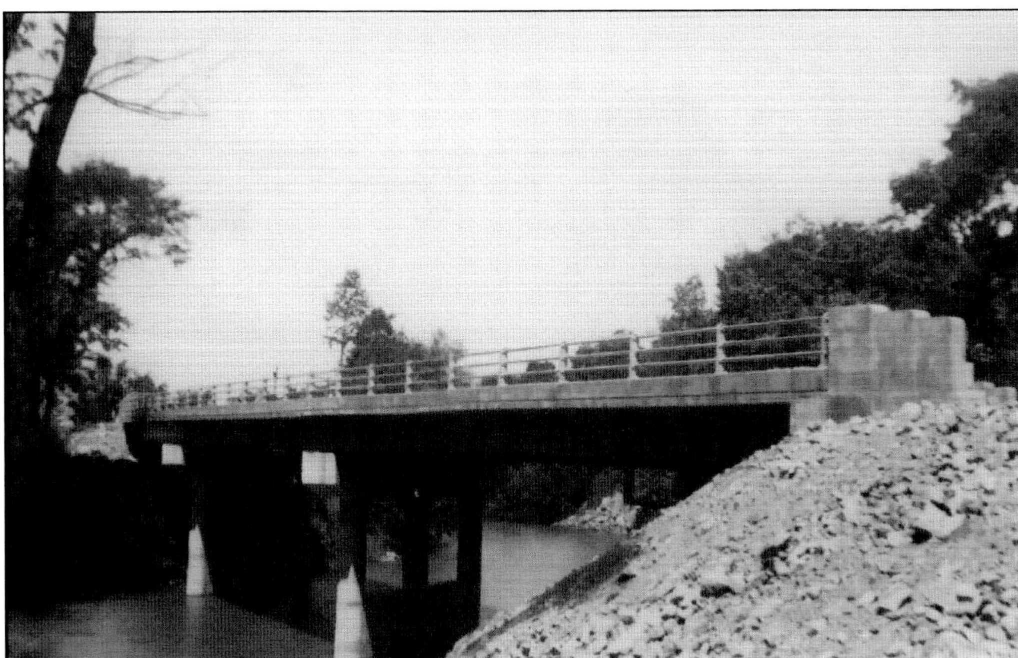

The completed bridge was much safer than the old bridge, able to bear the heavier loads of larger trucks and traffic.

Four

East Shoreham

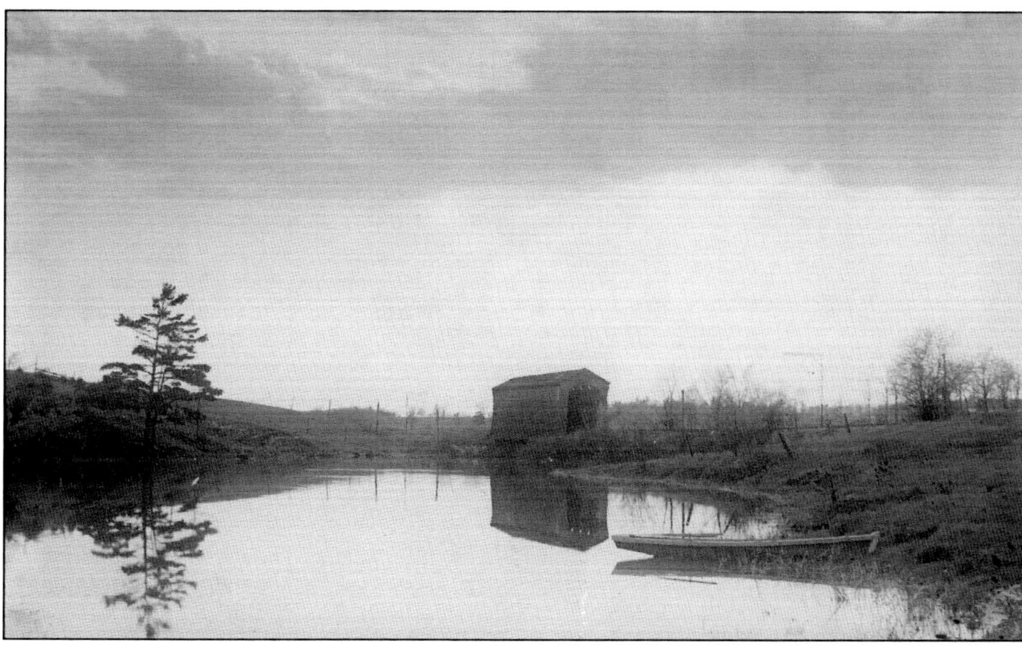

This covered railroad bridge was built in 1871 to allow trains to cross the Lemon Fair River. The Howe truss bridge is 109 feet long and 20 feet wide. Mail trains passed through without stopping, picking up and leaving bags of mail on poles with hooks outside of the station house. The last run was on May 21, 1951.

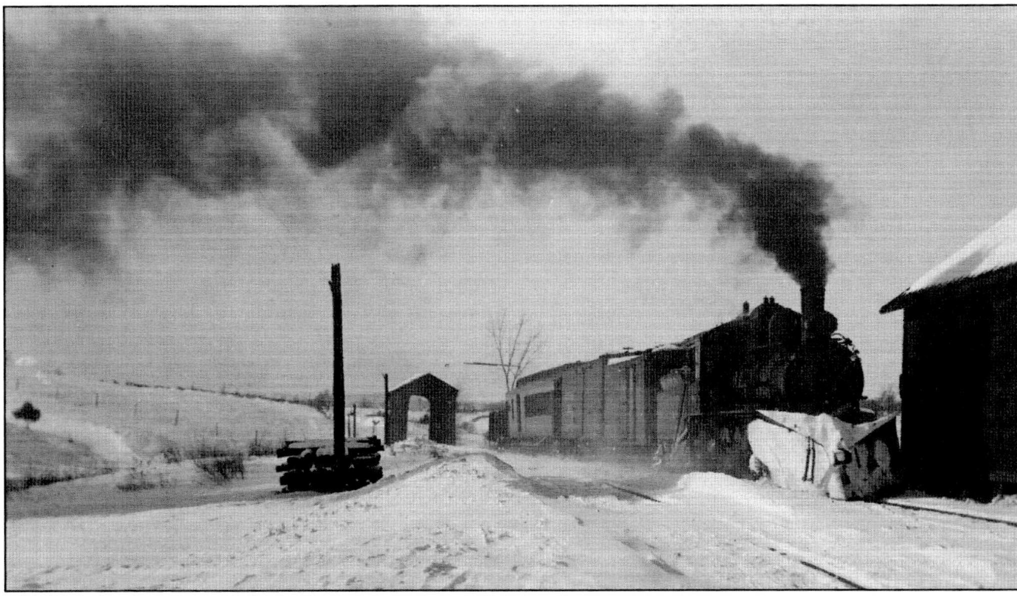

The Addison Branch train ran from Port Henry, New York, to Crown Point, to Ticonderoga, and then over a floating railroad bridge traversing Lake Champlain, with a barge swinging out to let boat traffic through. Reaching Vermont at Larrabee's Point in Shoreham, it then went to Orwell, East Shoreham, and Whiting, and ended at Leicester Junction. In the afternoon, it reversed the route, traveling back to Port Henry.

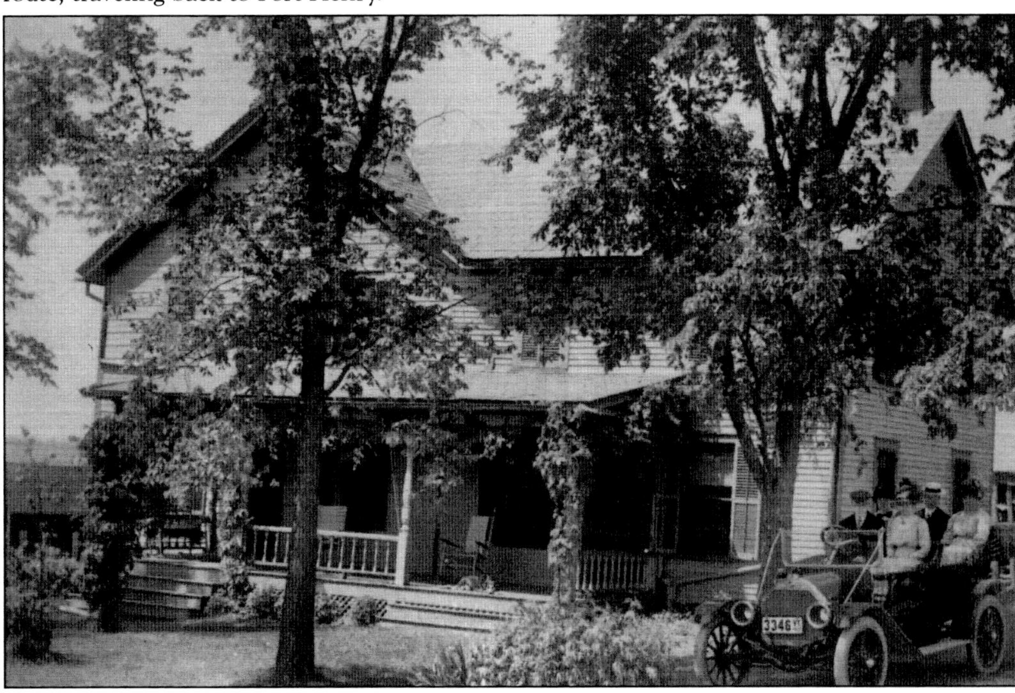

The Delano house was right next to the Shoreham depot. For many years, mail was left by the train and distributed from here. Clara (Brookins) Delano and then her son Arthur Brookins Delano served as the East Shoreham postmaster until that post office was transferred to Shoreham village in 1936.

Five generations of the Delano family posed for this photograph in 1908. They are, from left to right, (seated) Flora Delano and her mother, Adaline (Jennings) Delano (holding Doris Delano); (standing) Earl Delano and George Delano.

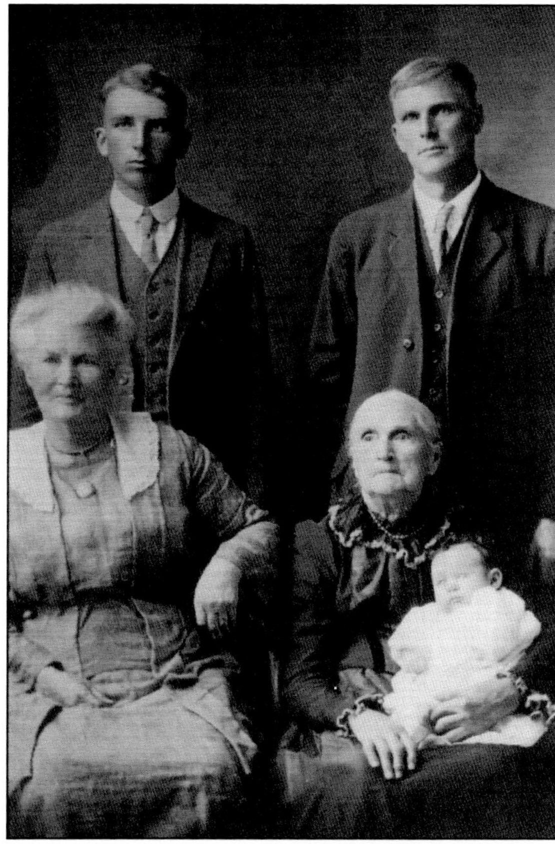

Below, an amazing party of hunters, dogs, and deer poses for a photograph at the Delano's hunting camp near the Lemon Fair River.

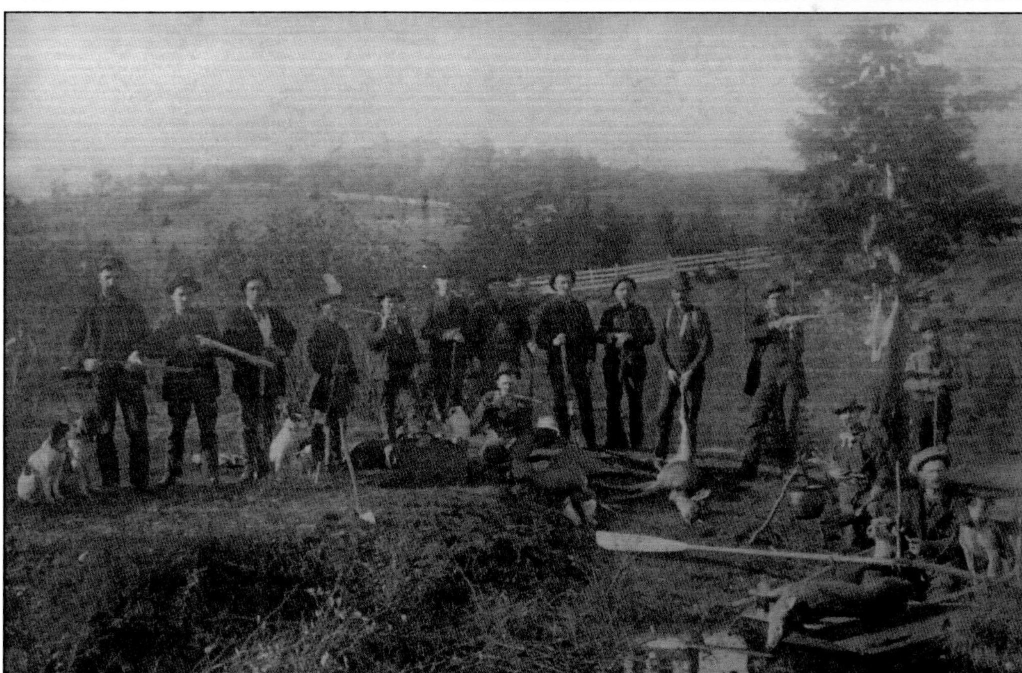

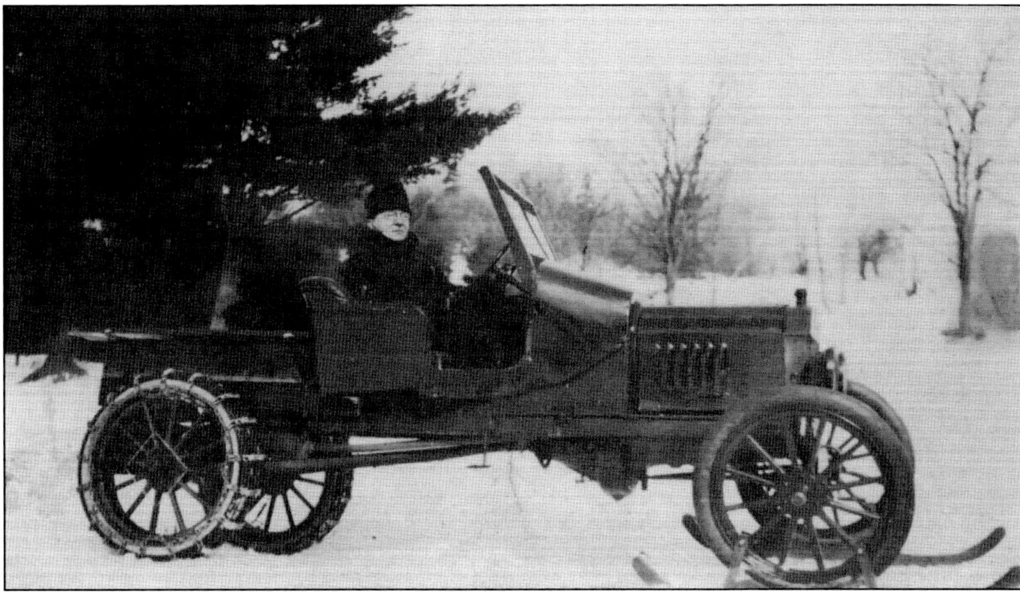

Adrian Birchard served as rural delivery mailman in East Shoreham for many years. In winter, he outfitted his automobile with skis in the front and chains on the rear wheels to traverse the hills. It must have been a chilly ride.

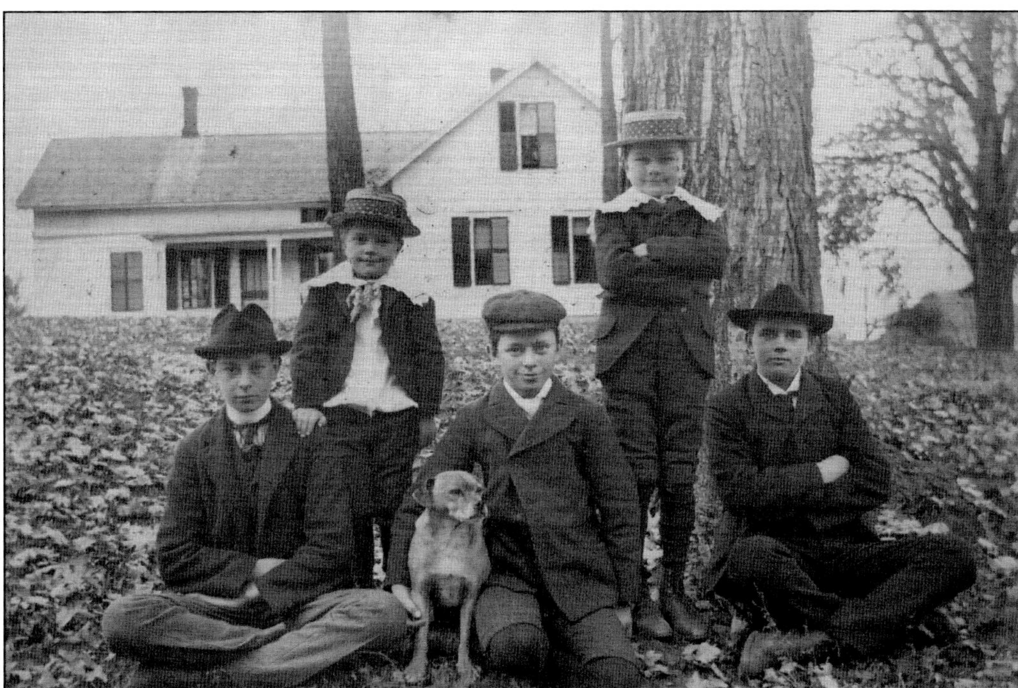

A group of East Shoreham cousins poses for a photograph around 1900. They are, from left to right, Herbert Treadway, Carl Birchard, Pug the dog, Raymond Birchard, Rollin Birchard, and Harry Birchard.

Five

Other Hamlets and Residents

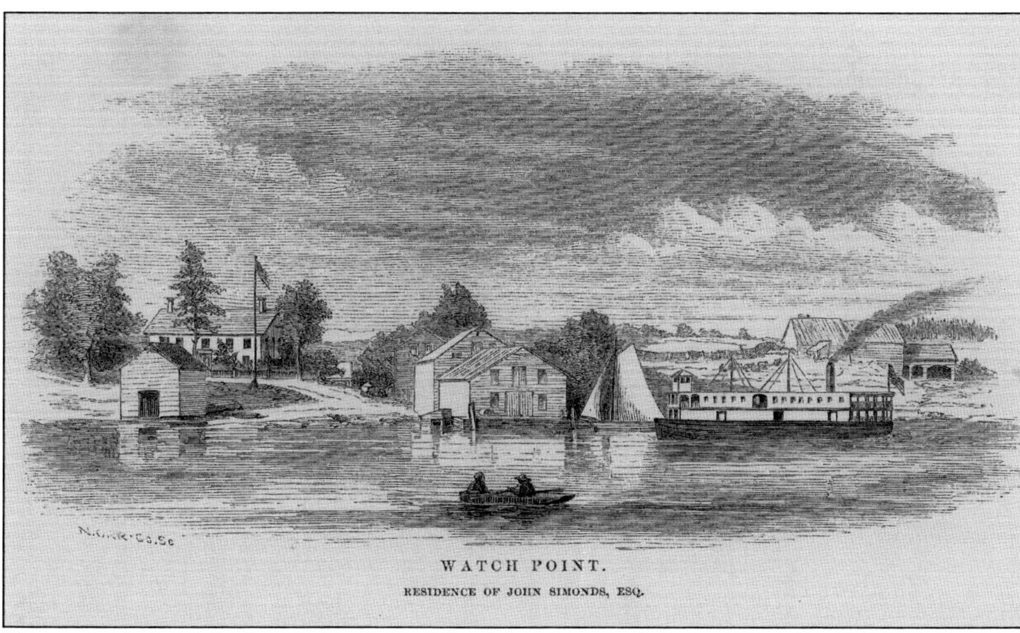

The once-thriving little community at Watch Point included a meat-packing plant and a store for local residents.

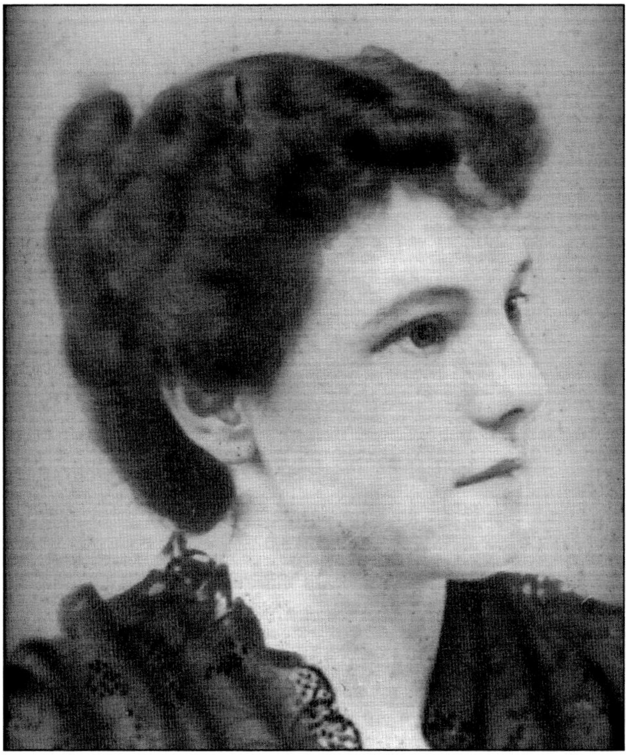

Catherine MacVicker (Hay) Lapham (1847–1921) was a farm wife and mother of five. She was one of the main organizers of the construction of the Episcopal church on the corner of Lapham's Bay Road and Basin Harbor Road. (Courtesy of H. Kent Wright III.)

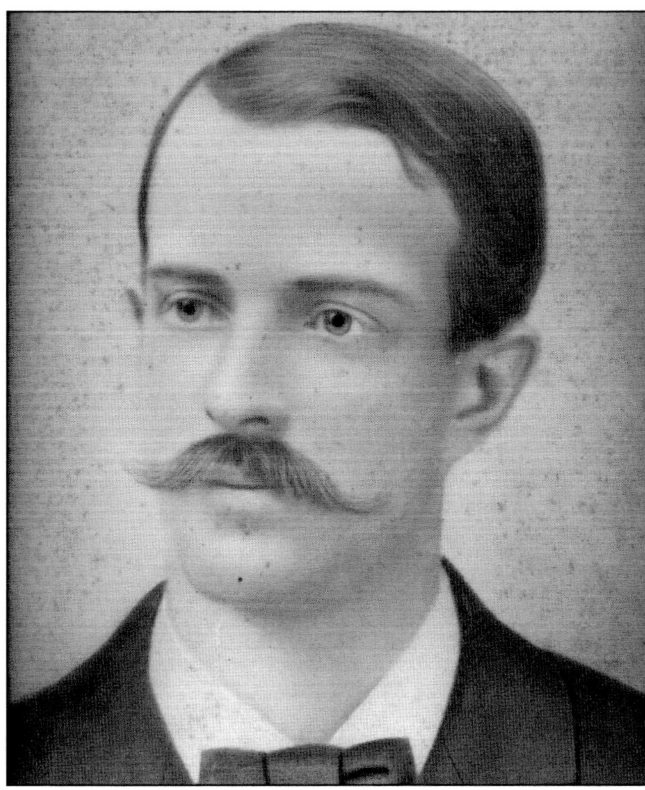

Horace Lapham II (1840–1915) was married to Catherine Hay. They farmed near Watch Point, by the lake. During the Civil War, he served as a corporal in Company K, 1st Vermont Cavalry, from June 29, 1864, to February 13, 1865. (Courtesy of H. Kent Wright III.)

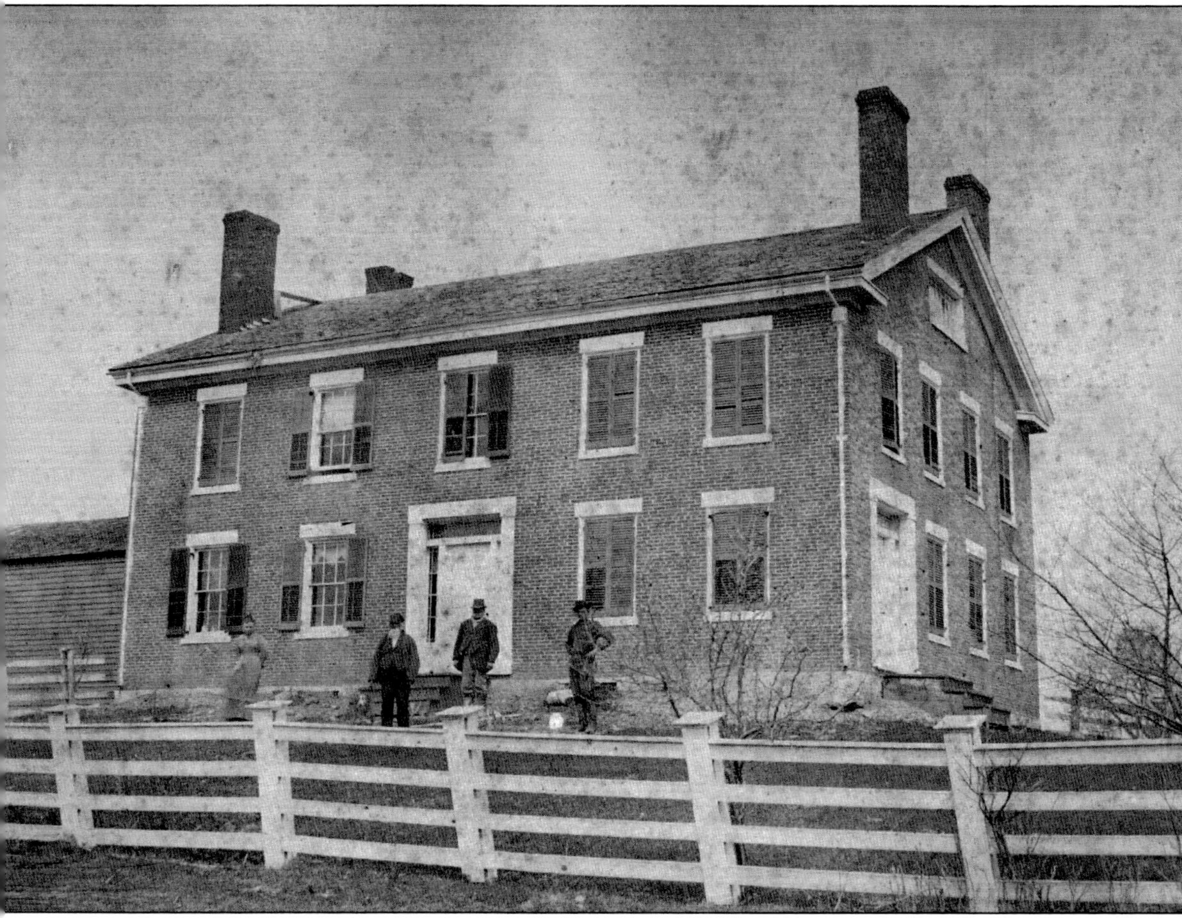

The Lapham farmhouse was at the west end of Lapham's Bay Road. Here, standing out front from left to right, are Catherine (Hay) Lapham; her father, Archibald Hay; Horace Lapham II; and their son Solon Francis Lapham. (Courtesy of H. Kent Wright III.)

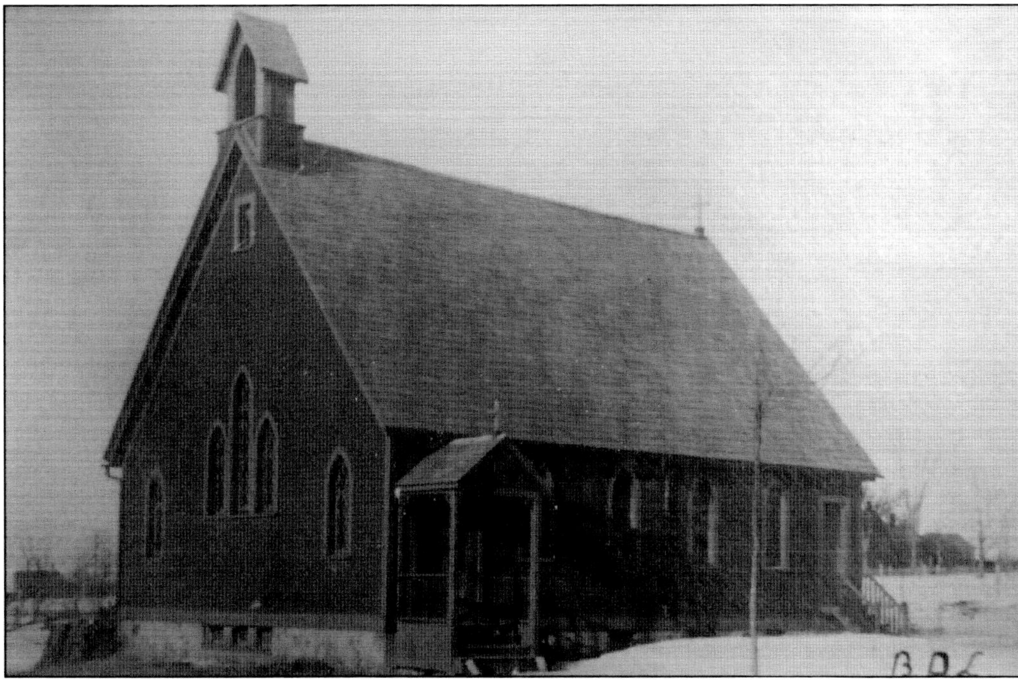

The Episcopal All Saint's Chapel was built in 1900 on land donated by John Holmes, who was also the contractor. Regular services were discontinued in 1950. The church was eventually torn down, and parts of it were used to build a chapel in South Burlington. All that remains today is the small cemetery that stood to the north of the church.

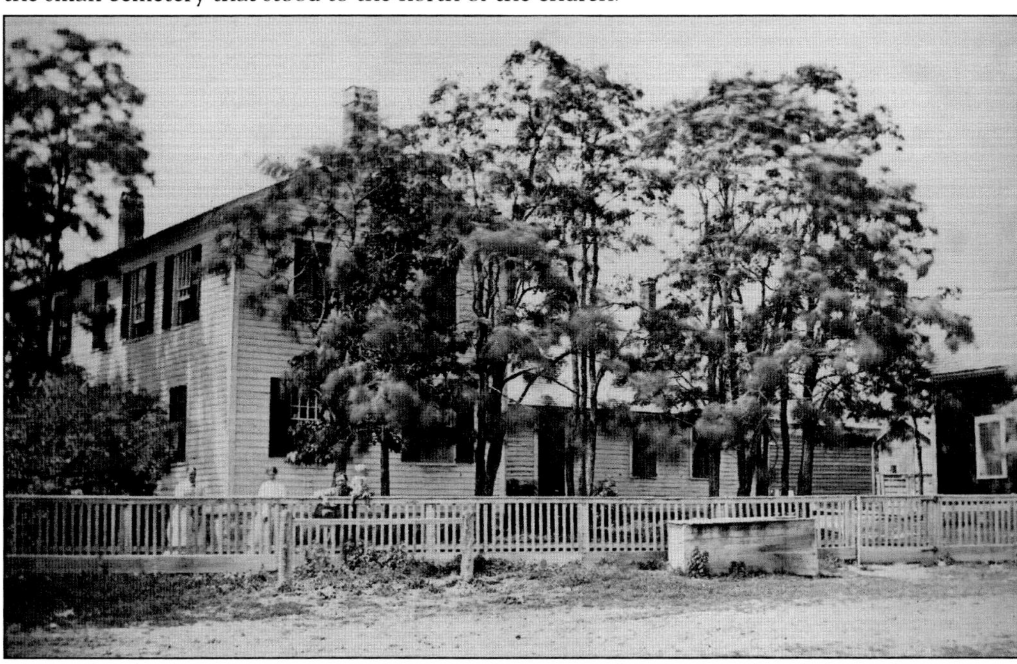

The Callender house, on Cream Hill, is seen here around 1850. Standing behind the fence are, from left to right, Sarah (Smith) Callender, the widow of Noah Callender; her son Clark Callender; his wife Eliza (Wicker); and their son Gustavius A. Callender.

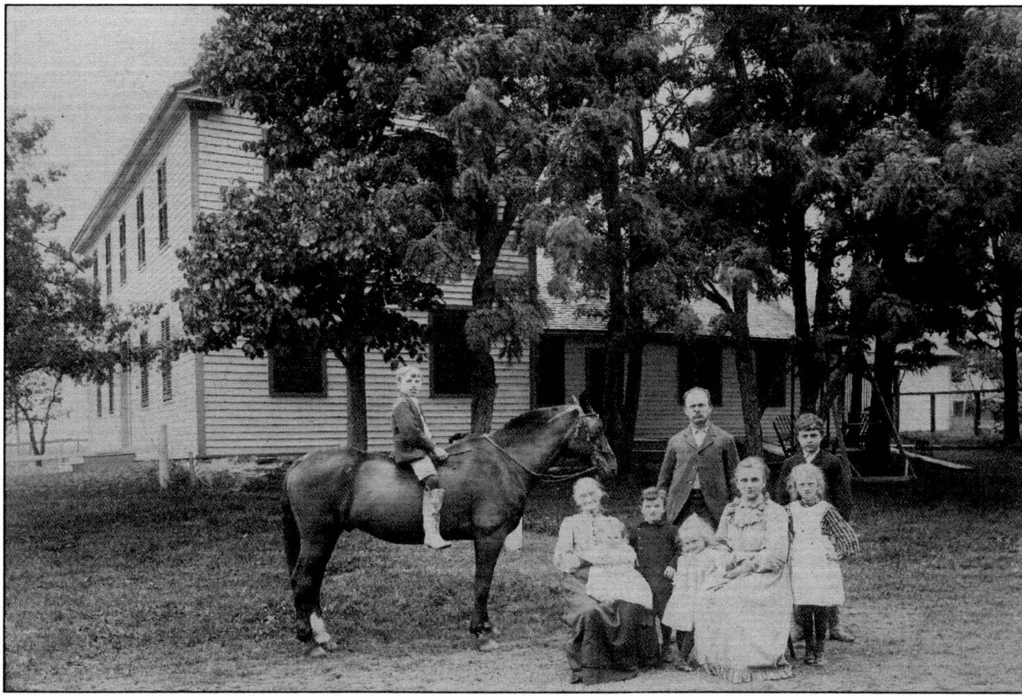

The same Callender house is seen here 55 years after the photograph on the previous page. At this time, it was home to the family of William and Mary (Duckett) Wisell. On the lawn from left to right are John Oliver Wisell, on the horse; Mary's mother, Anna (Scott) Duckett (holding Emory Wisell); Anna Wisell; William Wisell; Mary May Wisell; Mary (Duckett) Wisell; Amy May Wisell; and William A. Wisell.

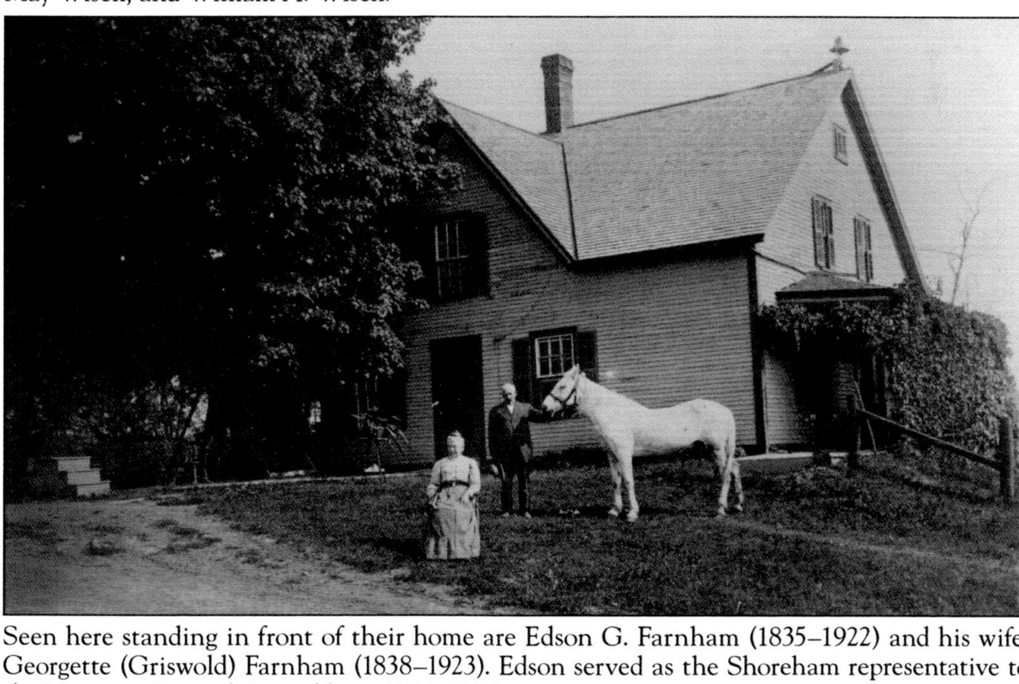

Seen here standing in front of their home are Edson G. Farnham (1835–1922) and his wife, Georgette (Griswold) Farnham (1838–1923). Edson served as the Shoreham representative to the Vermont General Assembly in 1884–1885.

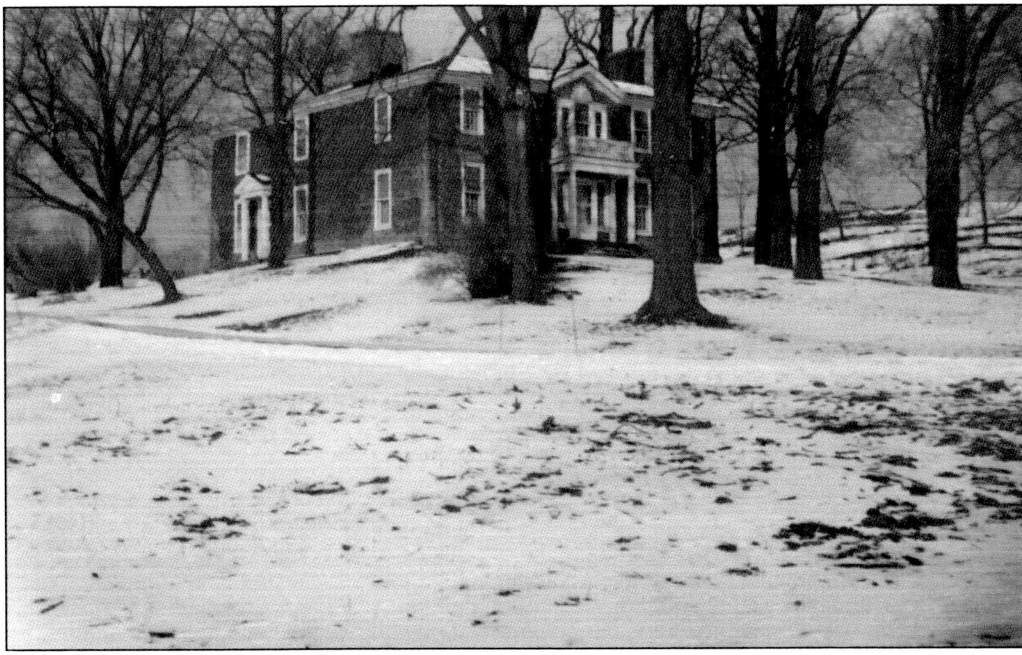

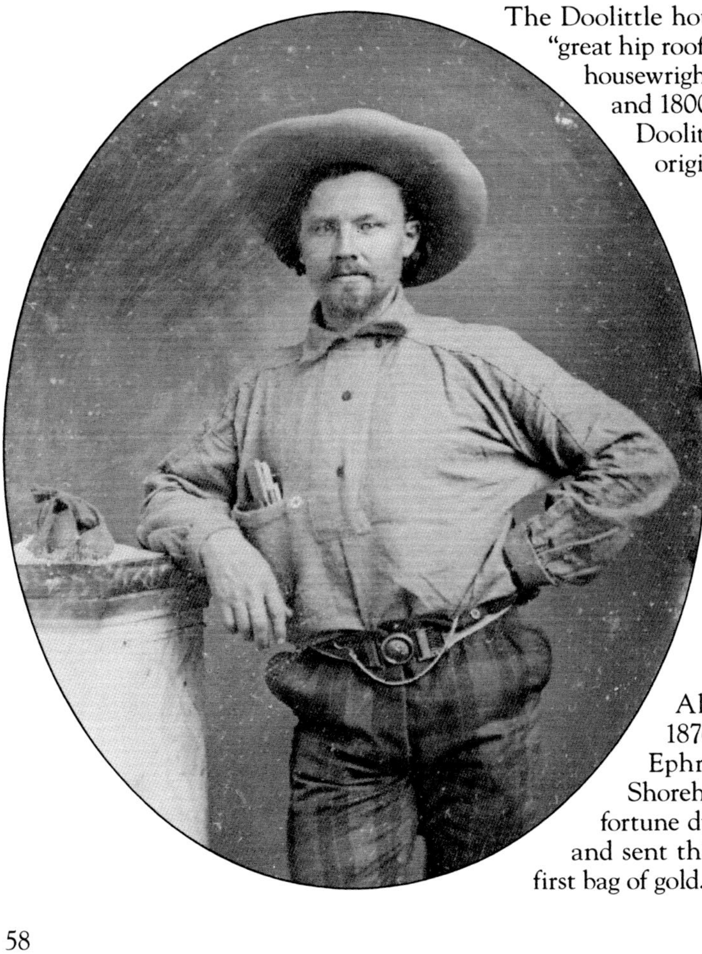

The Doolittle house (above) is one of the five "great hip roof houses" built in Shoreham by housewright Job Lane Howe between 1790 and 1800. It was built for Col. Ephraim Doolittle, who obtained Shoreham's original charter, and his family.

Alonzo Janes Doolittle (1821–1876), the great-grandson of Col. Ephraim Doolittle, was born in Shoreham. He went west to seek his fortune during the California gold rush and sent this photograph home with his first bag of gold.

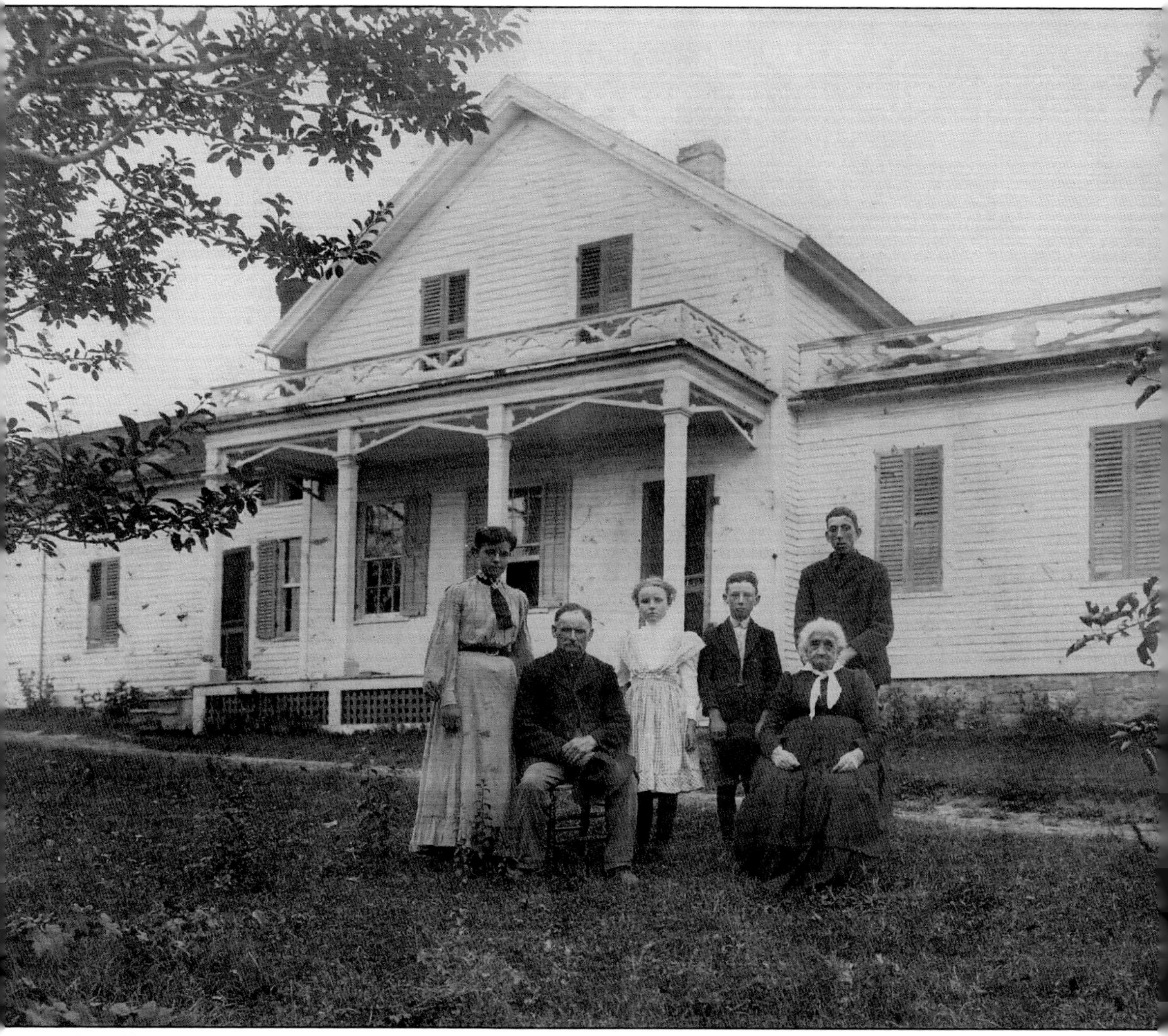

Orville Bigelow (1849–1921) and his wife, Mary (Chapman) Bigelow (1855–1929), lived with their children and Mary's mother, Lucretia (Huestis) Chapman, on Lapham Bay Road just west of Route 22A. Their house is still standing behind the Halfway House Restaurant.

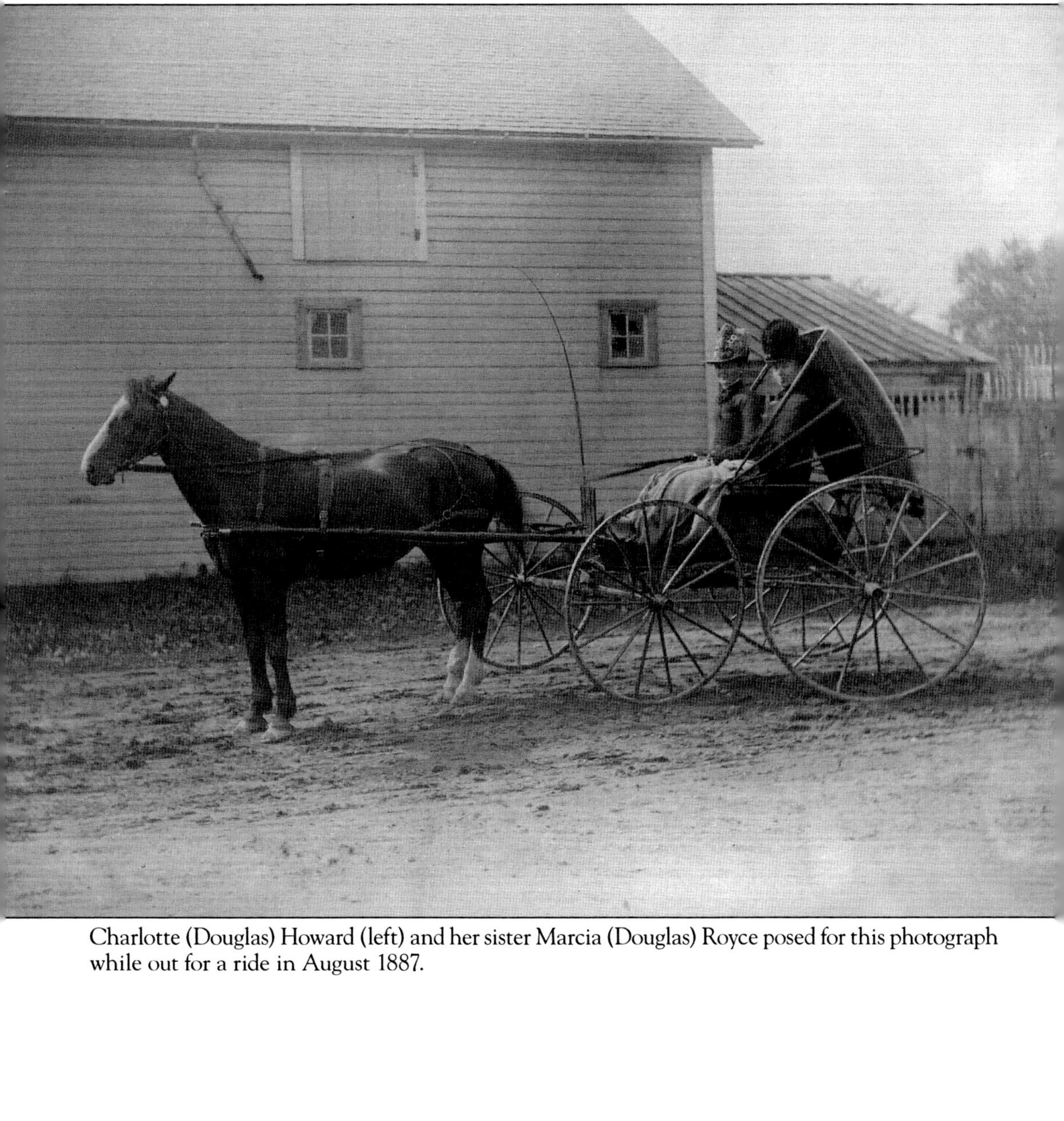

Charlotte (Douglas) Howard (left) and her sister Marcia (Douglas) Royce posed for this photograph while out for a ride in August 1887.

Alanson J. Towner (1843–1923) and his wife, Elizabeth Jones (1843–1928), were farmers on Smith Street. Alanson served in the Civil War as a private with Company D of the 14th Vermont Infantry from August 29, 1862, to July 30, 1863.

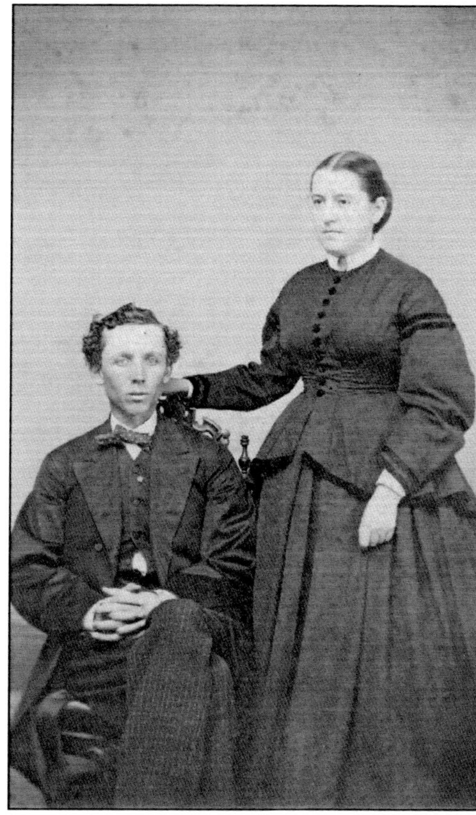

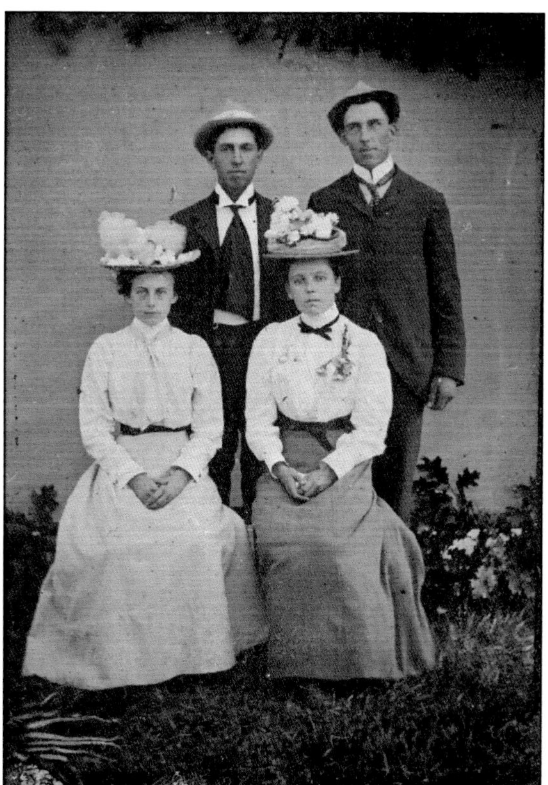

The daughters of Alanson Towner and their husbands remained in Shoreham. Maria Annette (left) married Charles D. Smith, who stands behind her. Mabel Eliza (right) married Wilbur E. Wisell, who stands behind her.

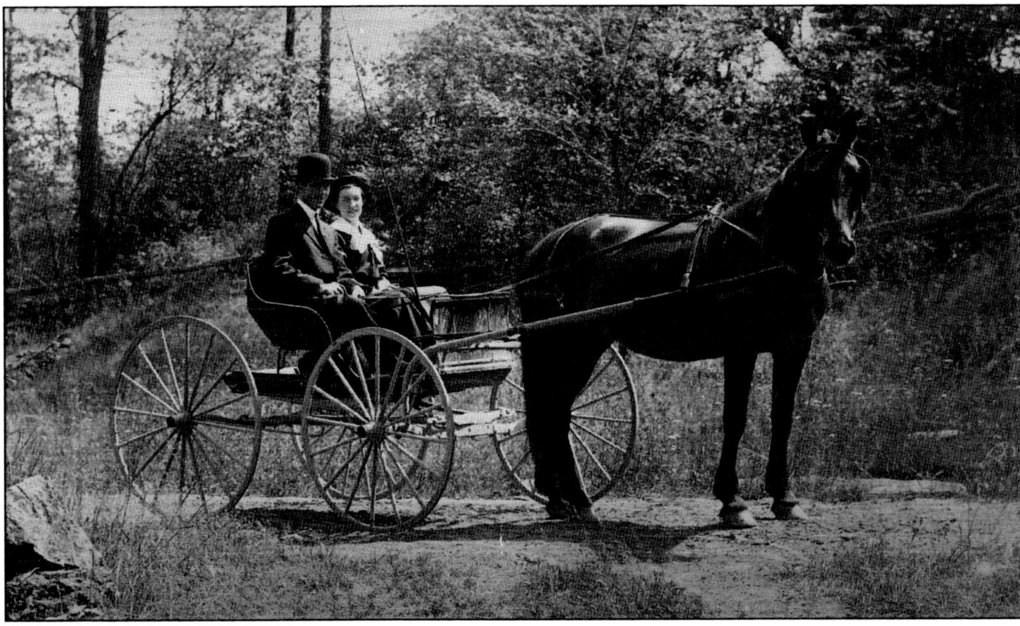

This photograph of Raymond Birchard (1889–1962) and his bride, Ruth (Webster) (1894–1989), was taken the summer after their wedding.

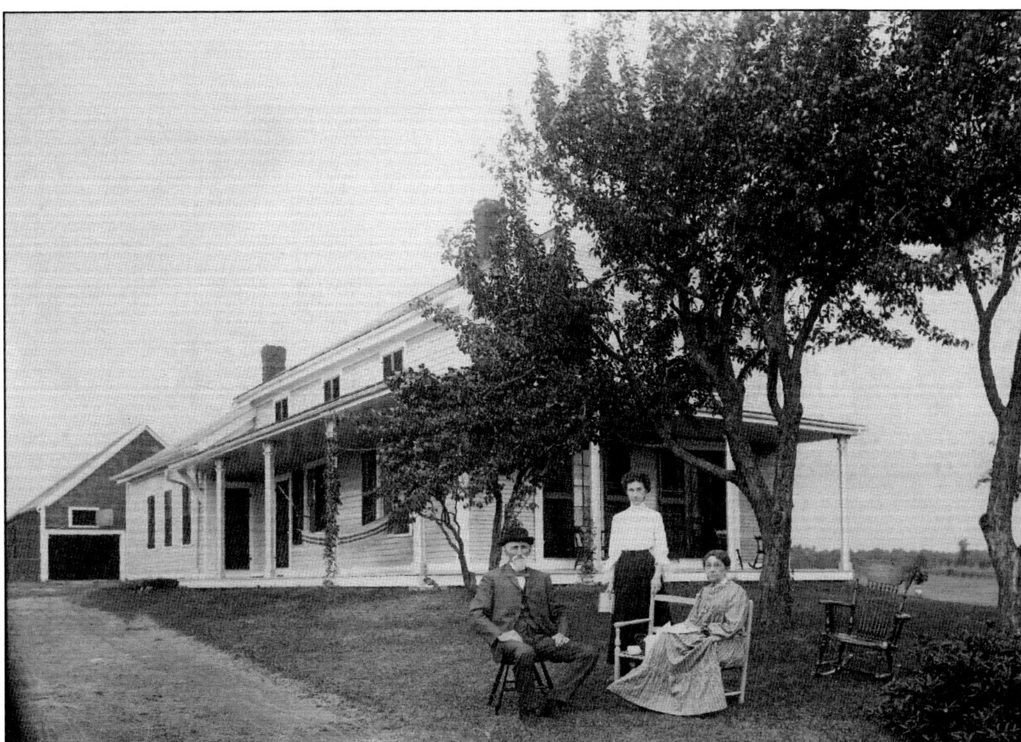

Dennis Ferguson Macauley (1855–1920) immigrated to Shoreham and married Mary Jane Carroll (1858–1923). They are seen here in front of their farmhouse with their daughter-in-law Nellie Mary Wisell, the wife of Thomas F. Macauley. (Courtesy of Halfway House Restaurant.)

Best friends (from left to right) Ina Smith, Maria Towner, and Margaret Burge had their photograph taken together on March 24, 1892.

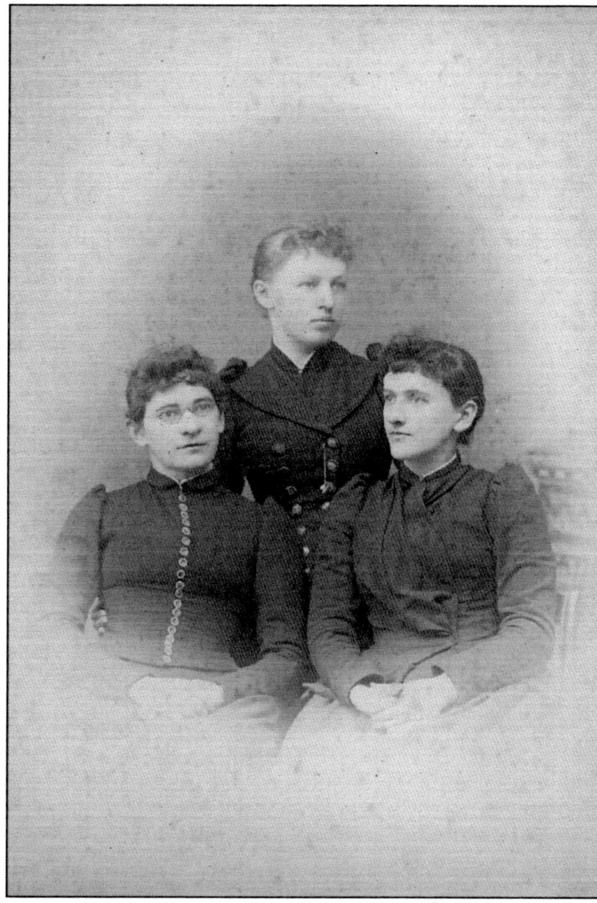

Four Smith brothers came to Shoreham from Nine Partners, New York, in the 1780s and settled on what became known as Smith Street. All built large Federal-style houses around 1820, two of which still stand. The one below was built by Nathan Smith.

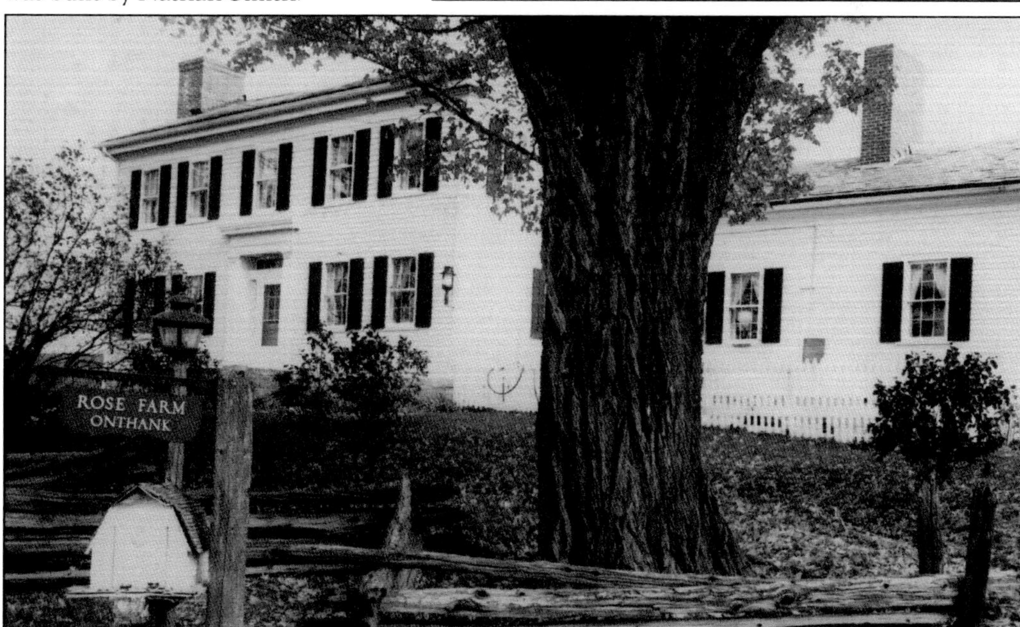

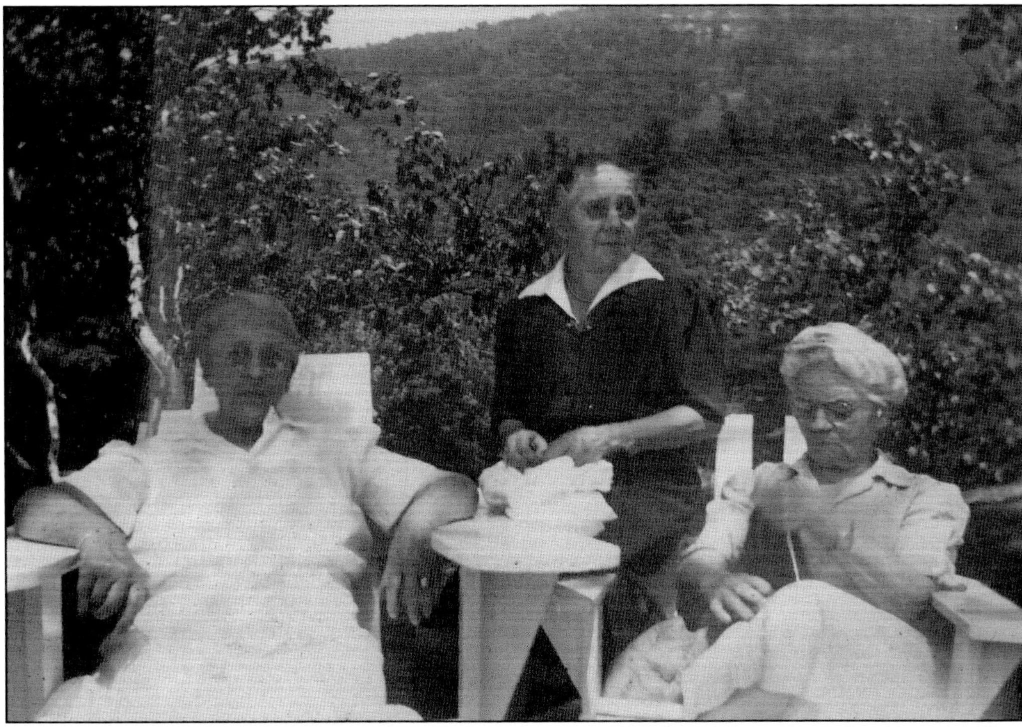

During World War II, civic-minded Shoreham women sewed bandages to help the war effort. Here, from left to right, Lillian Anderson, Mabel Wisell, and Lillian Larrabee work outside on a bright, sunny day.

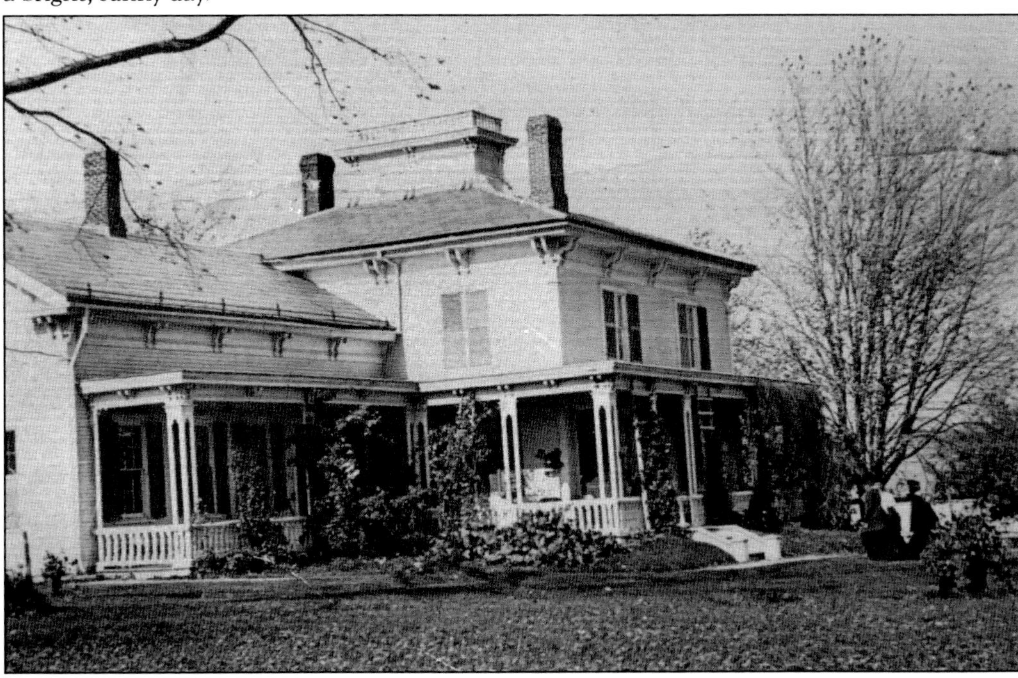

This house, known as the Birchard house, was first built by the Russell family, whose private family cemetery is still across the street. This photograph was taken around 1890.

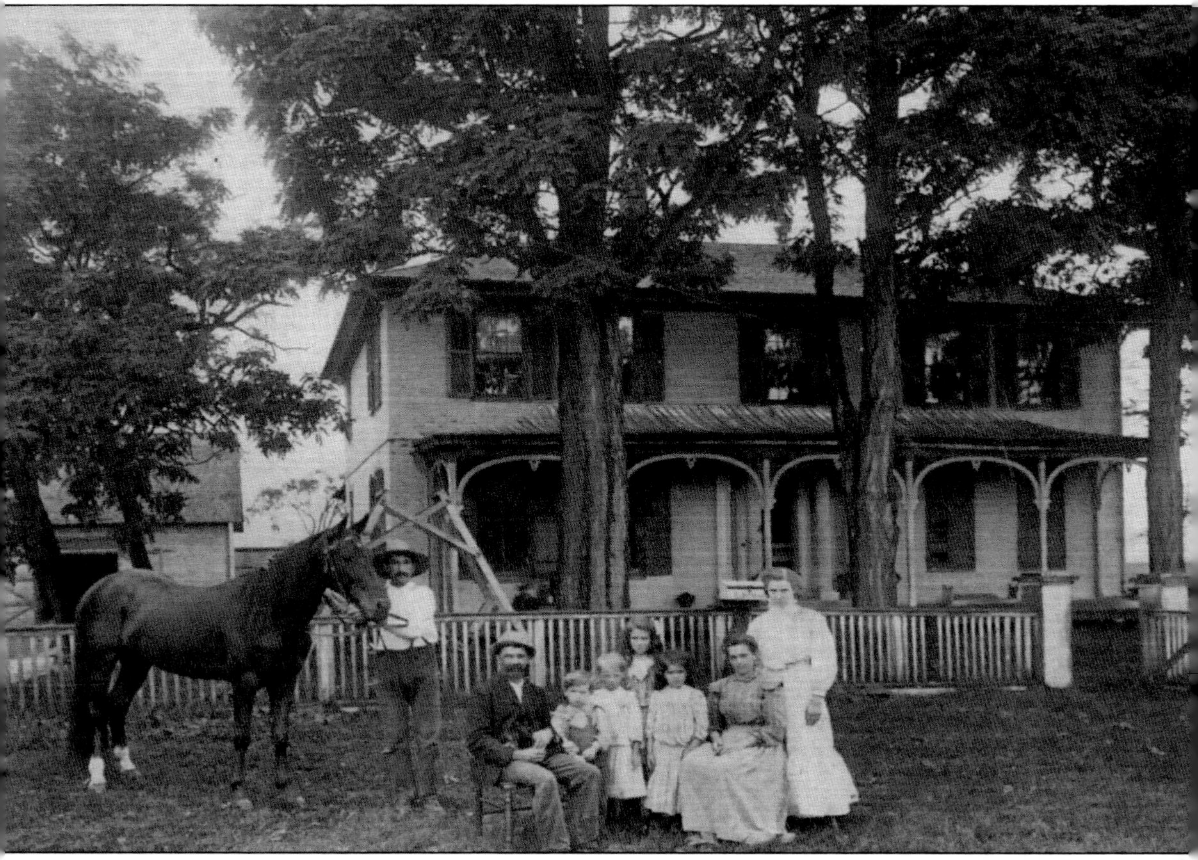

Another of the hip-roof houses designed by Job Lane Howe in Shoreham between 1790 and 1800, this house was first owned by Noah Callender. The two front rooms on the second floor have pocket doors that open into one large room, creating a "floating" dance floor, on springs, where many happy gatherings were held. When this photograph was taken, it was the home of the John Ephraim Wright family. From left to right are a hired man (holding the horse), John Ephraim Wright (holding a puppy), John Harold "Harry" Wright, Louisa Lapham, Mary Catherine Wright, Lois (Lapham) Wright, and the hired man's wife. (Courtesy of H. Kent Wright III.)

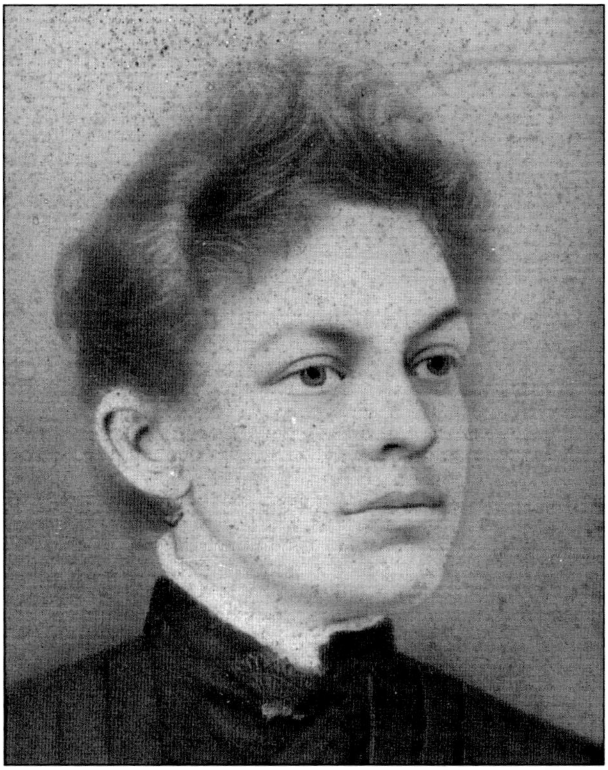

Lois Elizabeth (Lapham) Wright (1871–1951) was a farm wife and mother of five children. She was an active member of the Episcopal church across the street from her home. (Courtesy of H. Kent Wright III.)

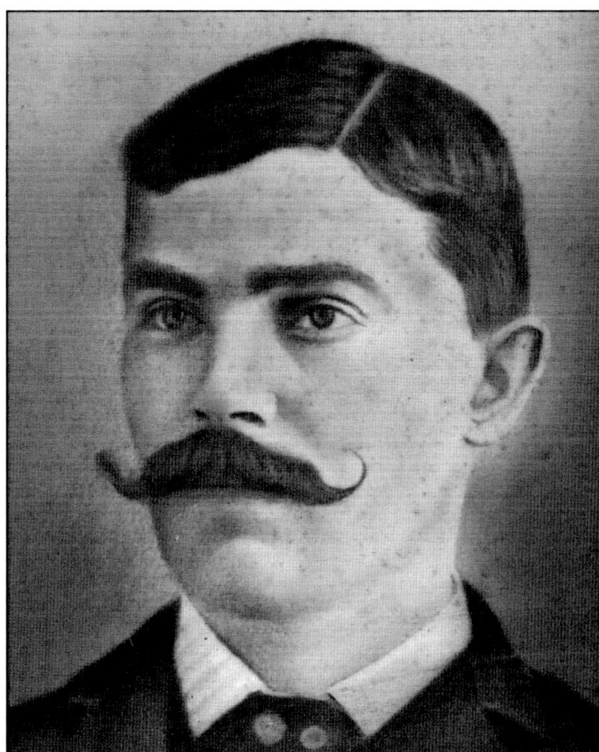

John Ephraim Wright farmed fertile acres in the Cream Hill section of Shoreham. He served the nation in World War I. (Courtesy of H. Kent Wright III.)

Six

AGRICULTURE

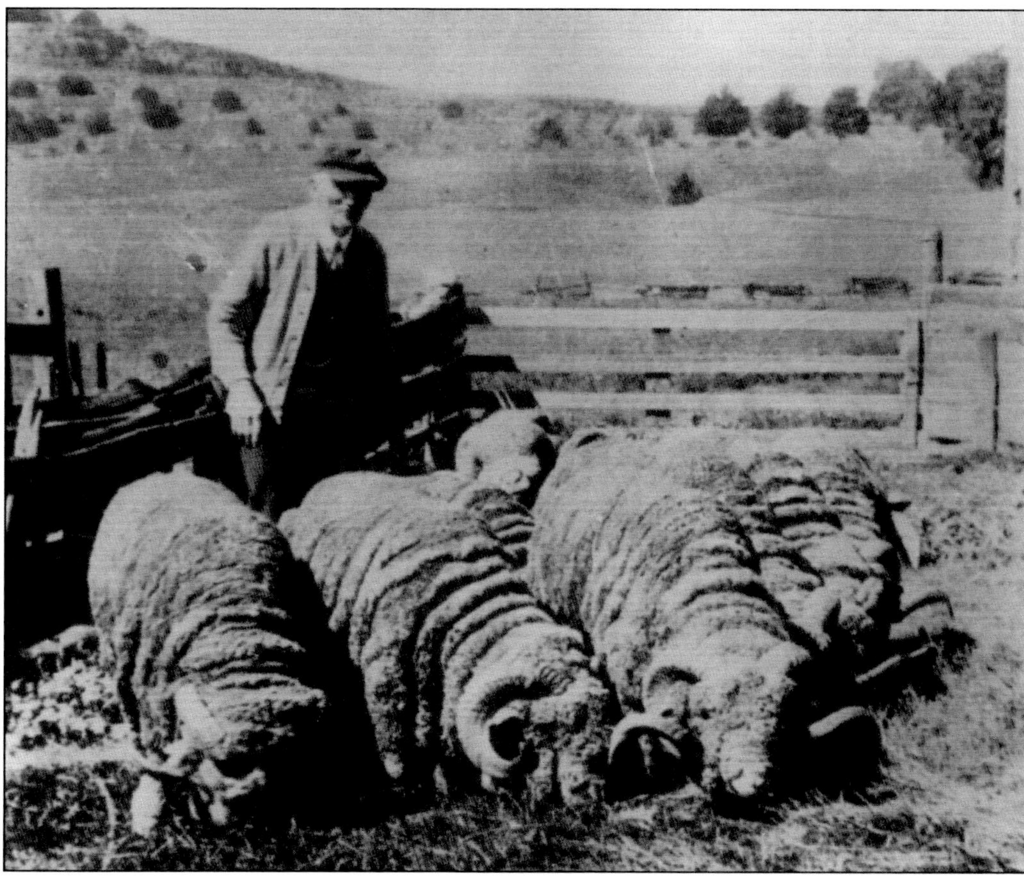

Merino sheep first came to Shoreham in 1816. Their soft, finely crimped fleece became the biggest moneymaking crop in Shoreham in the 1800s. Royal Witherell is seen here with some of his prize-winning rams. (Courtesy of Sanford S. Witherell Jr.)

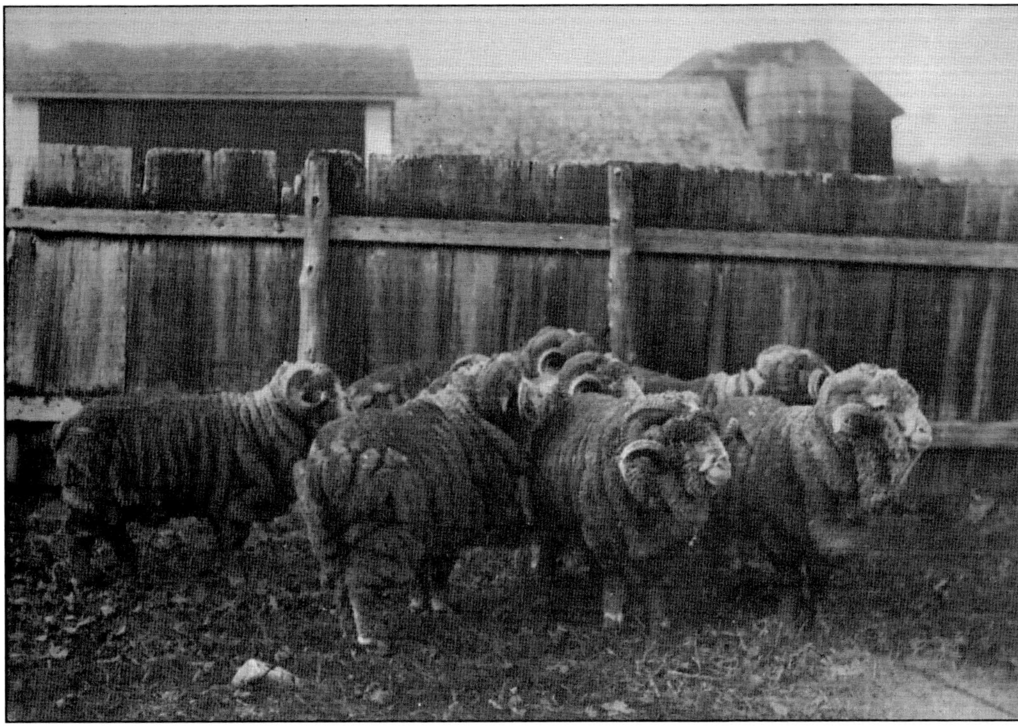

Most merino sheep were white, but some had darker-colored fleeces, as seen here.

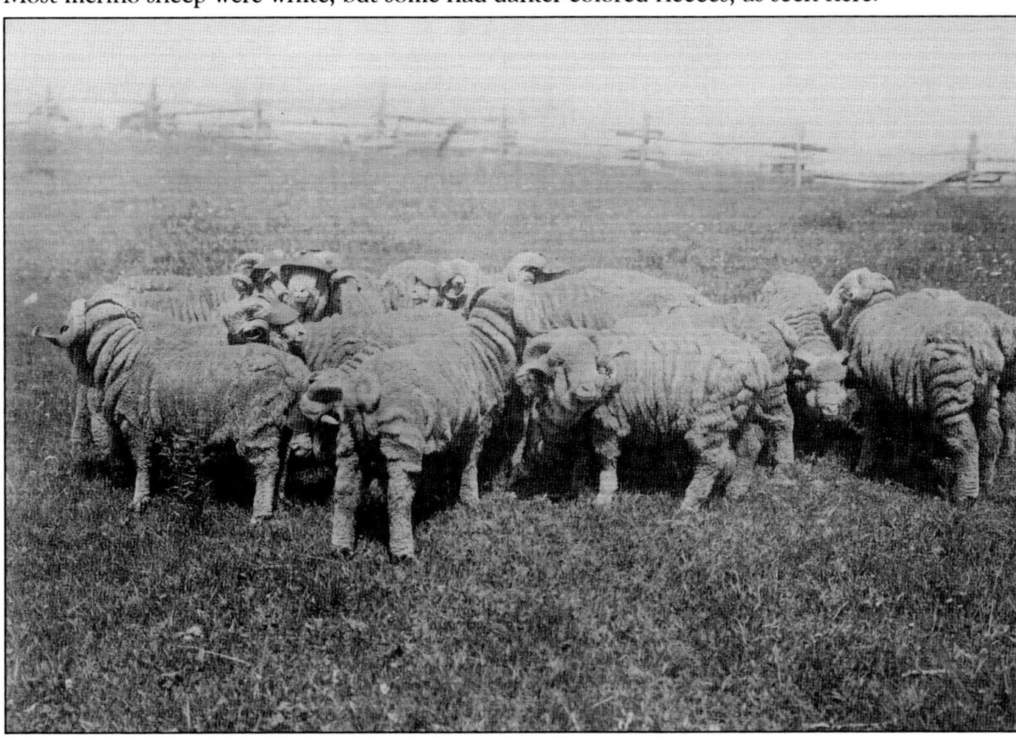

Some of the merinos in this group are wearing sun visors to keep the bright sun from bothering their eyes.

Charles Leslie Witherell (left) and his father, Charles Royal Witherell, are seen here in South Africa, where they went to auction off some of their sheep around 1900. They traveled by boat with the sheep around Cape Horn. (Courtesy of Sanford S. Witherell Jr.)

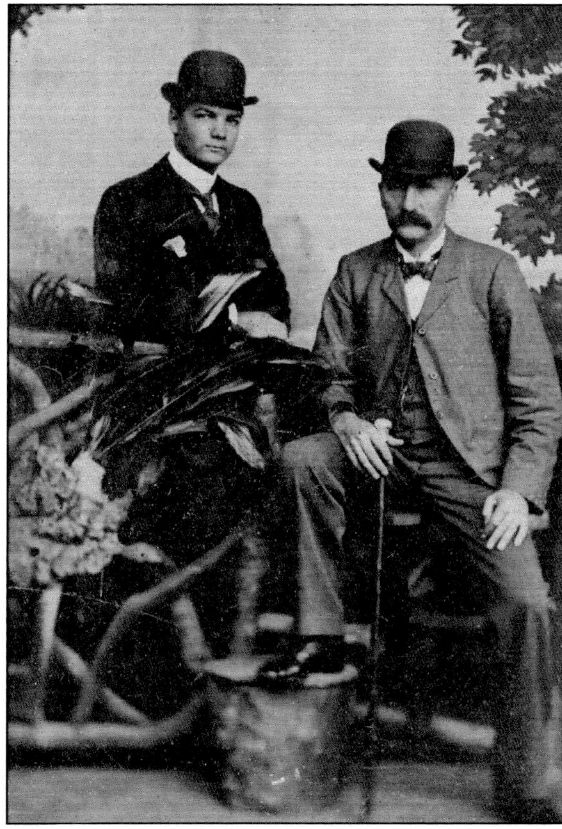

Charles Royal Witherell and some of his fancy racehorses are seen below at Stonehenge, in neighboring Cornwall. (Courtesy of Sanford S. Witherell Jr.)

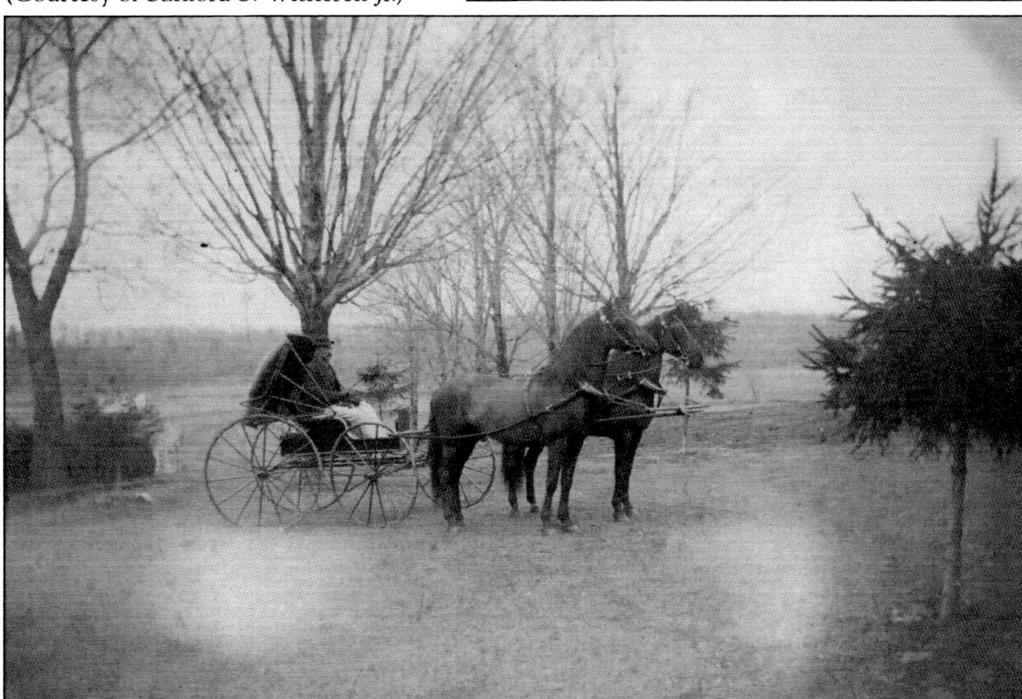

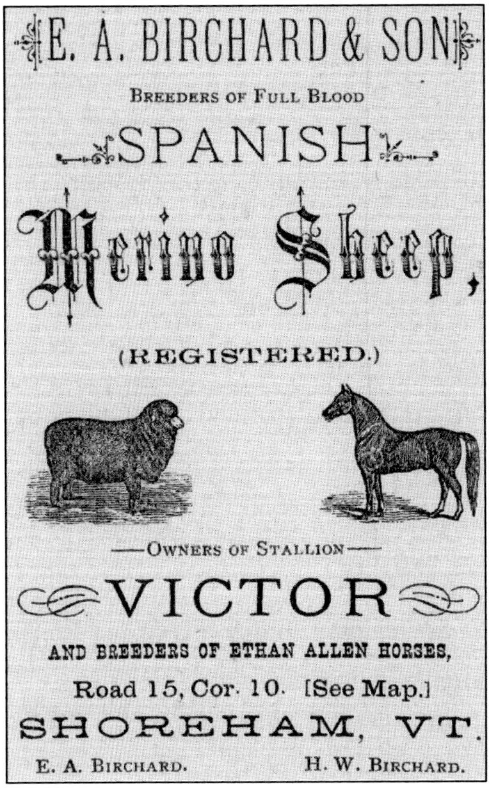

This advertisement, taken from Child's 1881–1882 *Gazetteer and Business Directory of Addison County*, shows that many farmers who raised sheep also raised racehorses for breeding purposes.

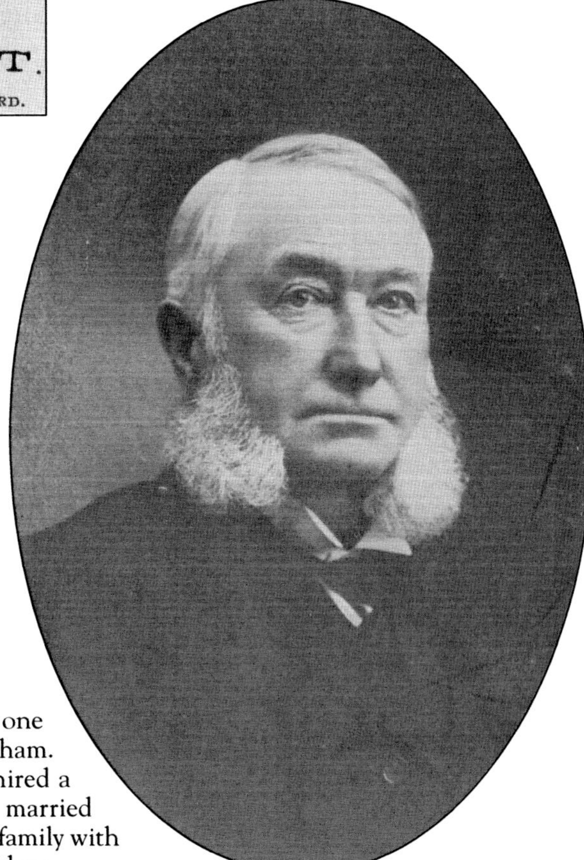

Edgar Nelson Bissell (1840–1917) was one of the largest sheep producers in Shoreham. He was drafted for the Civil War but hired a substitute to serve for him. In 1863, he married Sophia Needham, and they started their family with one adopted child and eight natural children.

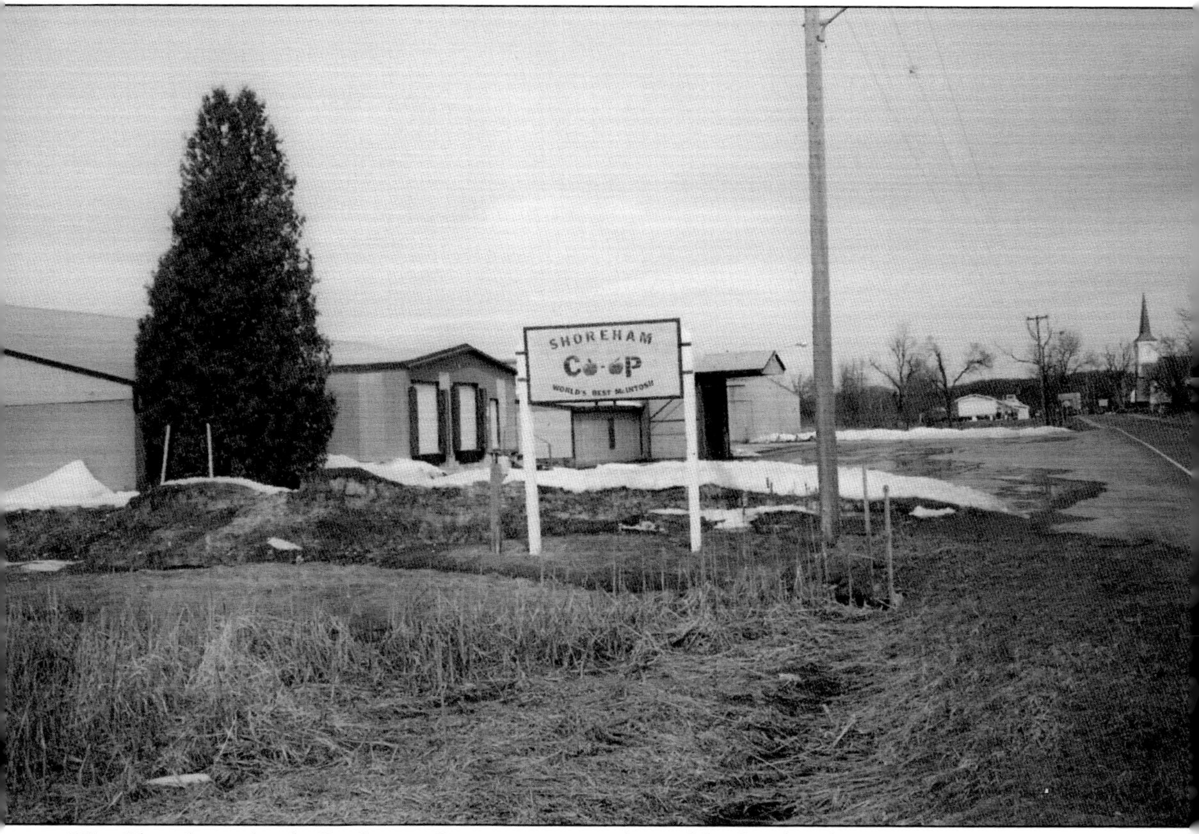

The Shoreham Apple Producers Cooperative was formed by five local growers, Norris Buxton, Thomas Cook, Jack Norinsberg, W.A. Stalker Jr., and Sanford S. Witherell, in 1946. It was the first cooperative of this type in Vermont. The original building was cement block and measured 140 feet by 100 feet. There were cork-lined, controlled-atmosphere storage rooms that held at three percent oxygen and five percent carbon dioxide, in order to put the apples to sleep and lengthen their shelf life. The building also had a packing room and could hold 11,000 bushels of apples. As the years progressed, building and equipment additions enhanced operations. (Courtesy of Sanford S. Witherell Jr.)

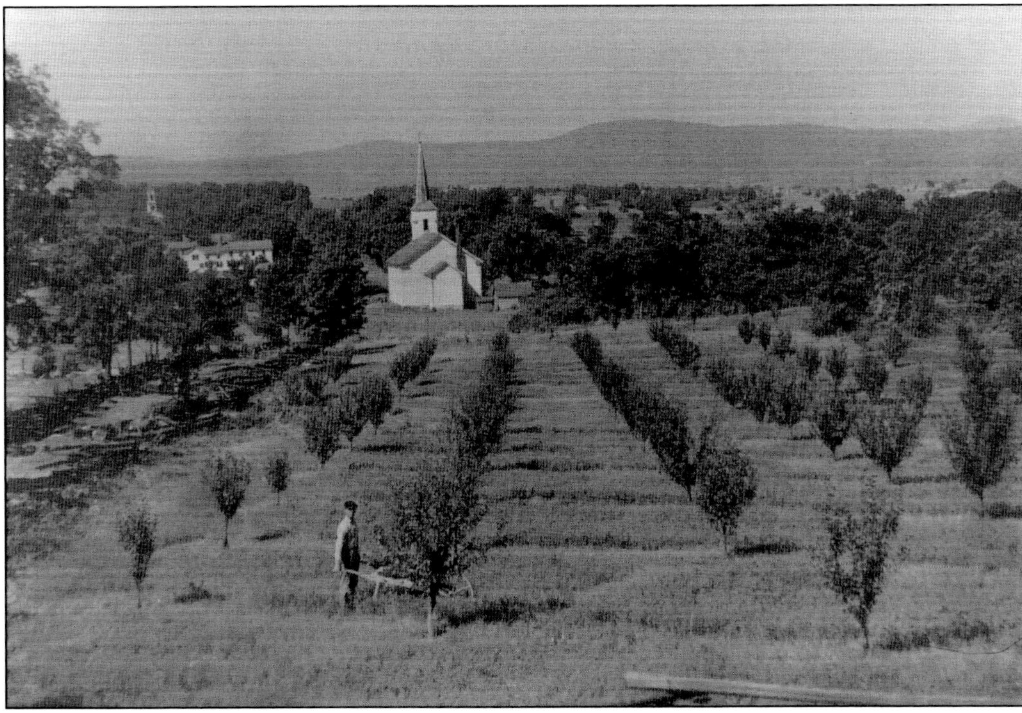

Diamond A Orchard was owned by William Anderson. Trees were set out in the village to the east of St. Genevieve's Catholic Church. He also had his own packinghouse on the north end of the orchard, across the street from his home.

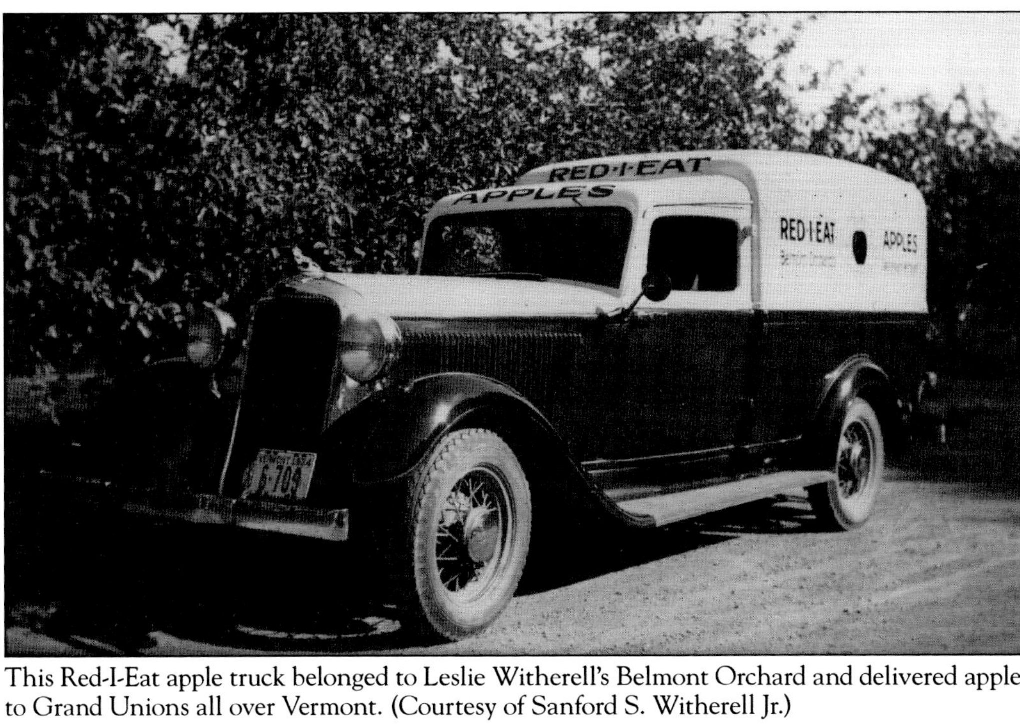

This Red-I-Eat apple truck belonged to Leslie Witherell's Belmont Orchard and delivered apples to Grand Unions all over Vermont. (Courtesy of Sanford S. Witherell Jr.)

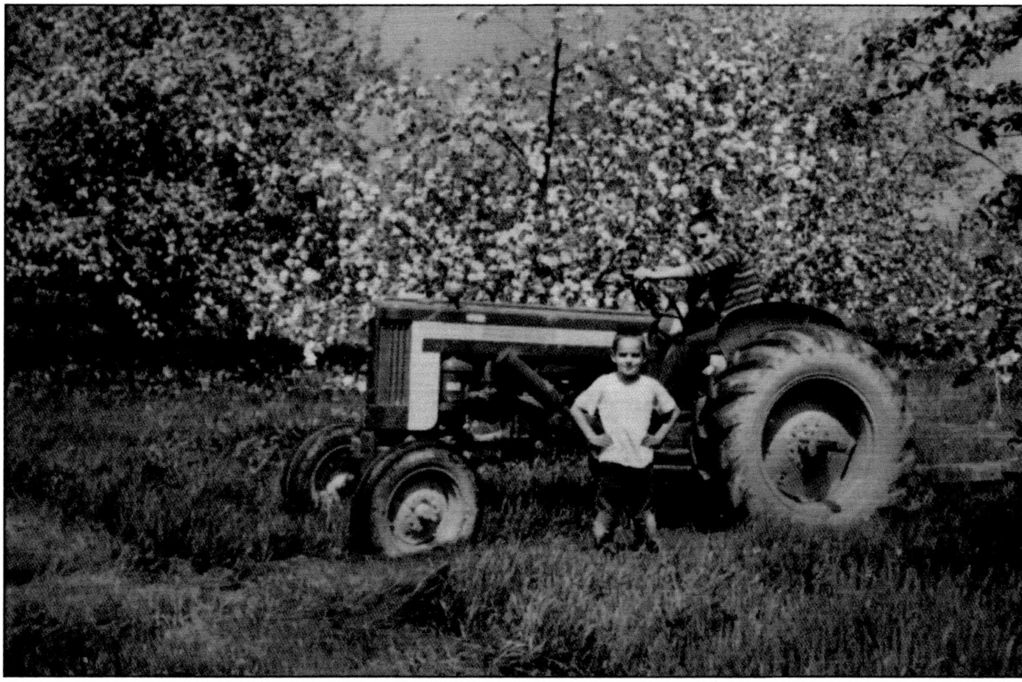

Harold Small (on tractor) and Steve Small posed for this photograph at Indian Trail Orchard as the apple blossoms were at their peak. (Courtesy of May Small.)

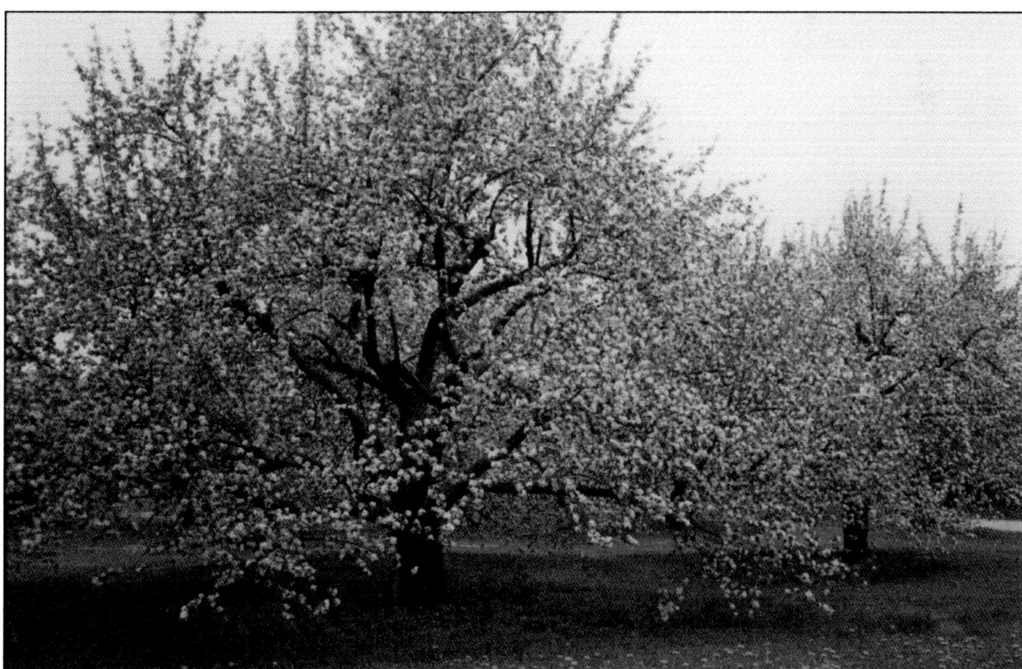

Not many things smell as sweet as McIntosh trees in full bloom. (Courtesy of May Small.)

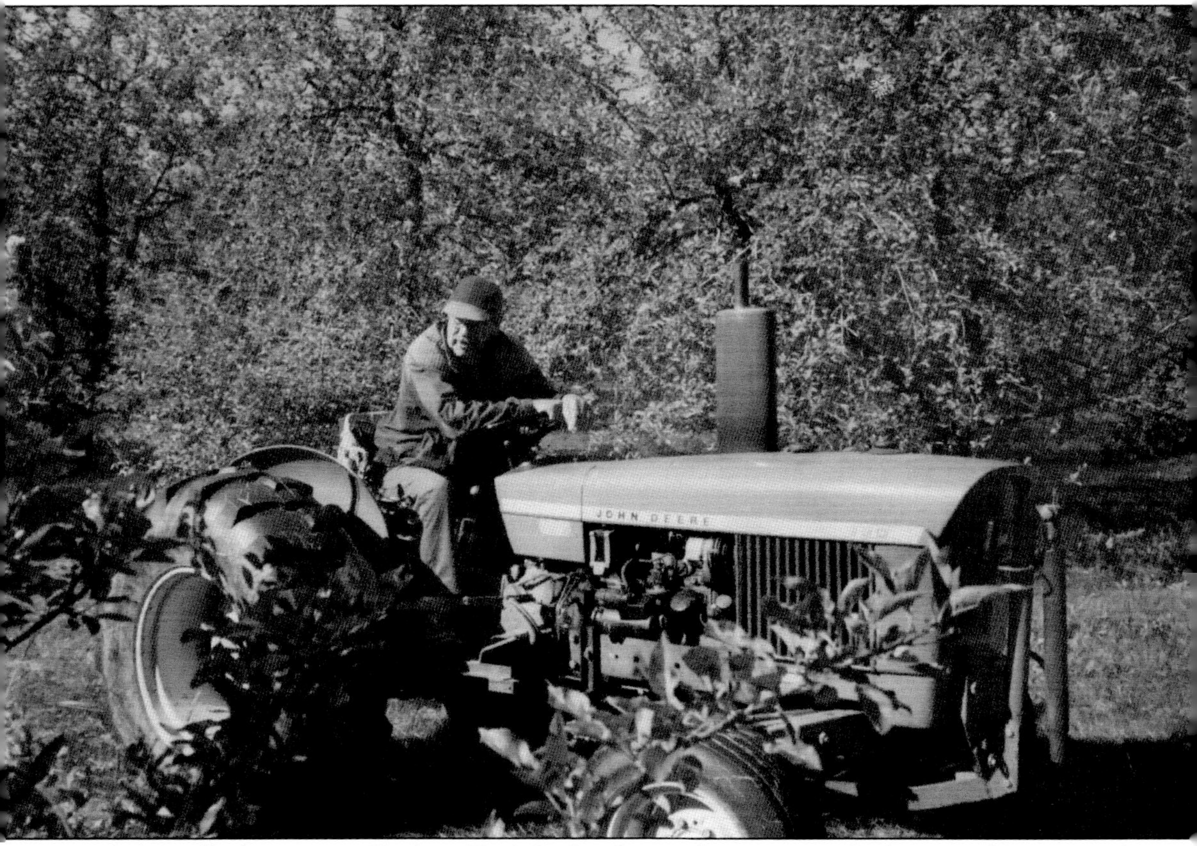

Phil Small, the owner of Indian Trail Orchard, gets things set up for harvest. (Courtesy of May Small.)

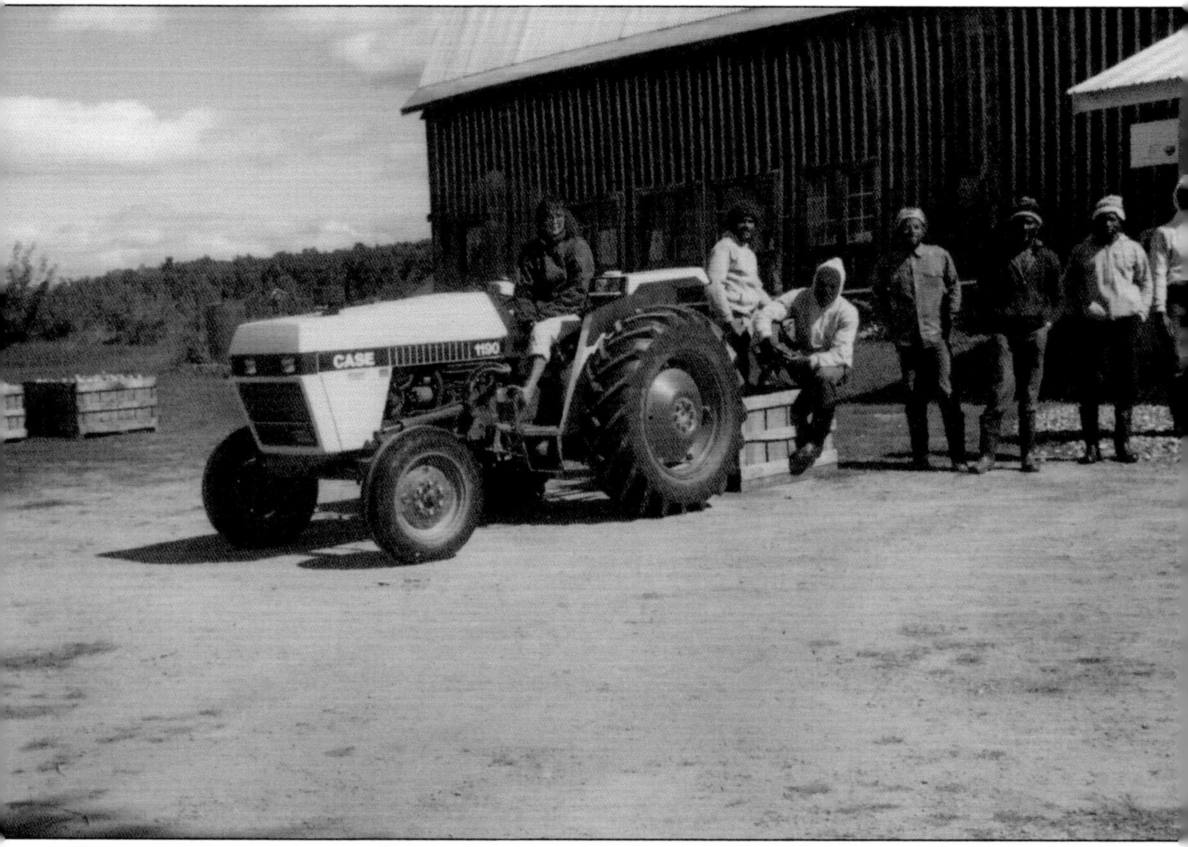

For many years, migrant workers from Jamaica have come to Shoreham each fall to help with the apple harvest. Here, Susan Small drives the tractor as the Jamaicans get ready for a day of work. (Courtesy of May Small.)

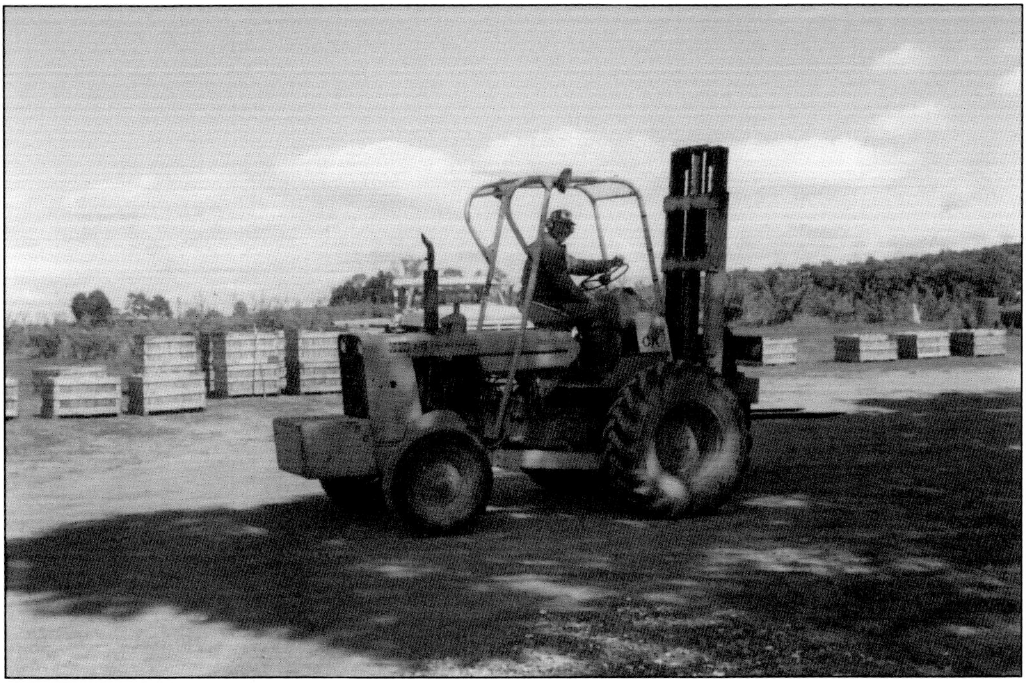

A forklift is used to move the 13 bushel bins that apples were placed in for shipment to storage. (Courtesy of May Small.)

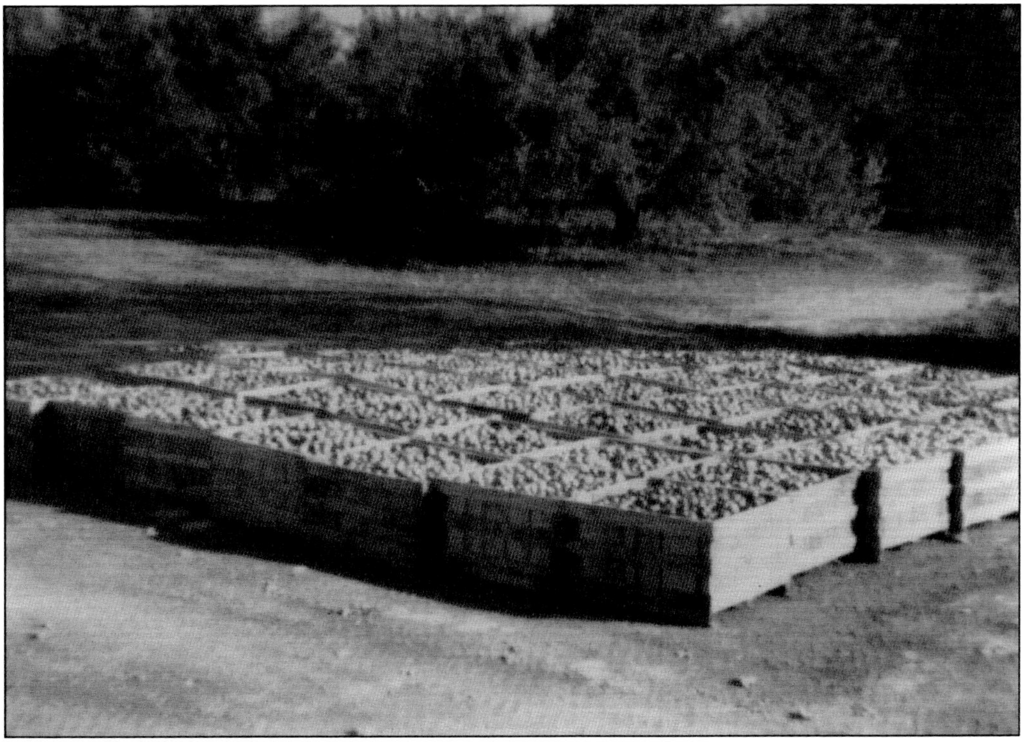

Bins are filled and ready for the ride up to the Shoreham cooperative on a flatbed truck. (Courtesy of May Small.)

George Severance packs apples in crates for shipment to grocery stores at Noggin Orchard. (Courtesy of Sanford S. Witherell Jr.)

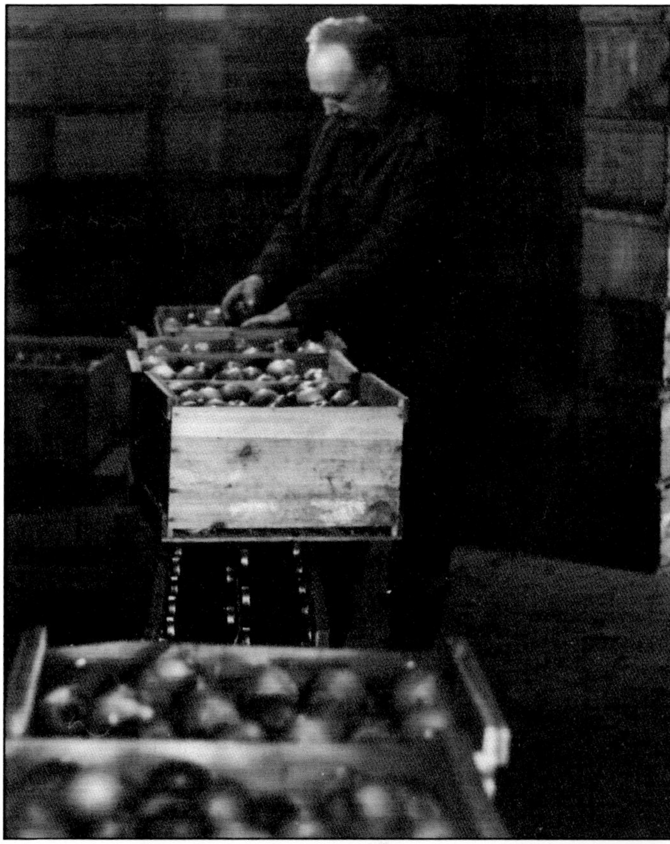

Below, patrons pick their own raspberries at Douglas Orchard around 1910. The orchard still offers pick-your-own apples, cherries, and raspberries today.

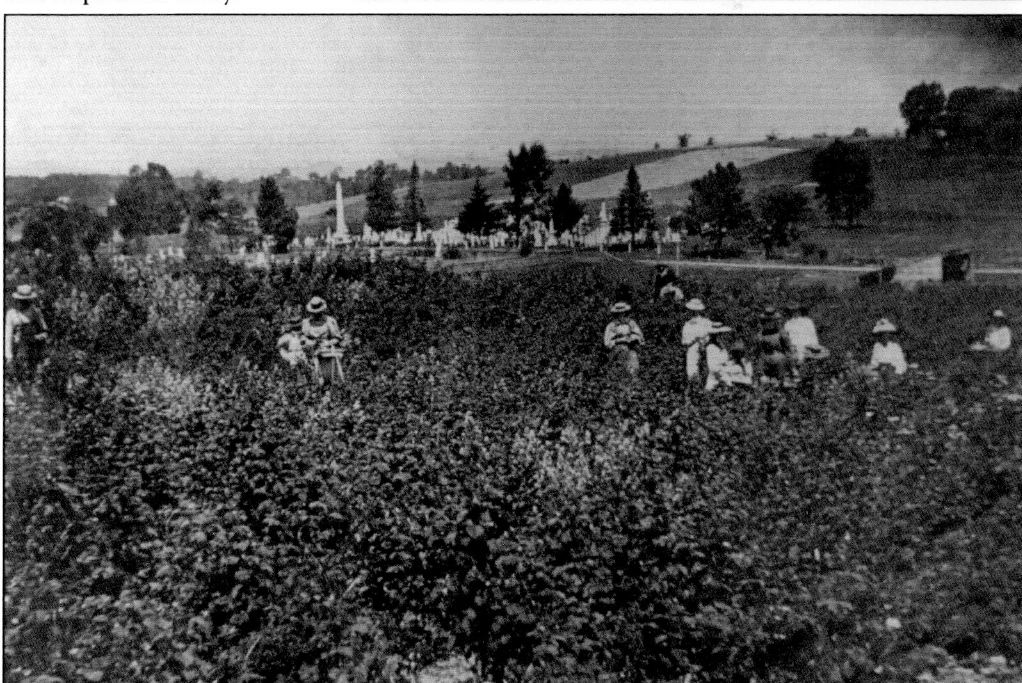

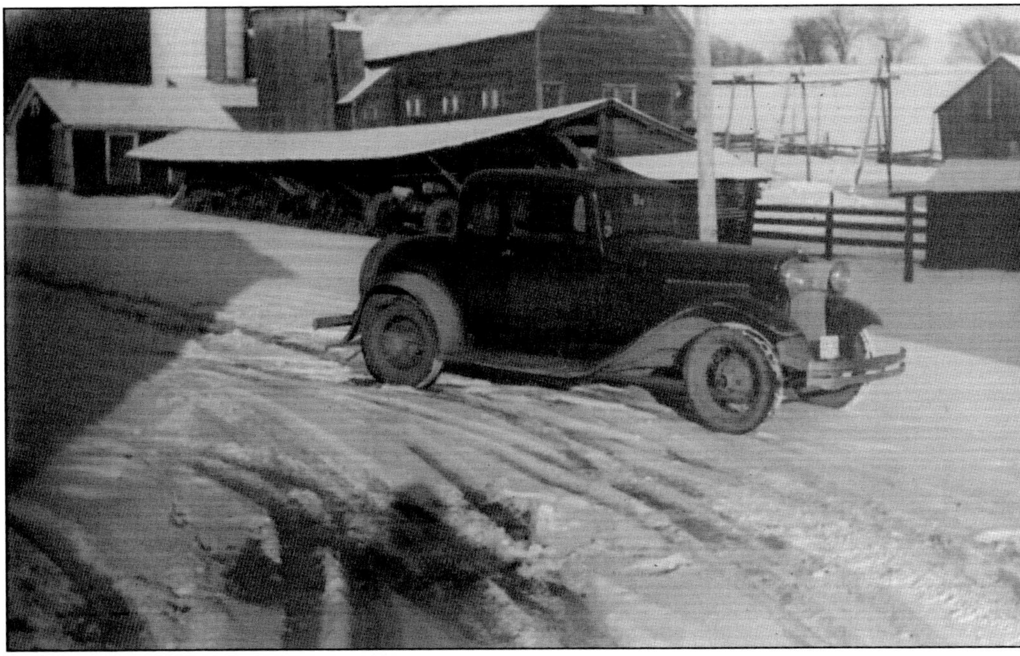

In addition to storing fruit, the barns at Douglas Orchard (pictured) also housed dairy cattle over the years.

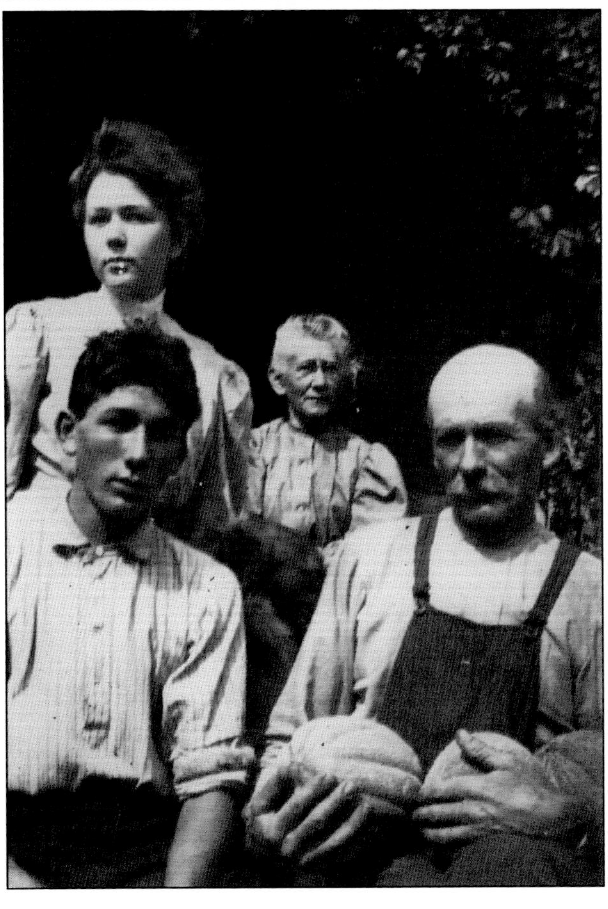

The Douglases grow a variety of crops. Seen here in front are Malcolm Douglas (1891–1980) and his father, Francis Edwin Douglas (1852–1924). Behind them are Bernice Naomi Douglas (1886–1977) and her mother, Helen Adelaide (Burge) Douglas (1855–1930).

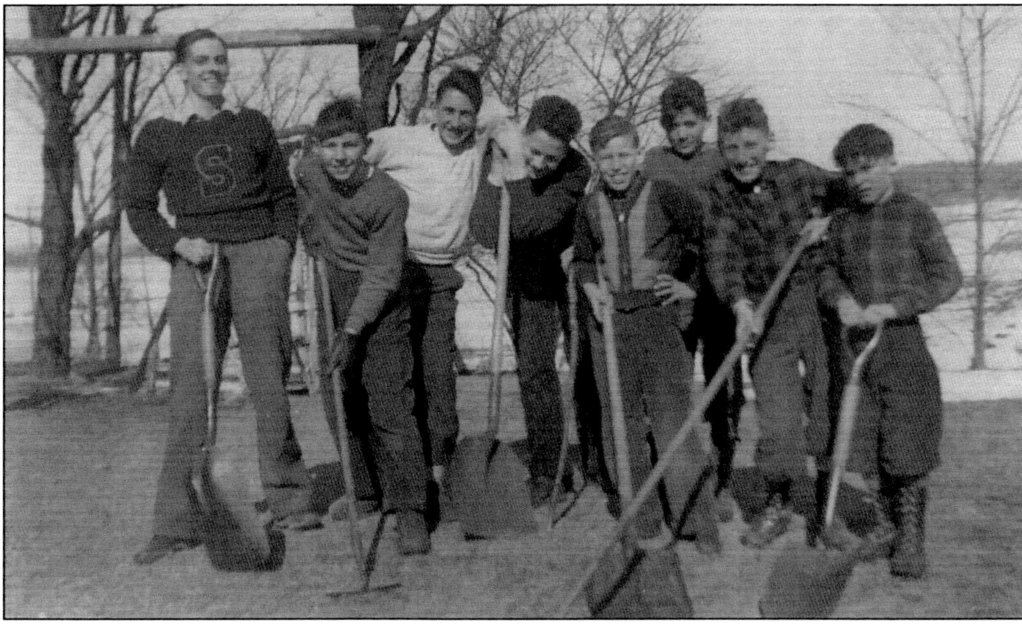

These Shoreham 4-H boys won the Champion Gardeners Award in 1941 under the guidance of their leader, Elsie Brisson. The boys are, from left to right, Wesley Larrabee, Wendael Hayden Jr., Philip Hayden, Robert Douglas, William Birchard, Harris Brisson, Kenneth Farnsworth, and Lucien Farnsworth. (Courtesy of Linda Larrabee.)

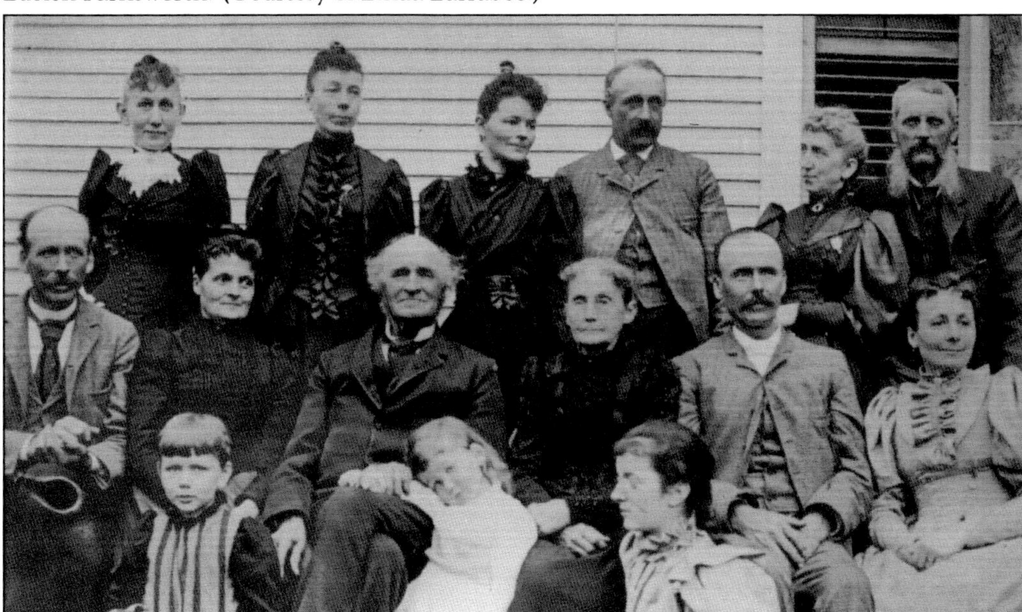

The entire Douglas clan got together in 1899 for this group photograph. They are, from left to right, (first row) Malcolm Burge Douglas, Bernice Naomi Douglas, and Florence Howard; (second row) Francis Edwin Douglas, Elizabeth (Douglas) Collins, Edwin Benajah Douglas, Naomi (Tupper) Douglas, Norman Douglas, and Charlotte Naomi (Douglas) Howard; (third row) Adelaide (Burge) Douglas, Marcia Ann (Douglas) Royce, Louise Amy (Douglas) Northrup, Samuel Northrup, Laura (Barnes) Douglas, and Charles W. Howard.

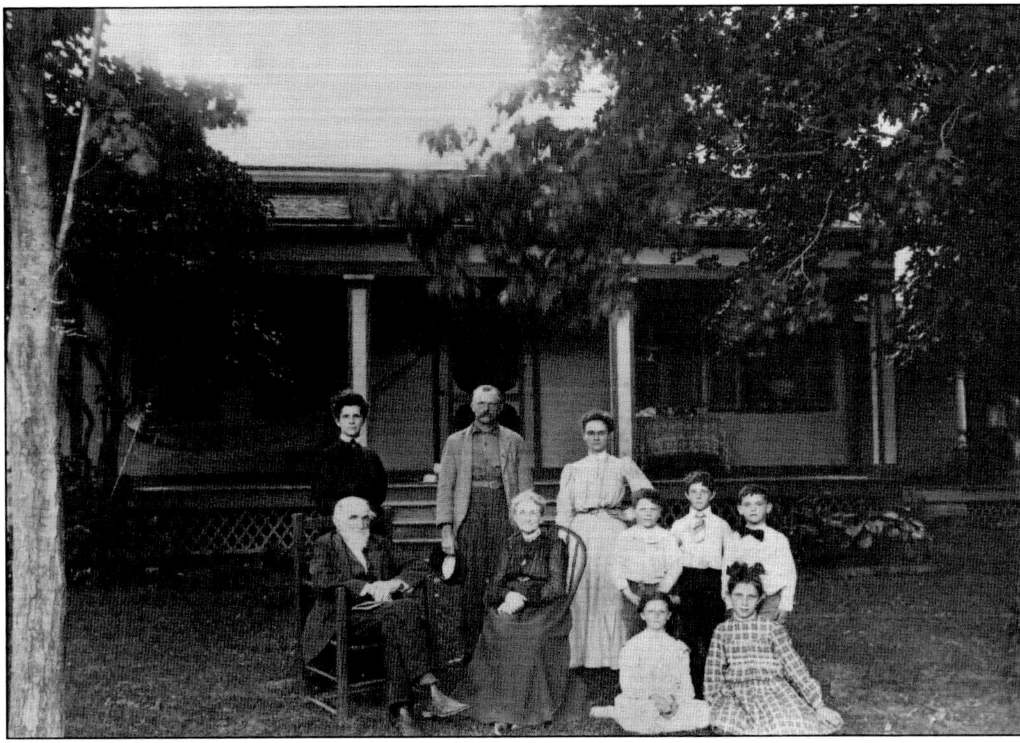

The Larrabee family gathers in front of their home at Larrabee's Point Orchard in 1904. They are, from left to right, (seated) Wesley Charles Larrabee, Mary Ellen (Hickox) Larrabee, and two unidentified young family members; (standing) Wallace Grover Larrabee, Lillian Baker Larrabee, unidentified, Ernest William Larrabee, and unidentified.

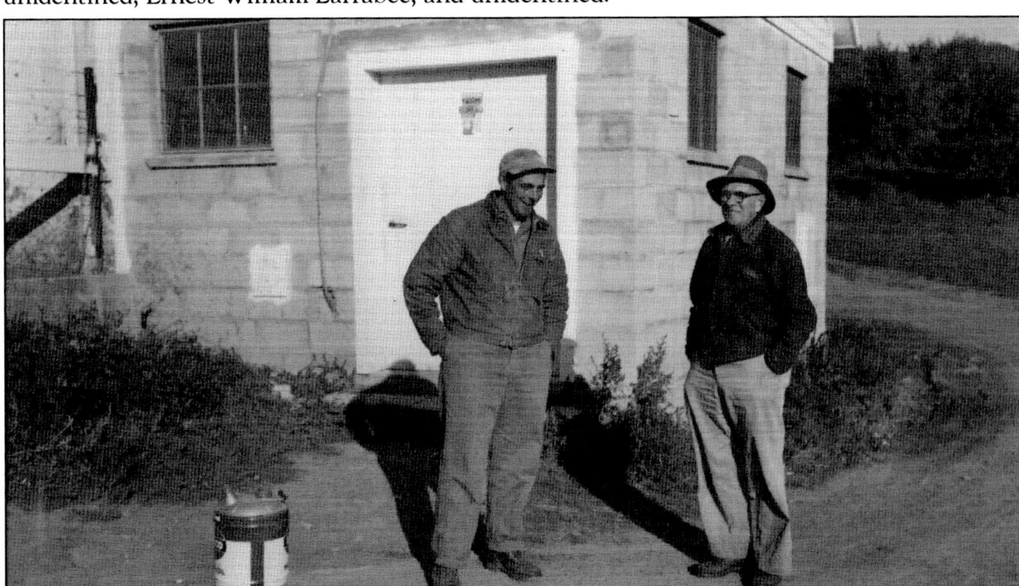

Wesley Campbell Larrabee (1923–2011) and his father Ernest William Larrabee (1896–1971) stand in front of their new milk house, which contained a bulk tank, in the late 1950s. (Courtesy of Linda Larrabee.)

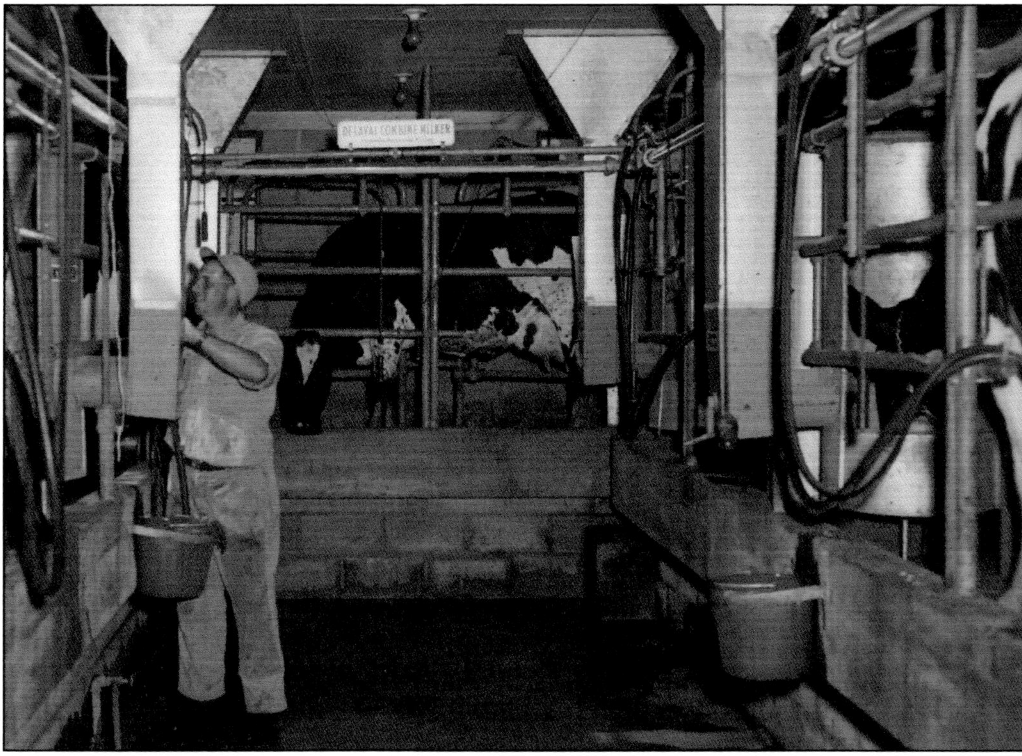

Wesley Larrabee milks in his state-of-the-art new milking parlor, built in the late 1950s. (Courtesy of Linda Larrabee.)

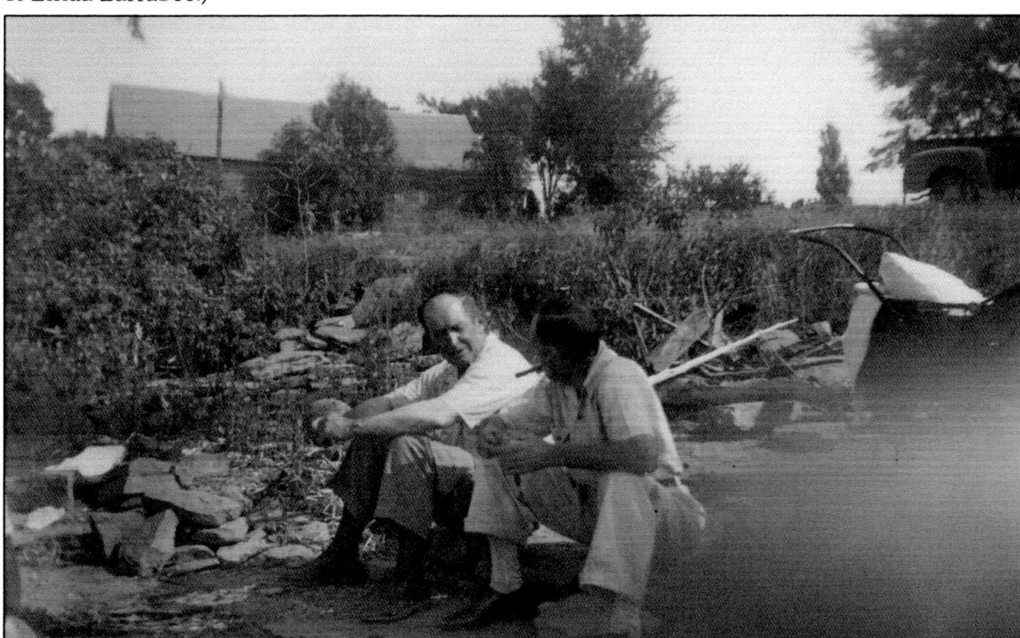

Homer Stewart (left) and Ernest Larrabee make plans for the day's work on the farm. (Courtesy of Linda Larrabee.)

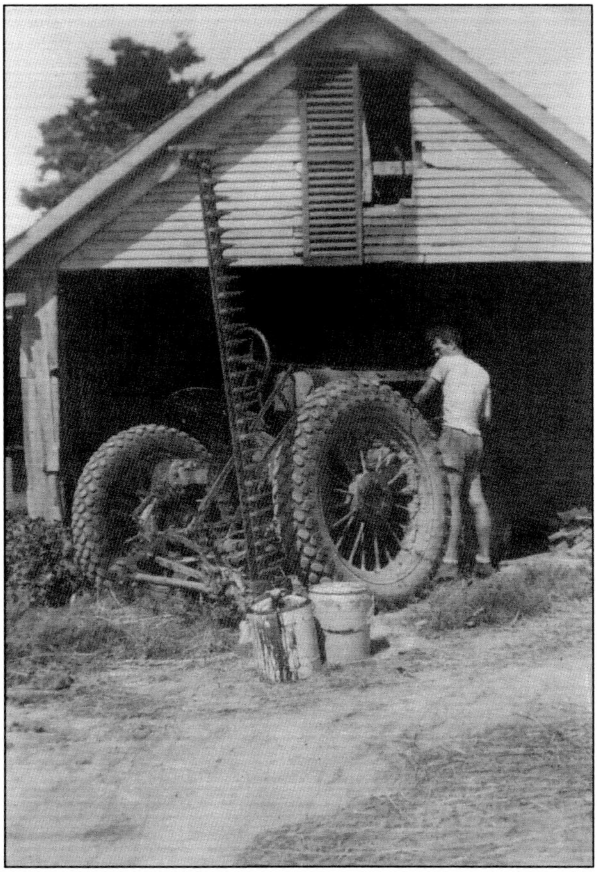

Joe Kivlin readies the new Farmall tractor for its first day of mowing on the farm. (Courtesy of Philip Kivlin.)

The invention of the sweep rake made for faster haying. Joe Kivlin is seen below on the tractor. (Courtesy of Philip Kivlin.)

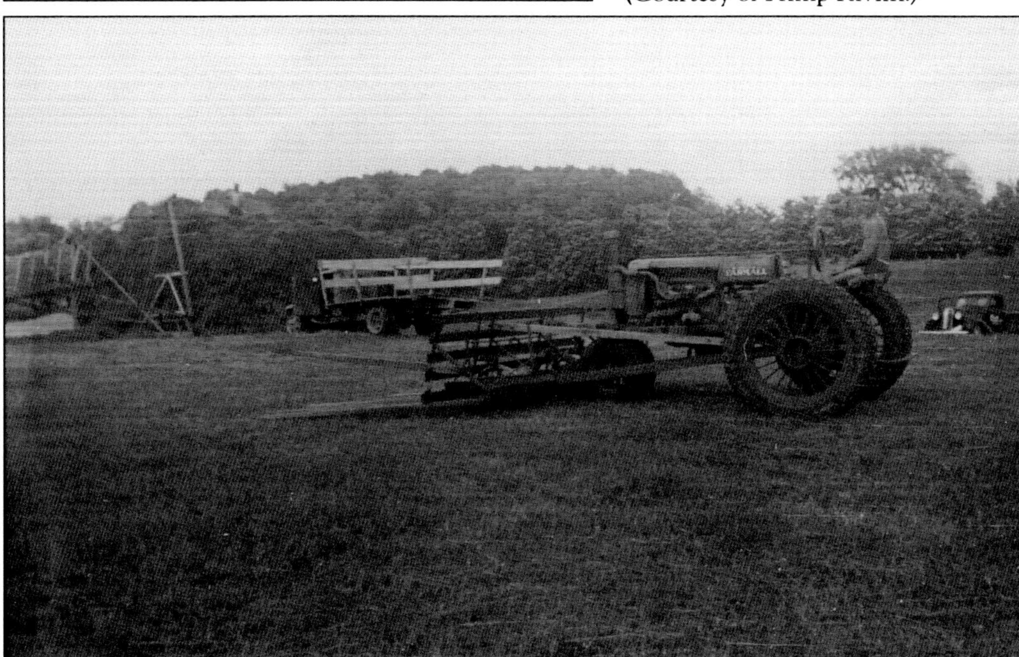

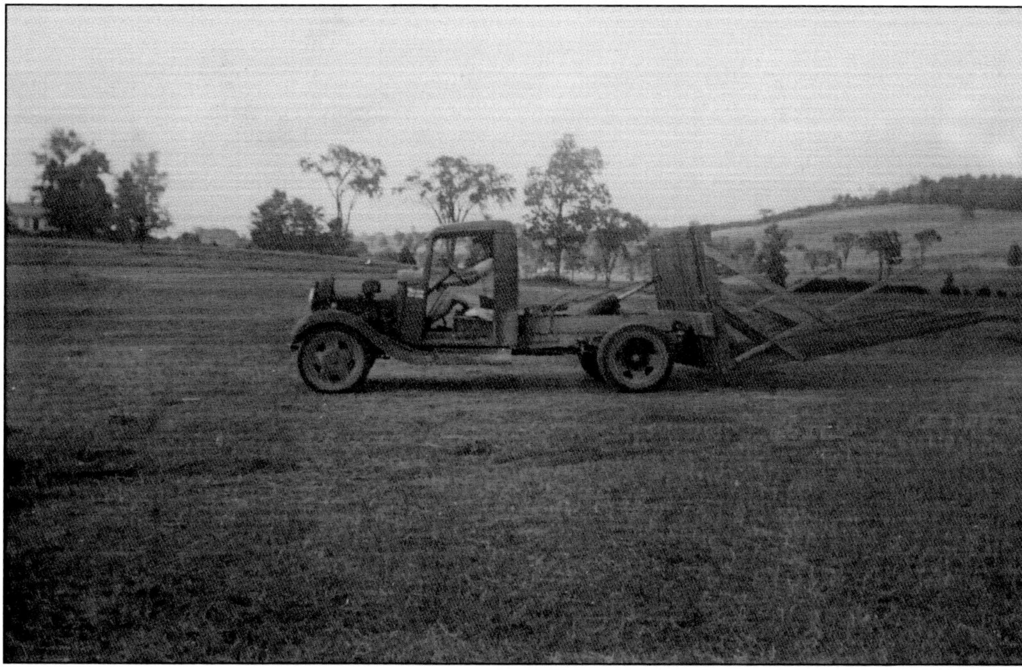

Robert Douglas moves the sweep rake from field to field with his old truck. (Courtesy of Philip Kivlin.)

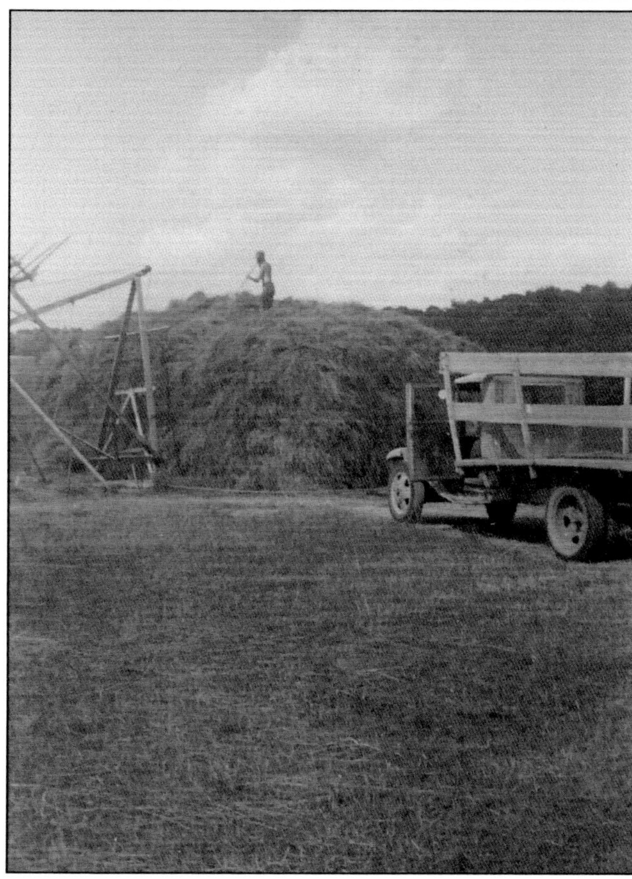

Malcolm Douglas is seen here atop a stack of hay. (Courtesy of Phil Kivlin.)

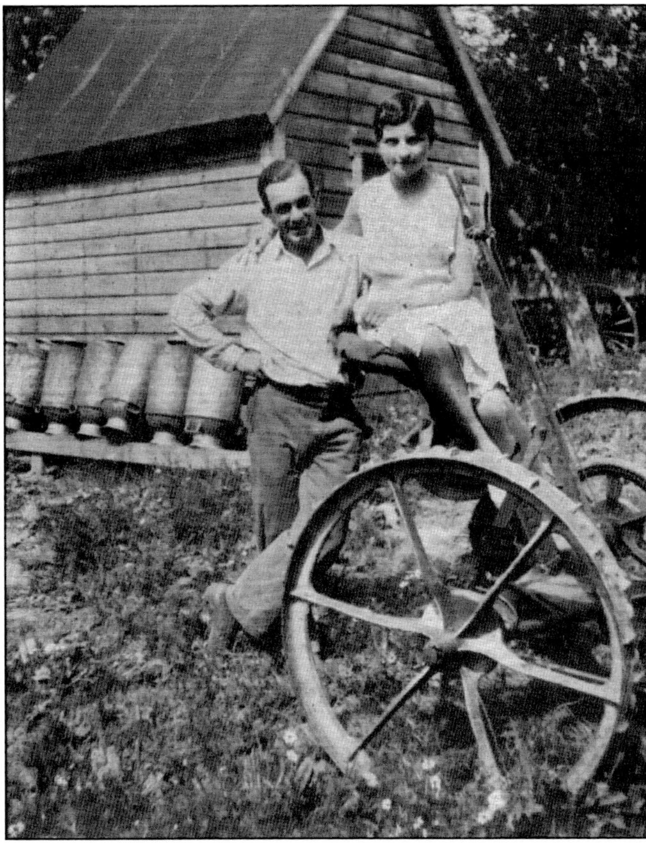

John Harold Wright (1900–1945) and his wife, Hildegard (Walker) Wright (1901–1968), are seen here with their horse-drawn mowing machine. They shipped milk in the milk cans against the shed, which are all labeled number 17. (Courtesy of H. Kent Wright III.)

Tapping maple trees and sugaring (pictured) were also done by most farmers in addition to their other pursuits. (Courtesy of John Sullivan.)

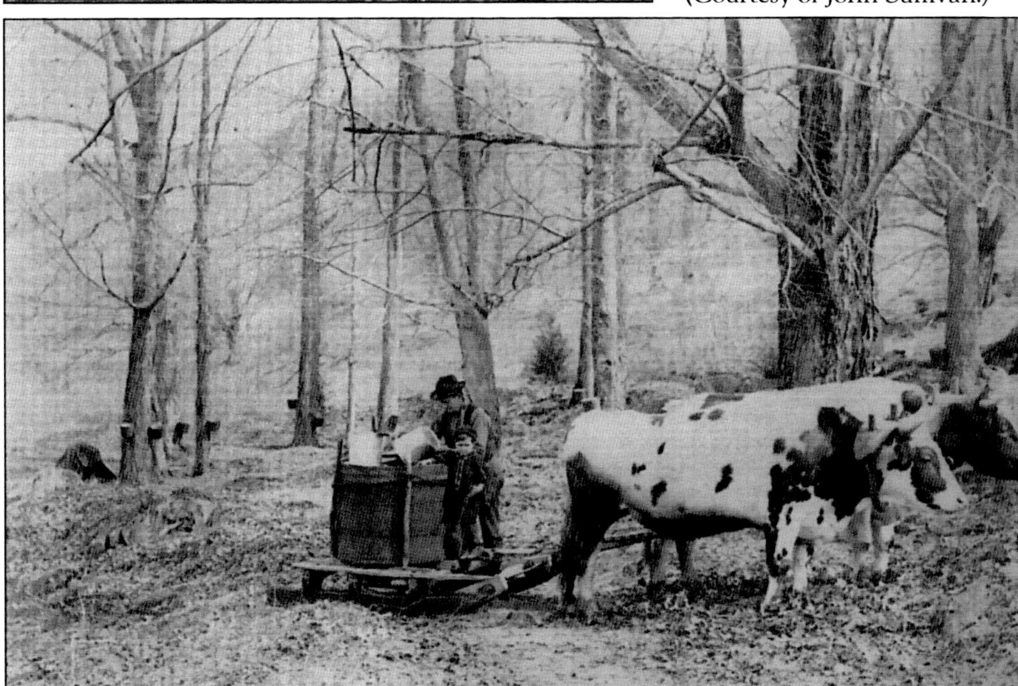

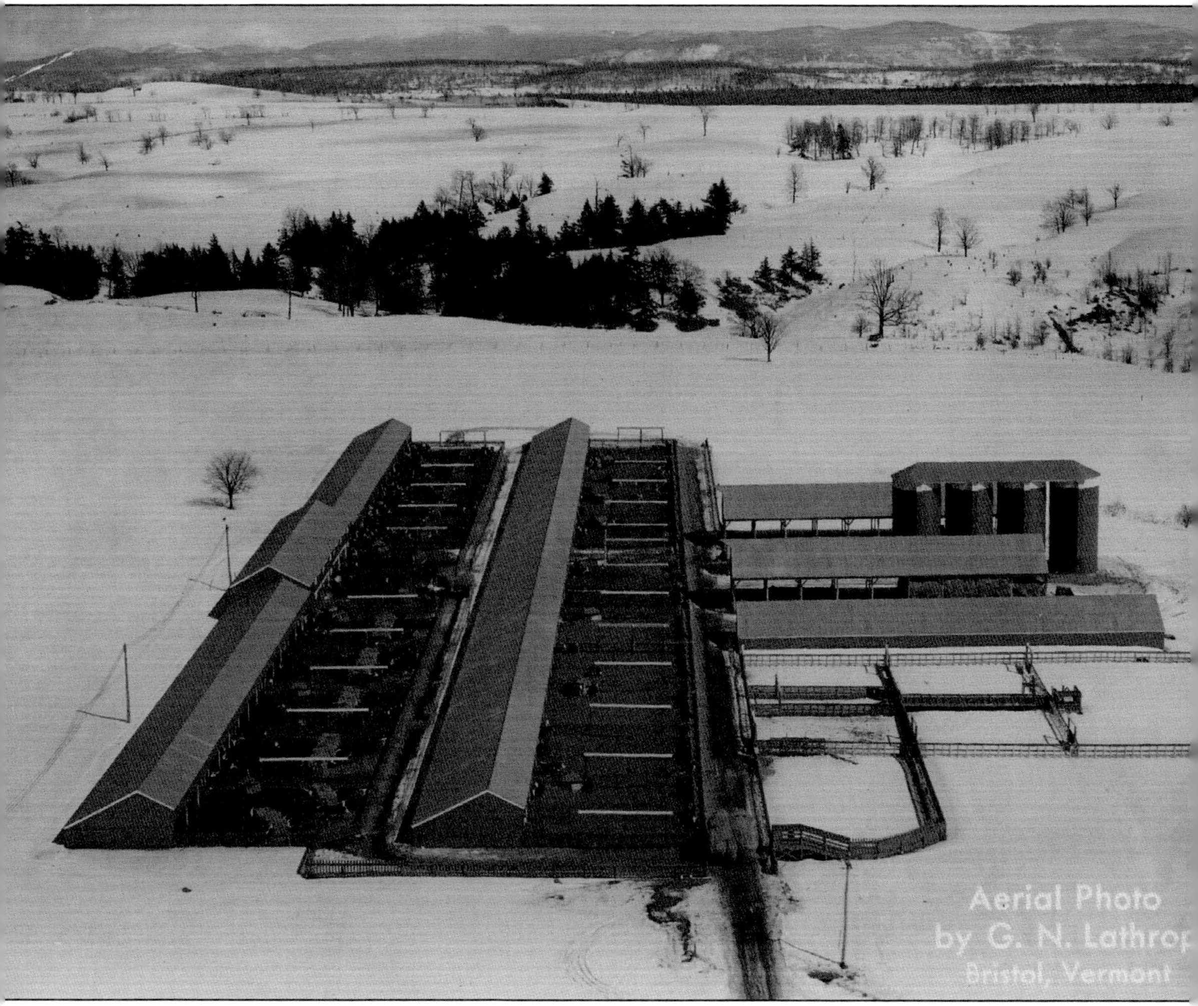

This photograph of Whiteface Ranch was taken in 1938 by George Lathrop. Richard Barlow bought up many of the small farms in the area when property values were low during the Depression. He then erected a 600-foot feeding station that could accommodate 1,000 head of cattle. Hereford cows were shipped in from Texas. They unloaded at Larrabee's Point, and local men gathered on Sunday morning to drive them up the roads to the ranch. The cattle were eventually phased out, and an Amish community rented the land. They grew vegetables, which they peddled around, selling out of their horse-drawn buggies. The ranch is now part of a large dairy farm owned by the Barnes family.

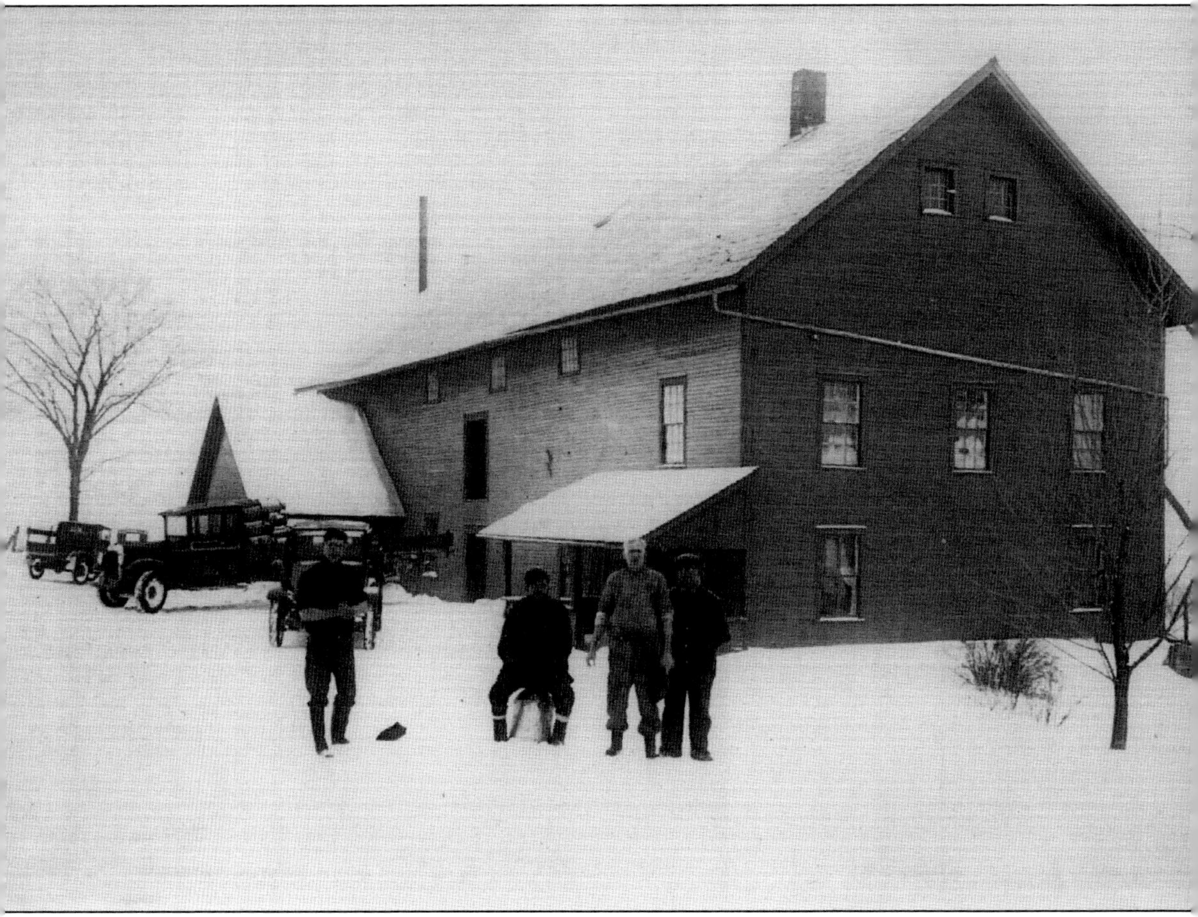

In the 1930s, this New England Dairies, Inc., creamery was the largest cheese-making plant in the state, and one of the largest east of the Mississippi River. These workers posing outside of the plant are, from left to right, Henry Betourney, two unidentified, and Joe Duffany. (Courtesy of Eleanor Brisson.)

Seven

Notable Citizens

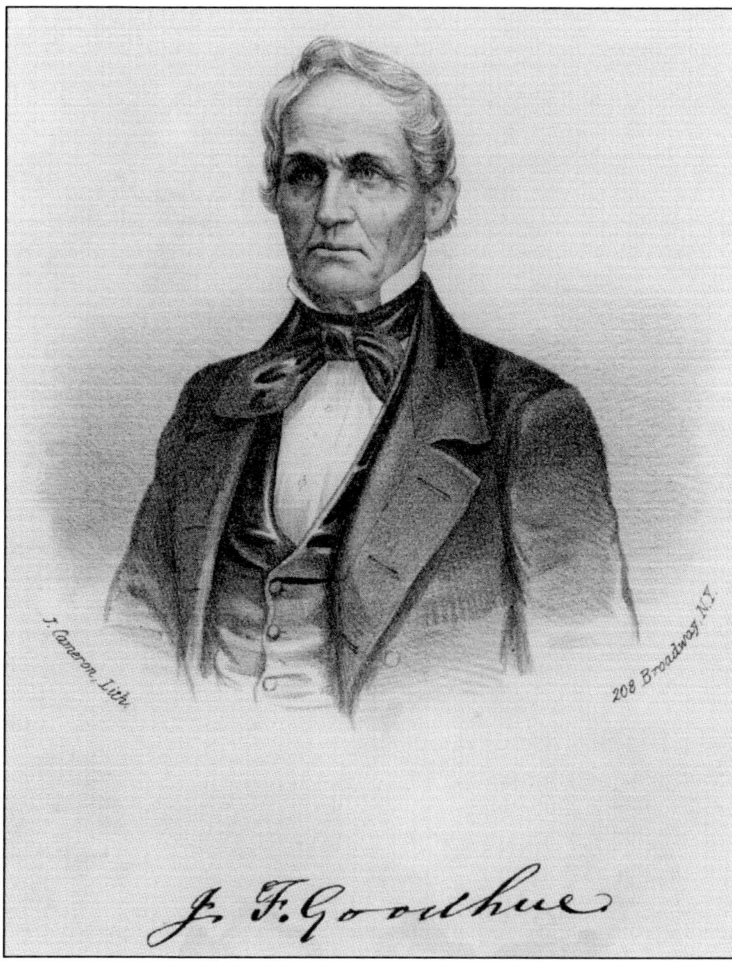

Josiah F. Goodhue served as the Congregational minister in Shoreham from September 1833 until September 1857. He began to write a history of the town in 1859, and completed it in 1861 after he had moved to Whitewater, Wisconsin.

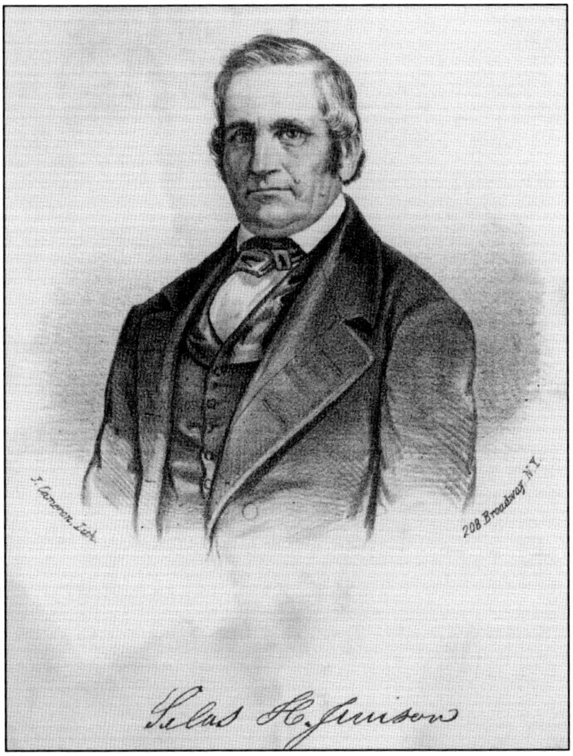

Silas Hemenway Jenison was born in Shoreham on May 17, 1791. His father died when he was one year old. Raised by a single mother, he was needed at home to help her run the farm, so he had limited education. He was, however, a voracious reader. In 1826, he was elected to represent Shoreham in the state legislature. He held that position for six years before serving as the assistant justice of the county court for six years and as a member of the state council for three years. After that, he served as lieutenant governor for two years, and, in 1836, he was elected governor of Vermont by popular vote, and he remained in that office for three terms.

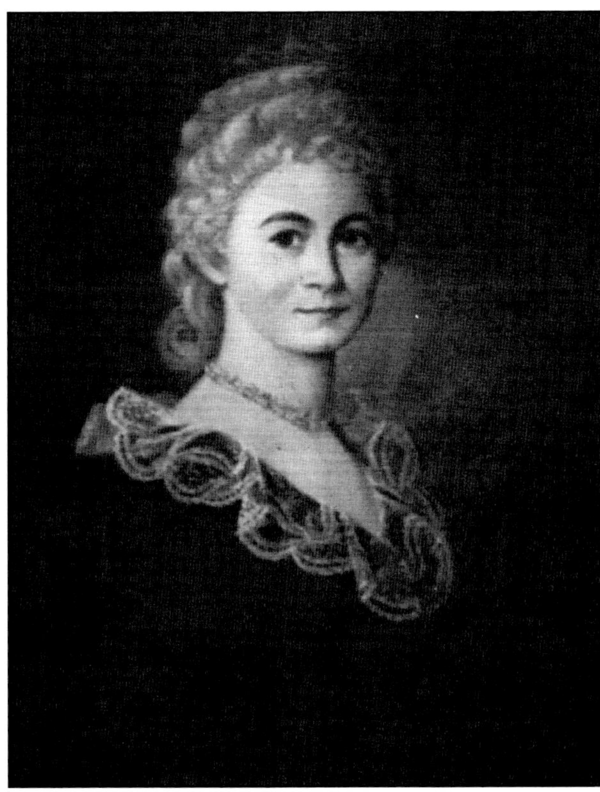

Lydia (Maltby) Larrabee was the wife of John S. Larrabee. They moved to Shoreham in 1787. Although a ferry had been running since the 1750s at this narrow stretch of Lake Champlain, Larrabee applied for and was granted the first official franchise for the ferry in 1799. It is the franchise that the ferry still operates under in the 21st century.

Lucia Hemenway, born in 1810, was the granddaughter of Samuel Hemenway (1755–1813), the famed Windsor Chair maker. He lived in Shoreham and made many chairs that are in museums around the country today. The Shoreham Historical Society also has a barn loom he made for his wife, which is still in working order.

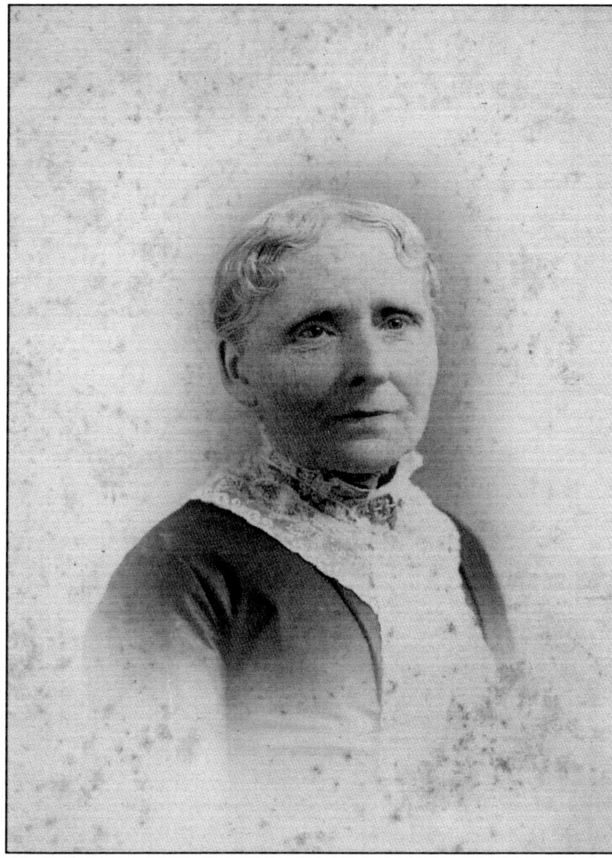

The three chairs below were made by Samuel Hemenway at his shop in Shoreham.

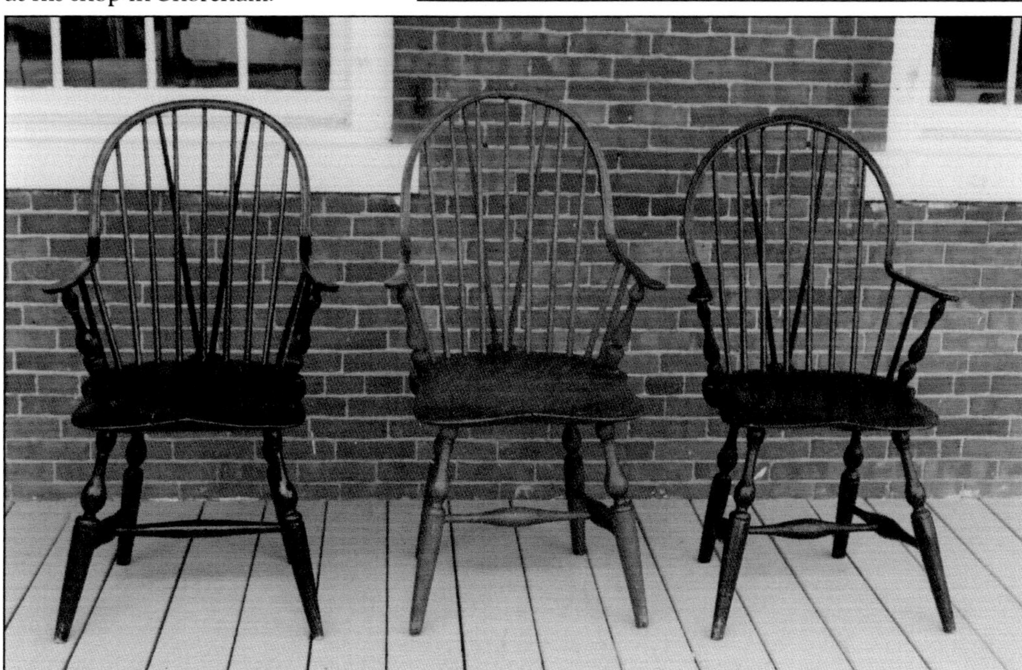

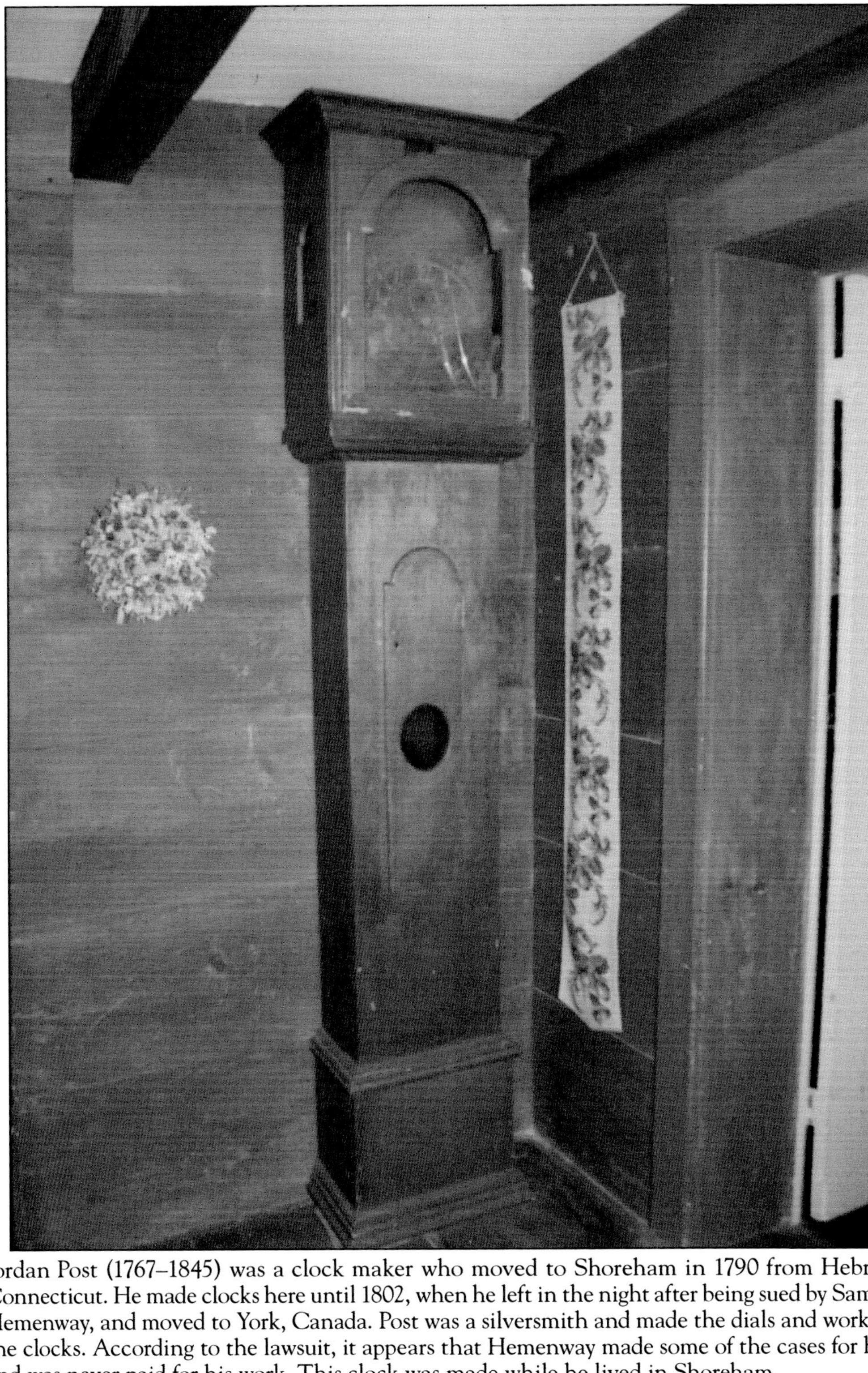

Jordan Post (1767–1845) was a clock maker who moved to Shoreham in 1790 from Hebron, Connecticut. He made clocks here until 1802, when he left in the night after being sued by Samuel Hemenway, and moved to York, Canada. Post was a silversmith and made the dials and works of the clocks. According to the lawsuit, it appears that Hemenway made some of the cases for him and was never paid for his work. This clock was made while he lived in Shoreham.

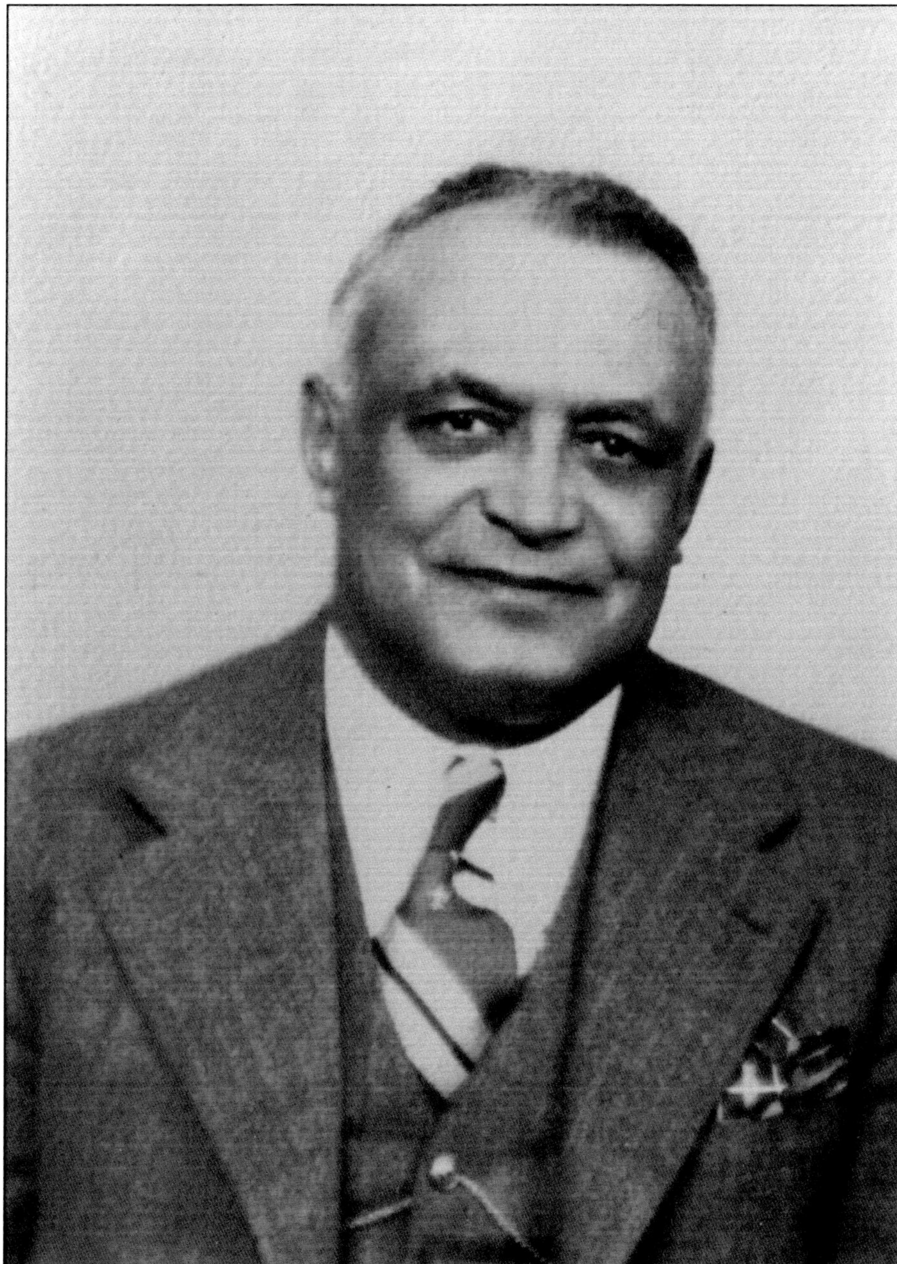

William John Anderson Jr. was born in Shoreham on February 14, 1876. He was educated in village schools and then attended Mt. Hermon School for Boys in Massachusetts. In 1911, he set out apple trees on land his father owned east of St. Genevieve's Church. By 1920, the orchard had grown and became Diamond A Orchard. He became very ardent about growing fruit and was elected president of the Vermont Horticultural Society in 1935. He was also elected to represent Shoreham in the Vermont Legislature for two terms. During World War I, he served in military intelligence and was chairman of the Selective Service board. When World War II threatened, he proposed a separate training academy for black men, which became the Tuskegee Advanced Flying School.

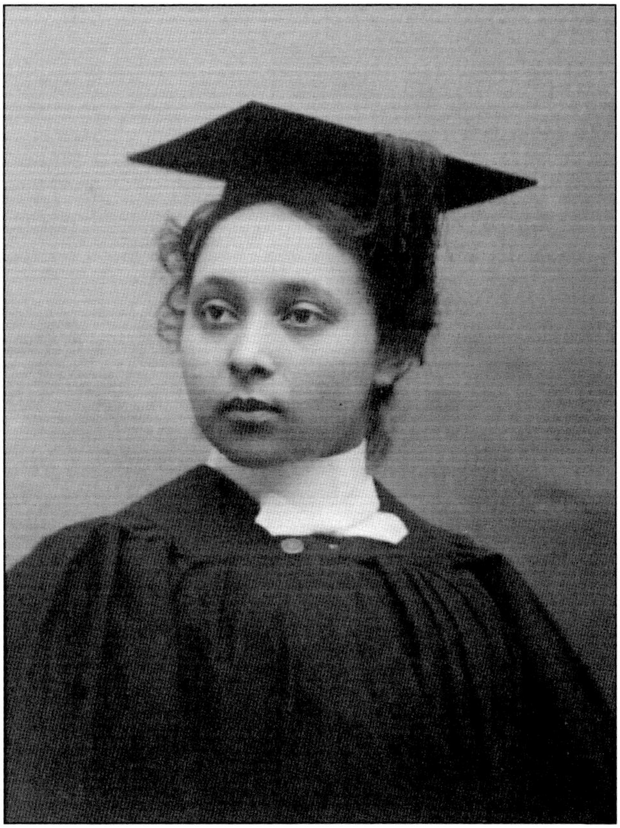

Marion Annette Anderson was born in 1874 in Shoreham and was the older sister of William Anderson Jr. After attending schools in Shoreham, she was sent to Northfield Seminary for Young Ladies. She graduated as valedictorian of the class of 1899 at Middlebury College, and was the first black Phi Beta Kappa. She taught English and history at Howard University until she married Walter Smith. They maintained homes in Washington, DC, and in Shoreham, where she died in 1922 at the age of 47.

Charles Byron Kendall (left, 1854–1927), and his son Edward Charles Kendall (1883–1913) lived in Shoreham village and ran a general store on Main Street. The wood-frame store burned in 1906, and they rebuilt it as a brick building, which still stands today and houses three apartments.

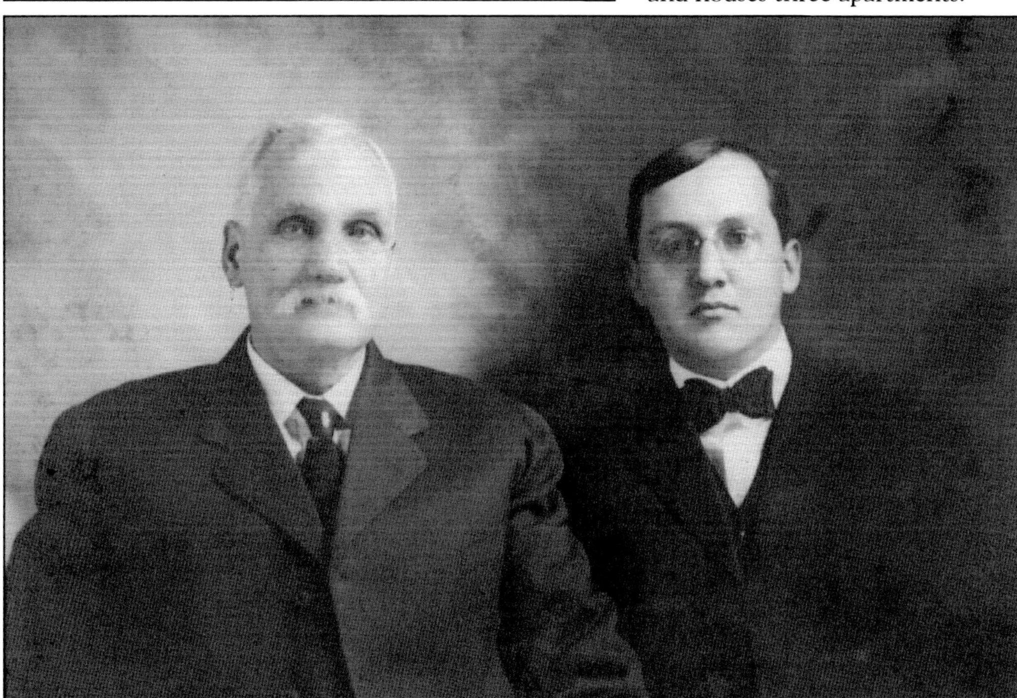

Dr. Charles Willard Howard (1846–1917) served the town of Shoreham as a physician. He also served as town clerk from 1881 to 1917 and represented Shoreham in the Vermont General Assembly in 1908.

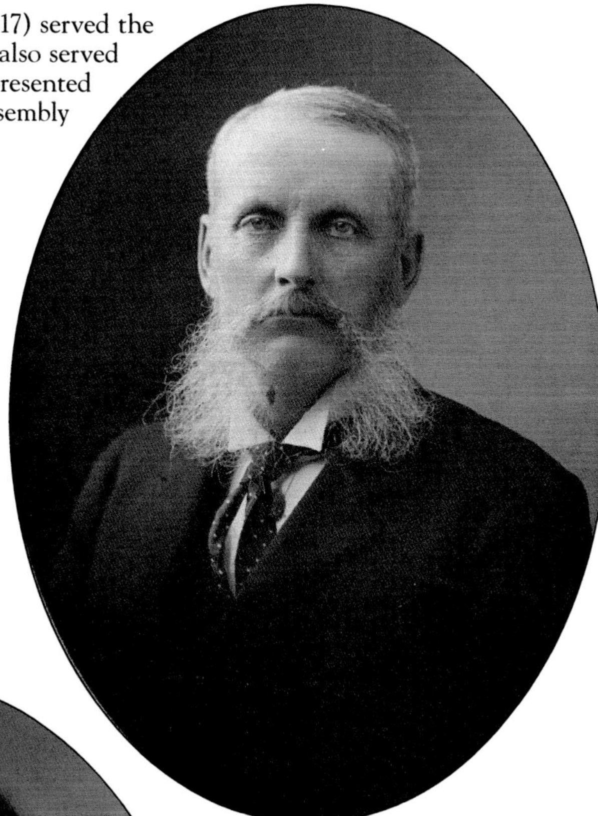

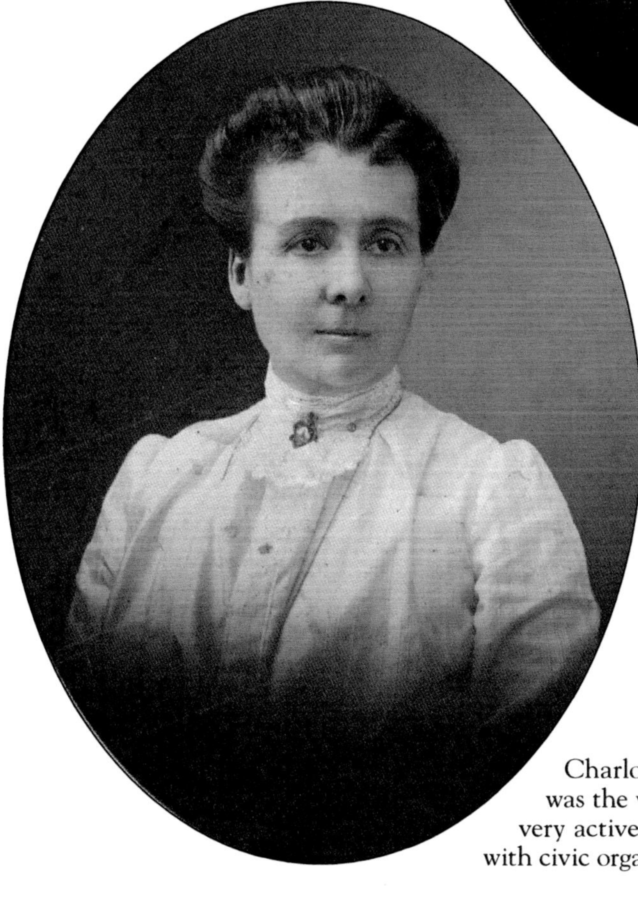

Charlotte (Douglas) Howard (1846–1924) was the wife of Charles W. Howard. She was very active in the Congregational church and with civic organizations in town.

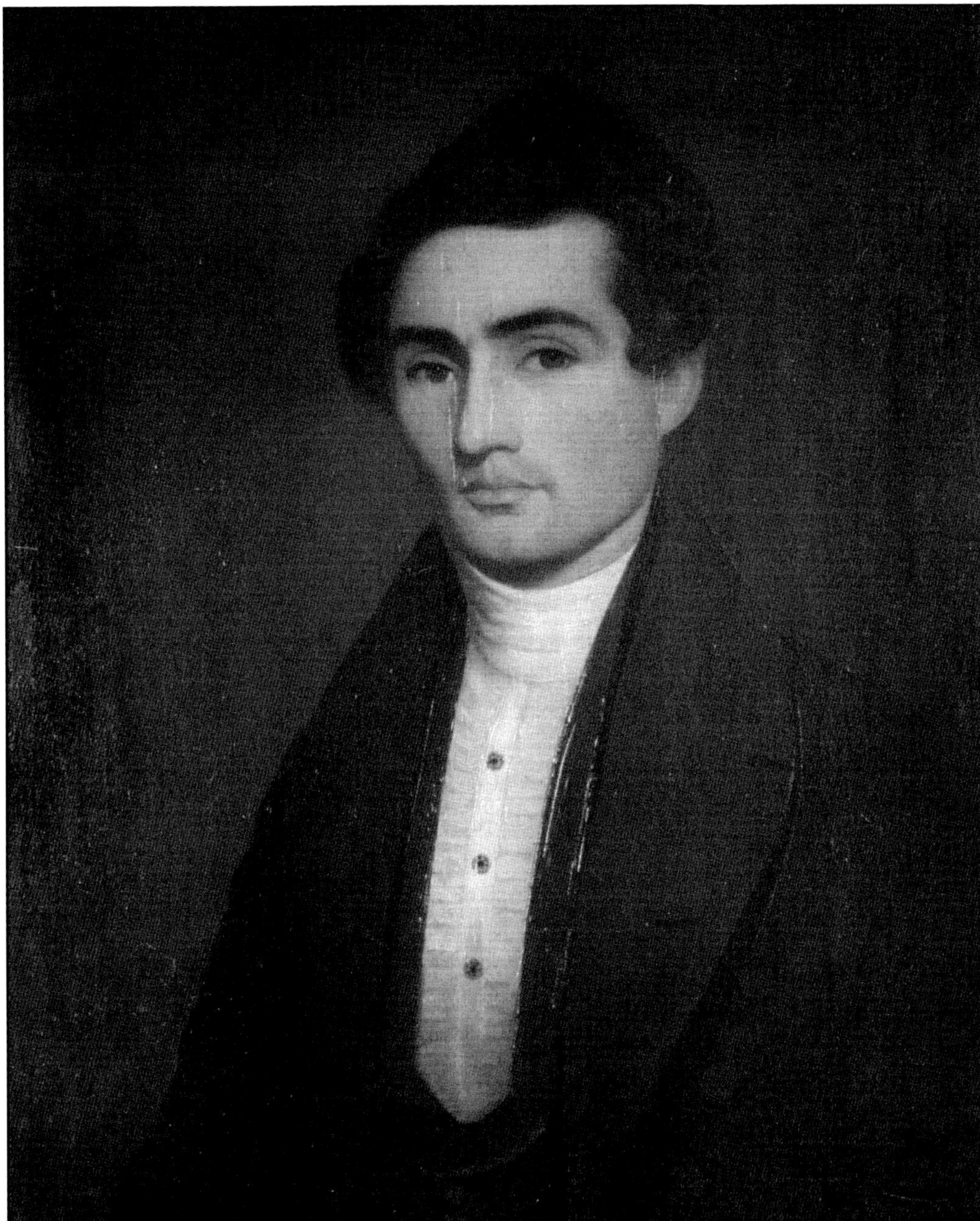

Charles Maris Baker (1804–1872) attended Newton Academy in Shoreham and then Middlebury College. He became smitten with Martha Washington Larrabee, the daughter of John S. Larrabee, who ran the ferry. But wanderlust eventually struck him, and when the Erie Canal opened in 1823, he headed west. Unlike other young men of his day, he wrote letters home to Shoreham regularly, which were all saved. In 1928, they were all published as *Charles Minton Baker and the Pioneer Trail*, edited by Edward Larrabee Baker. It is a marvelous glimpse into what life was like during that time period.

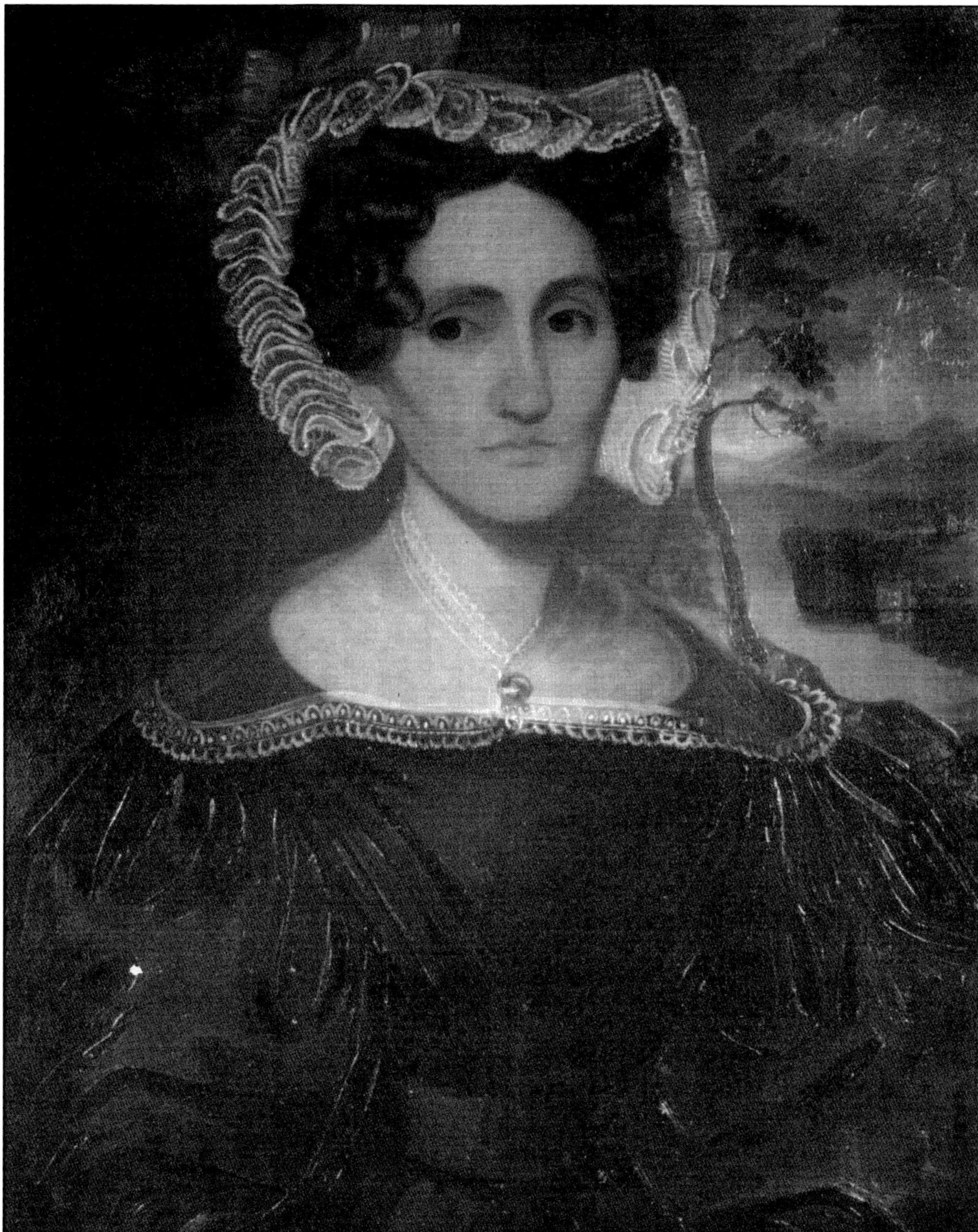

Martha Washington (Larrabee) Baker (1806–1843) did indeed marry her sweetheart, Charles Baker. They settled in Lake Geneva, Wisconsin. Unfortunately, she died giving birth to her seventh child at the age of 37.

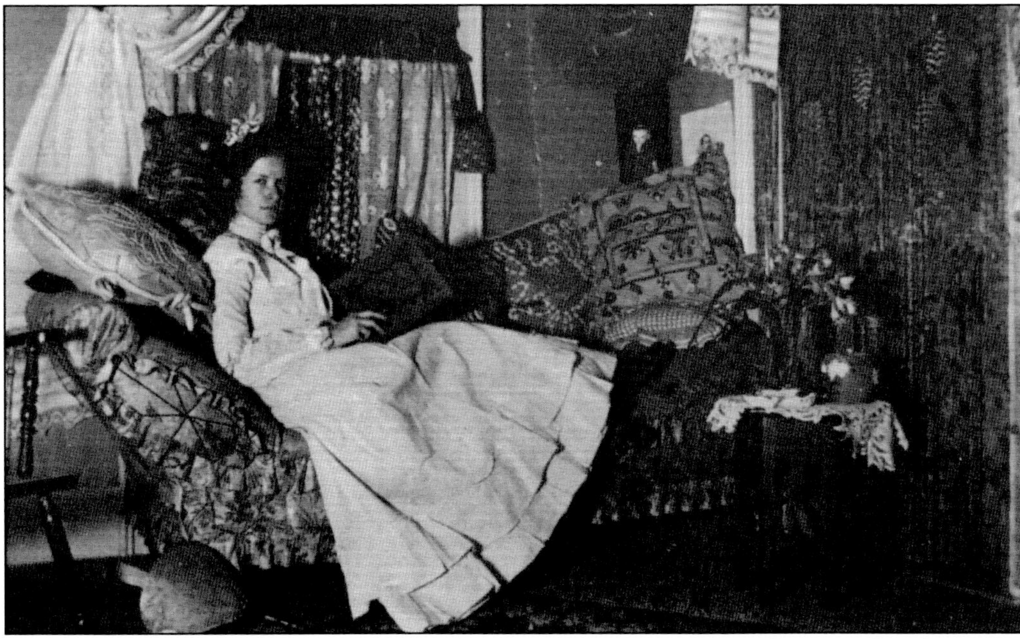

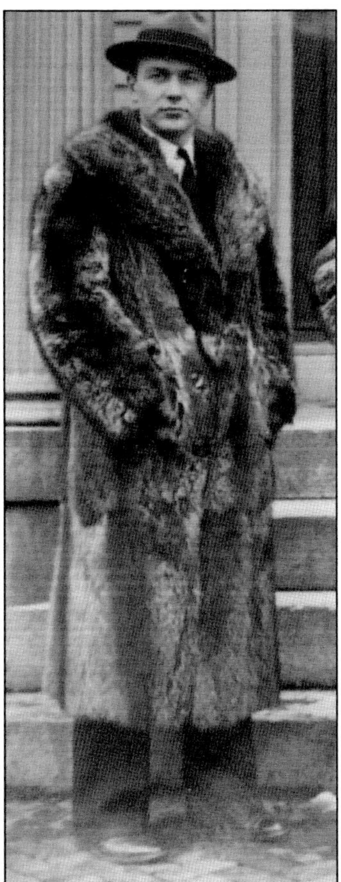

Elizabeth Clark (North) Sharon was born in Shoreham in 1881 to Clayton Nelson North and Anne Elizabeth Bascom. She grew up in the village, where her father ran a store. She was instrumental in getting a monument put up in the village for veterans of World War I.

Dr. Isaac Paul Sharon served as a physician in Shoreham for many years. He married Elizabeth North, practicing medicine and living in the house where she grew up.

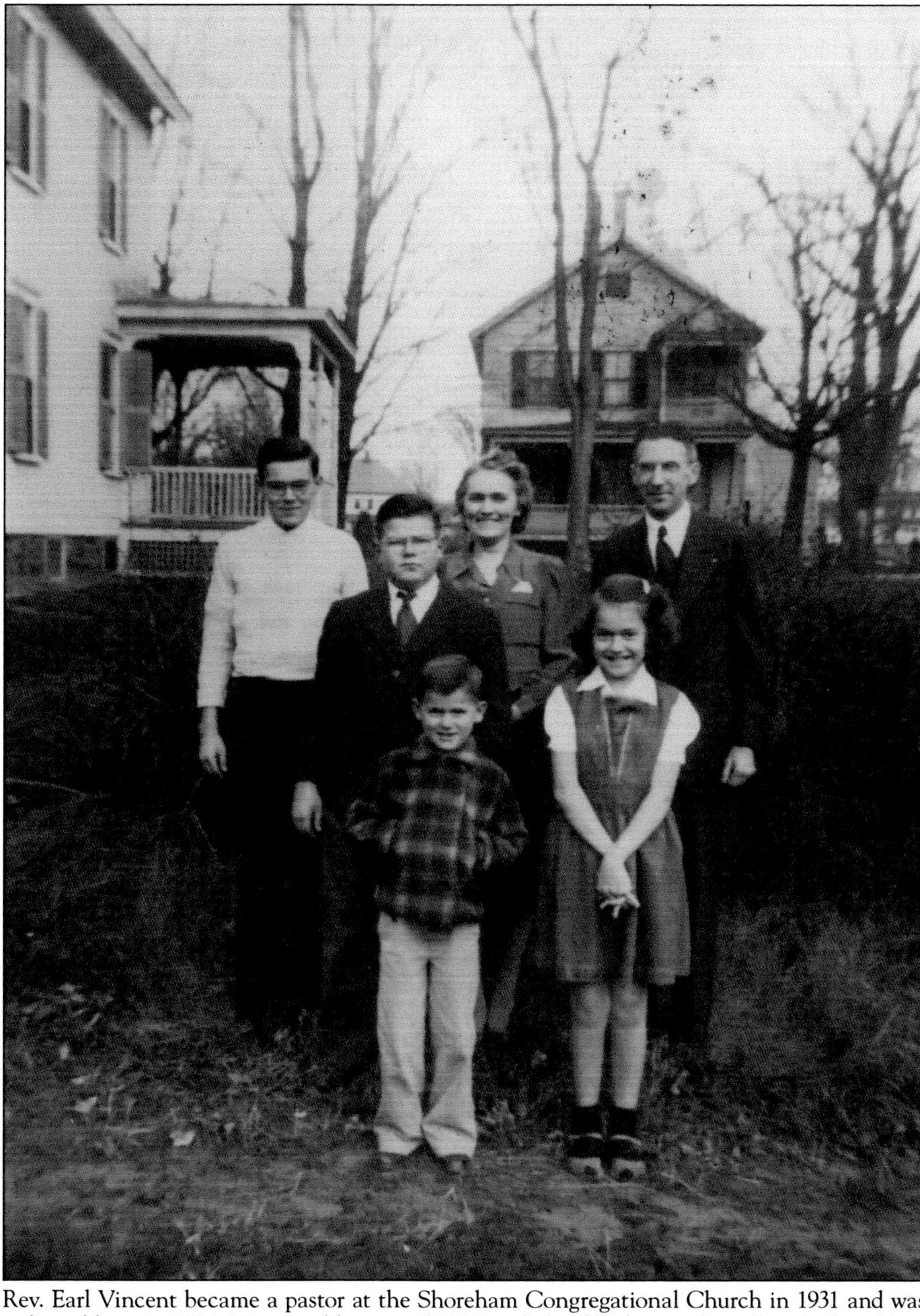

Rev. Earl Vincent became a pastor at the Shoreham Congregational Church in 1931 and was ordained here in 1934. He served here until 1939 and also filled in as the village barber. He is seen here with his family. They are, from left to right, Robert Vincent, Richard Vincent, Sonny Vincent, Gladys Vincent, Ruth Vincent, and Rev. Earl Vincent.

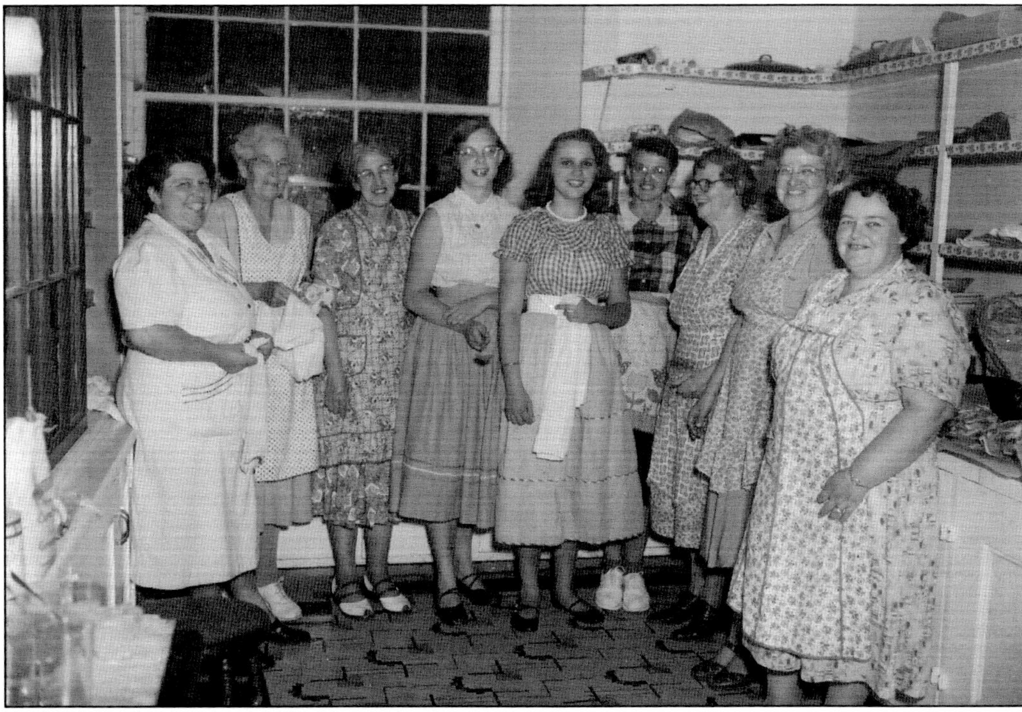

Known for those fabulous New England church suppers, the ladies above, in the kitchen of the Congregational church, produced some very fine meals. They are, from left to right, Mary Hutchins, Florence Brown, Clara Stanley, two unidentified women, Winifred Birchard, Esme Cook, Veda Orvis, and Ureka Sunderland.

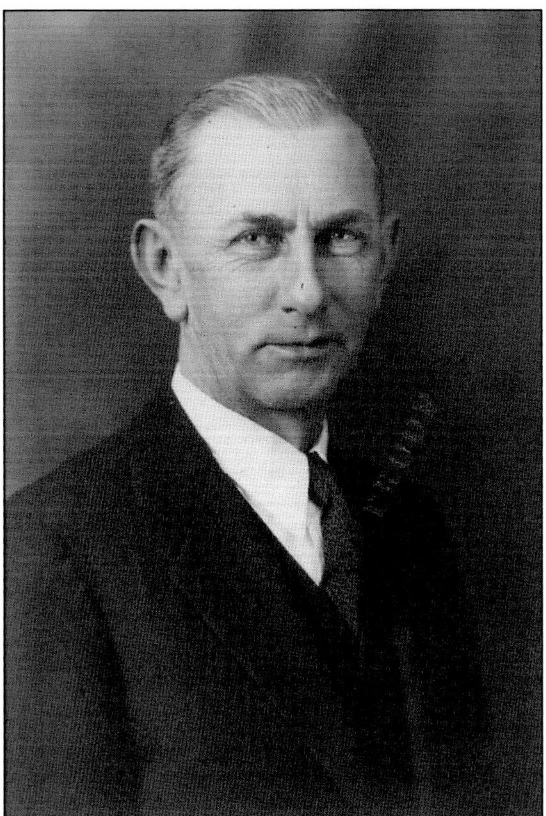

John Loren DeWitt (1888–1971) was the son of an immigrant from Holland. He became an insurance agent and kept a book of the properties he insured sketched out on graph paper. The Shoreham Historical Society now has this book, with homes, outbuildings, and barns all carefully documented.

Levi Parsons Morton (1824–1920) was born in a small house on Route 22A. His father was the pastor of Shoreham Congregational Church. When he was two years old, the family moved into the village. He lived here until 1830, when his father was transferred to another church; however, he always listed Shoreham as his hometown. He became a New York congressman in 1879. He was the US ambassador to France from 1881 to 1885 and even drove the first rivet into the Statue of Liberty. He went on to be the vice president under Pres. Benjamin Harrison and then served as governor of New York from 1895 to 1897.

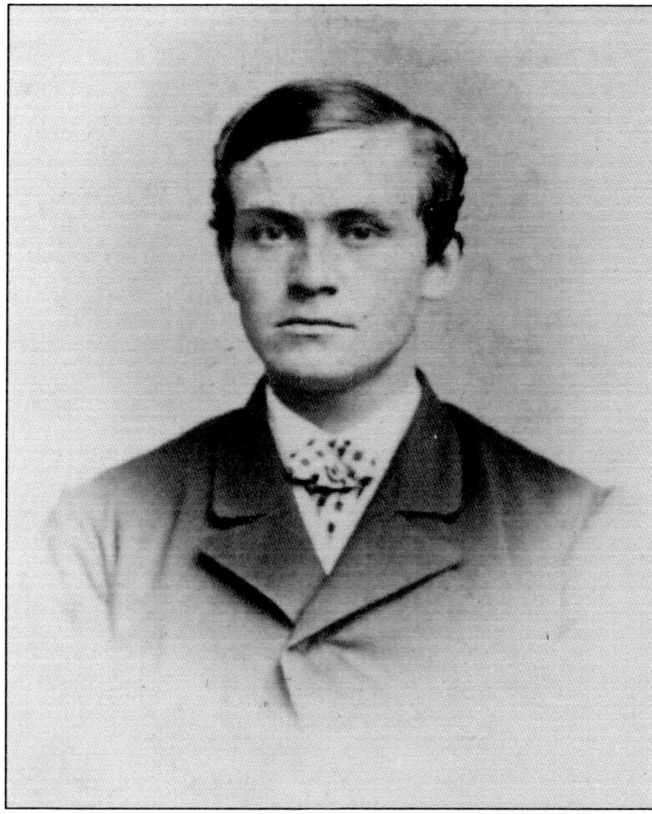

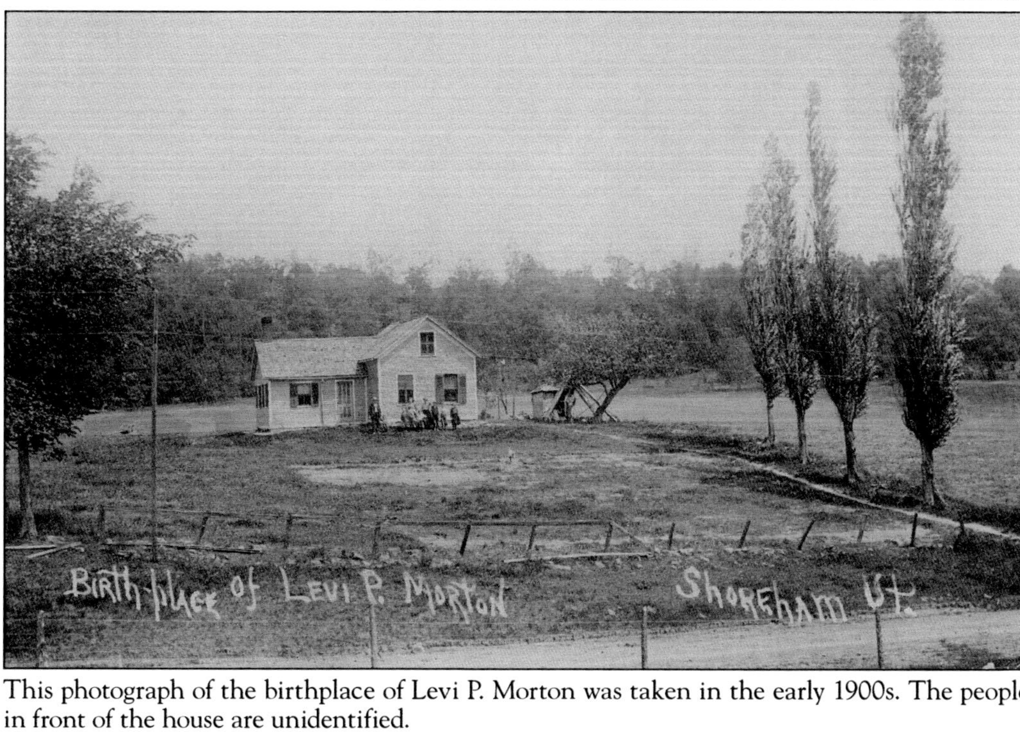

This photograph of the birthplace of Levi P. Morton was taken in the early 1900s. The people in front of the house are unidentified.

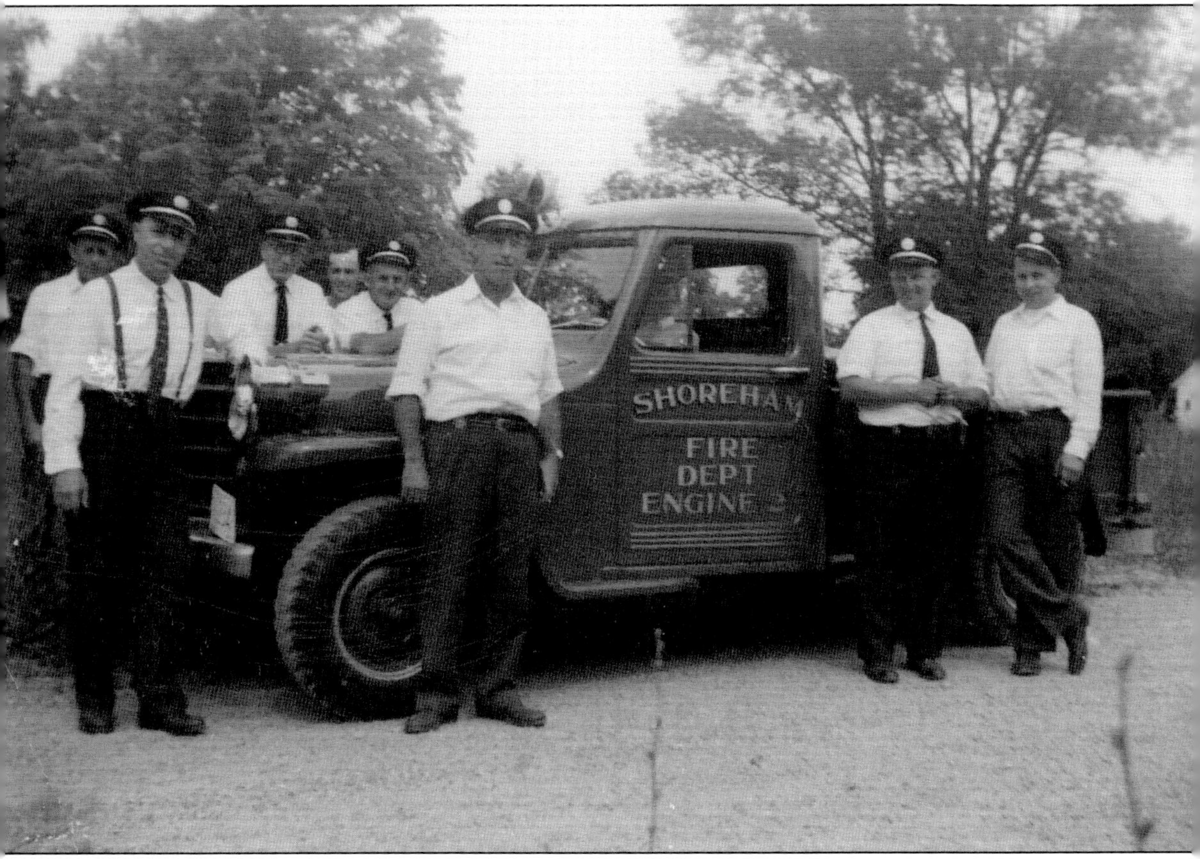

The Shoreham Fire Department came into being after a 1939 town meeting. Voters authorized a sum of $500 to purchase a used fire truck. Prior to that time, fires were fought by bucket brigade, baking soda, and acid fire extinguishers. This photograph includes, from left to right, (obscured), Paul Blair, Quentin Shackett, John Elithorpe, Robert Brisson, Donald Treadway, Buster Edwards, Norman Treadway, and Clifford Valley. (Courtesy of Kirk LaDuke.)

A small-town fire department has to do what is needed to get by. Quentin Shackett's old Renault was outfitted with a fire extinguisher holder and carried other equipment when it went on fire calls. Barbra (Shackett) Fitzpatrick is seen here walking by the car. (Courtesy of Kirk LaDuke.)

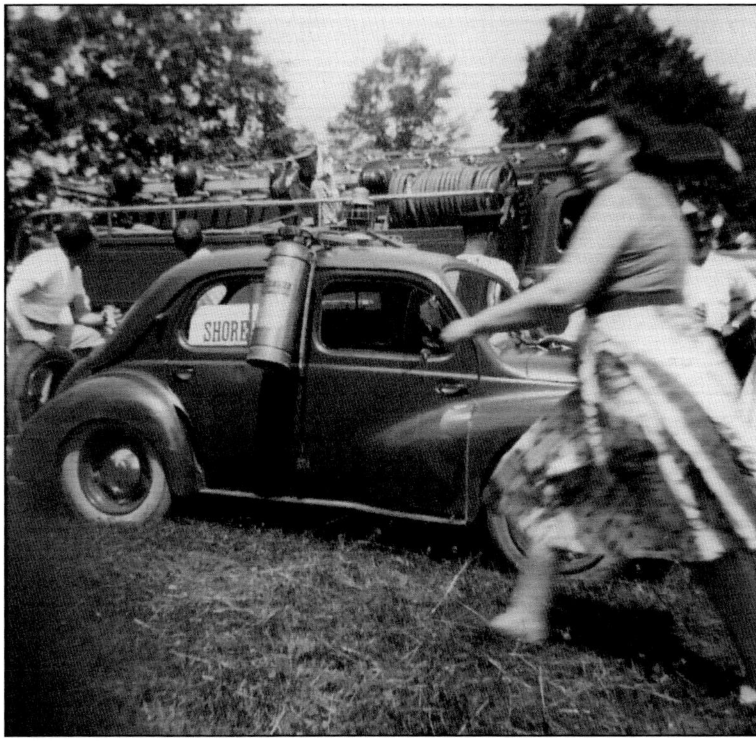

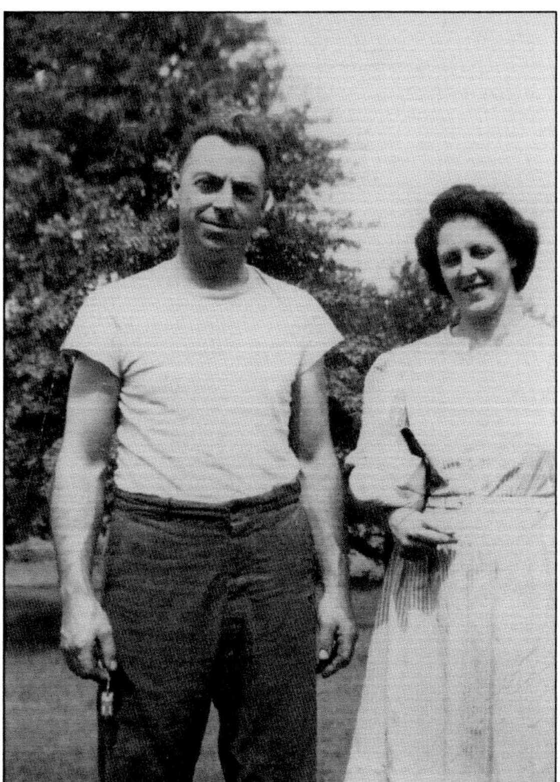

Quentin and Clarice Shackett contributed much time and energy to the betterment of Shoreham over the years. Quentin, a mechanic, had a shop behind his house. He was in charge of the road crew for many years. He also served on the select board. Whenever an iron fence at a cemetery needed repair, he was the man to call, and he never charged for doing that work. Clarice worked as an aide at Porter Hospital. She was active with the altar society of St. Genevieve's and dispatched calls for the fire department and rescue squad. (Courtesy of Kirk LaDuke.)

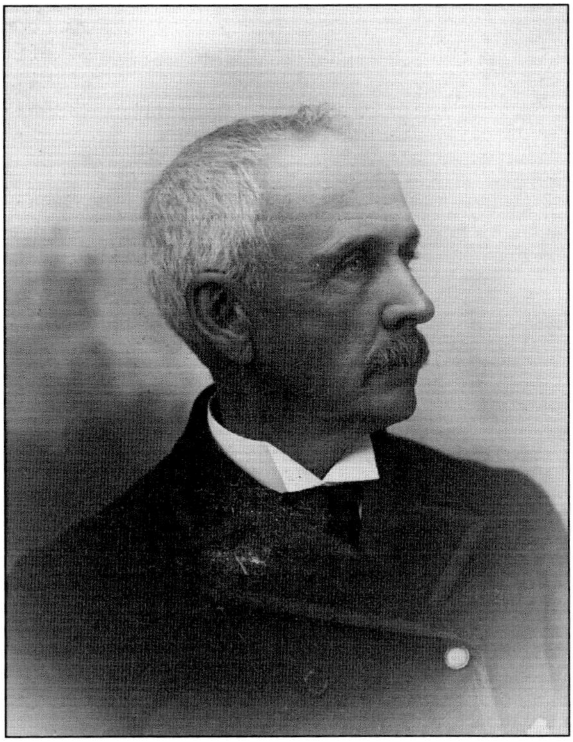

Samuel G. Moore, the son of William Walker Moore and Jane Hammond, was born in December 1863. He married Gertrude Samantha Hall in Shoreham. He farmed in Shoreham for a time but later worked as a machinist at a bicycle factory in Ticonderoga, New York.

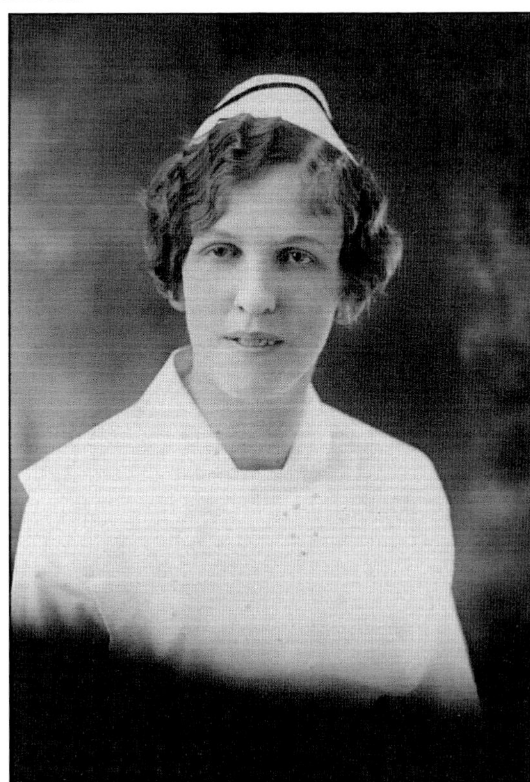

Dorothy Mabel Smith, the daughter of Charles D. Smith and Maria Towner, was born in Shoreham in February 1899. She married Dexter Henry Cross and became a nurse.

This photograph of Eva (Parker) Cook (1852–1955) was taken the day after her 100th birthday. The wife of Milan P. Cook, she was active in many Shoreham women's groups and was one of the founders of the Moravian Club, a group that met monthly and gave scholarly reports on situations around the world.

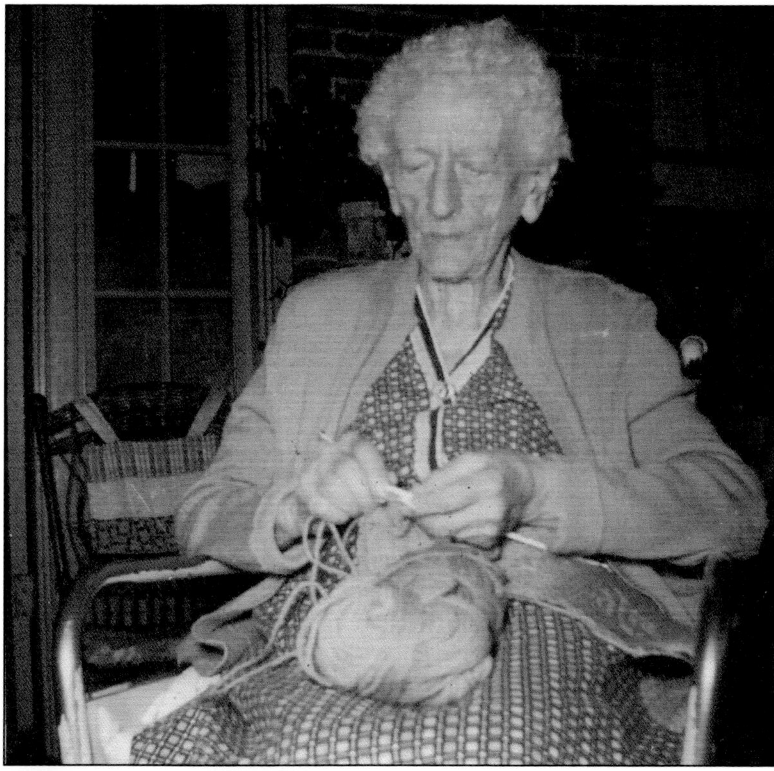

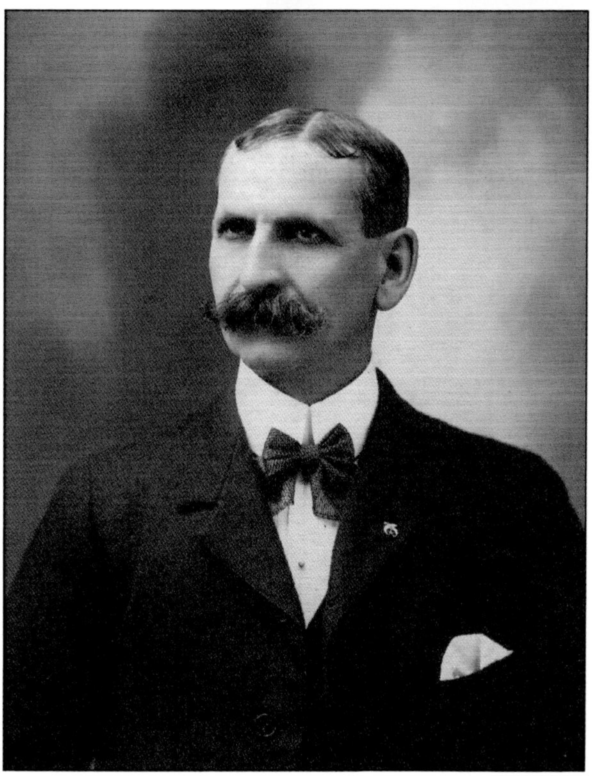

Richard Preble (1847–1926) married Emma Towner, the sister of Alanson Towner. In 1885, Preble was appointed postmaster in Shoreham. He was later elected to represent Shoreham in the state legislature, in 1902 and 1906.

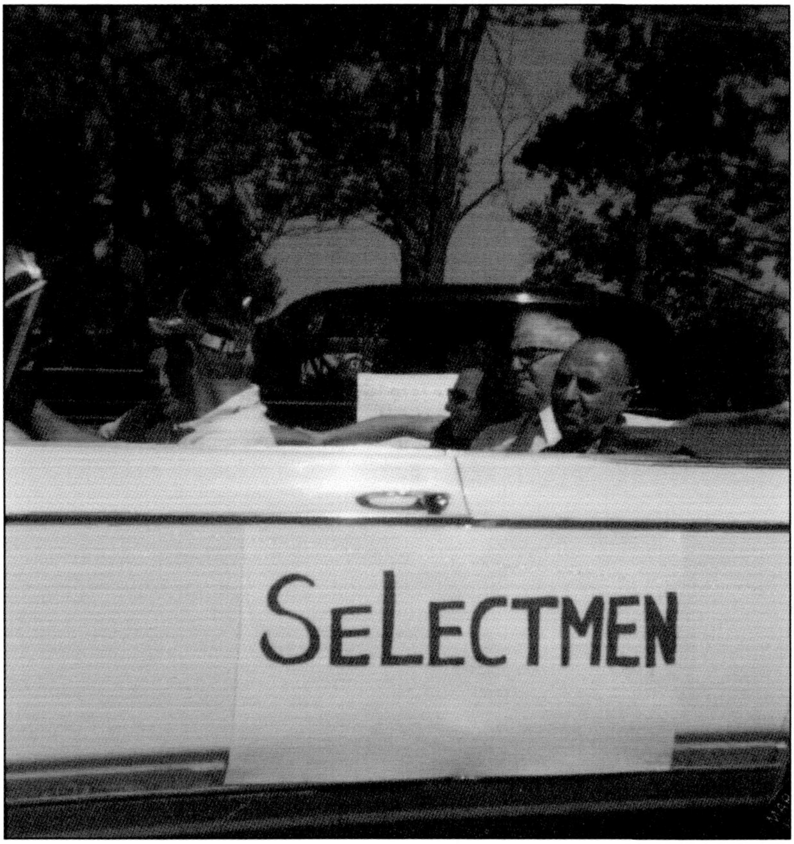

Over the years, many men and a few women have served on the Shoreham select board. This governing body of the town puts in many hours of work for the benefit of all who live here. This parade photograph includes selectmen, from left to right, (front seat) S. Whitney Blodgett and Donald Treadway; (back seat) Frederick Lapham, Edwin T. James, and Quentin Shackett. (Courtesy of Kirk LaDuke.)

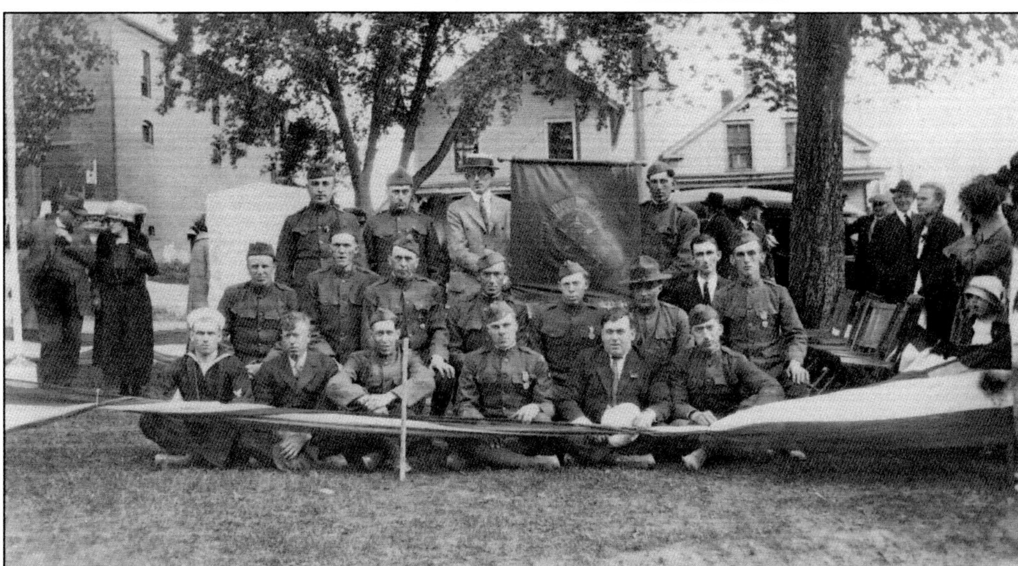

This group of Shoreham World War I veterans is seen here at the unveiling of their monument on the green in front of the Shoreham Inn. Most are unidentified, but Wilfred Brisson is in the second row, fourth from the left, and William Macauley is on the far right of the second row. (Courtesy of Mary Esther Macfarlane.)

These veterans of the Korean War came home to greet their grandmother. From left to right are William Shackett, Lucia Shackett, and Robert Shackett. (Courtesy of Kirk LaDuke.)

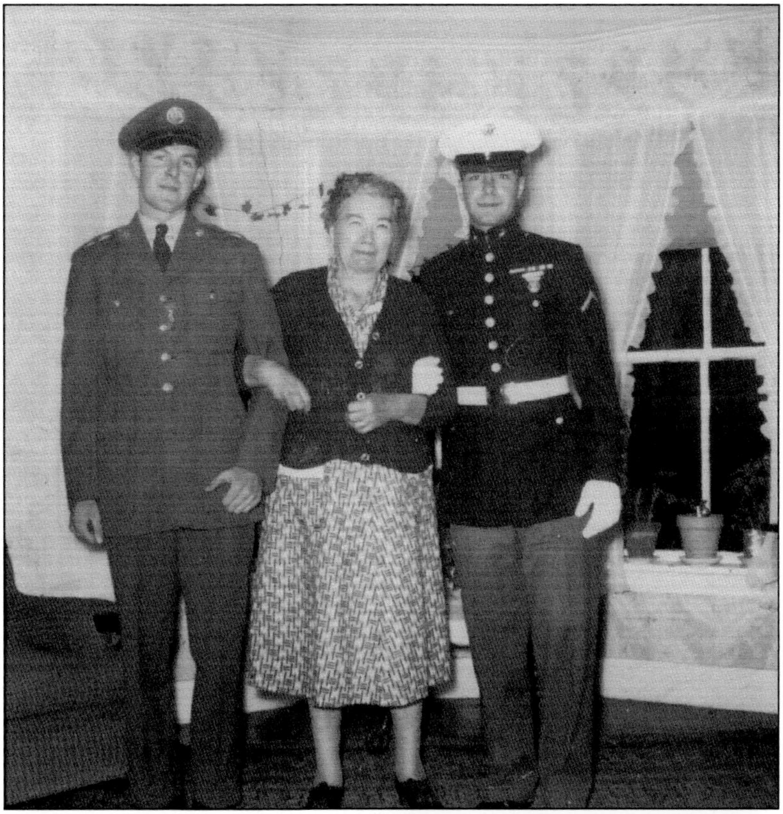

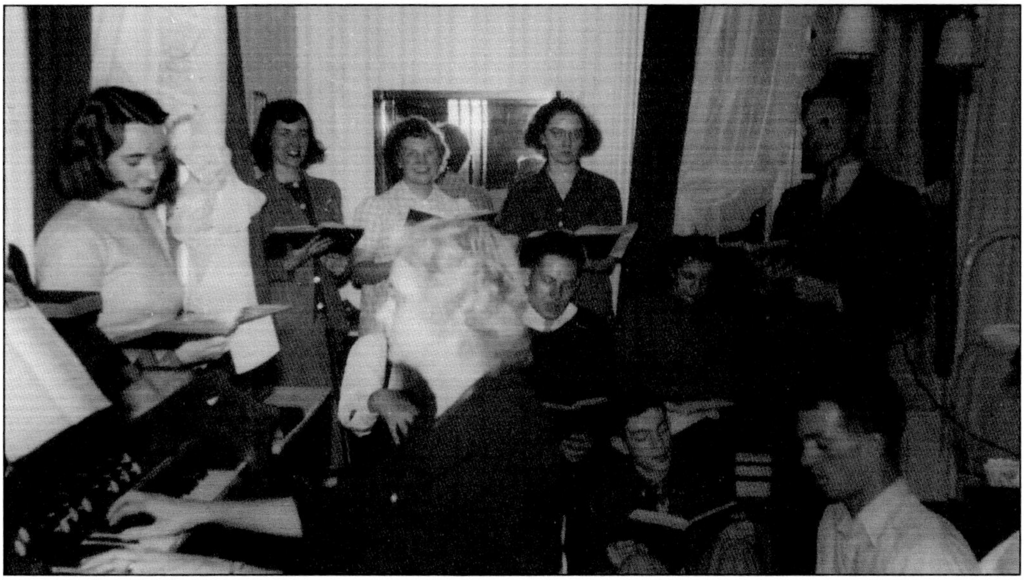

Many folks helped make the community a more pleasant place to live. Here, the Christmas choir of 1947 practices carols at the home of Joe and Laura Kivlin. The choir included, from left to right, (seated on floor) Theodore Sanders and Joseph Kivlin; (seated in chairs) organist Florence Easton, Robert Douglas, and Mary Ann Fuller; (standing) Betty Douglas, Audrey Stewart, Virginia Stewart, Marjorie Douglas, and Rev. Louis Turner. (Courtesy of Linda Larrabee.)

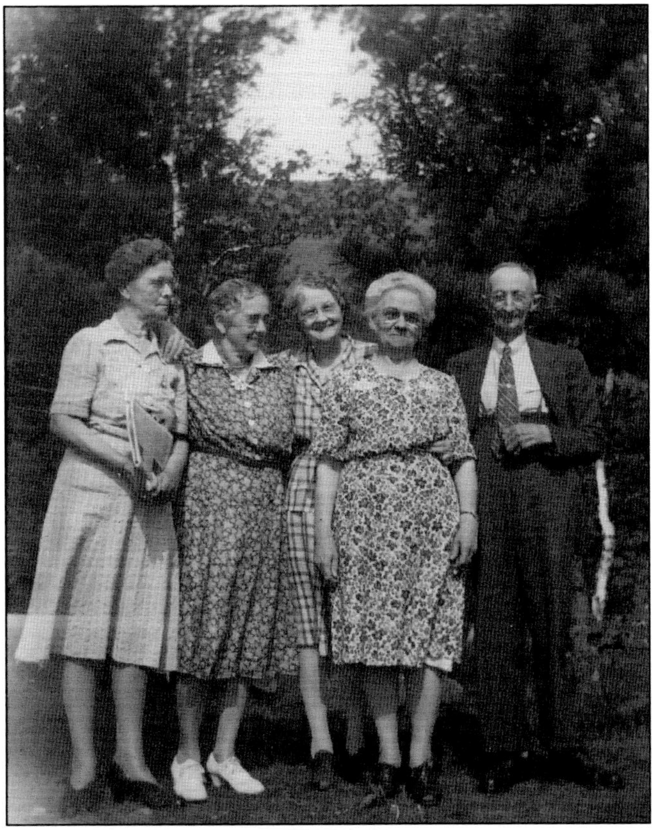

Sherrie Mead was born in Shoreham in 1873, the son of Henry Charles Mead and Louisa Harriet Fuller. He was postmaster in the village from 1912 to 1943. He is seen here on the far right with some of his adoring lady fans: (from left to right) Hattie M. Dudley, Mabel T. Wisell, Sarah Mead (his wife), and Lillian (Baker) Larrabee.

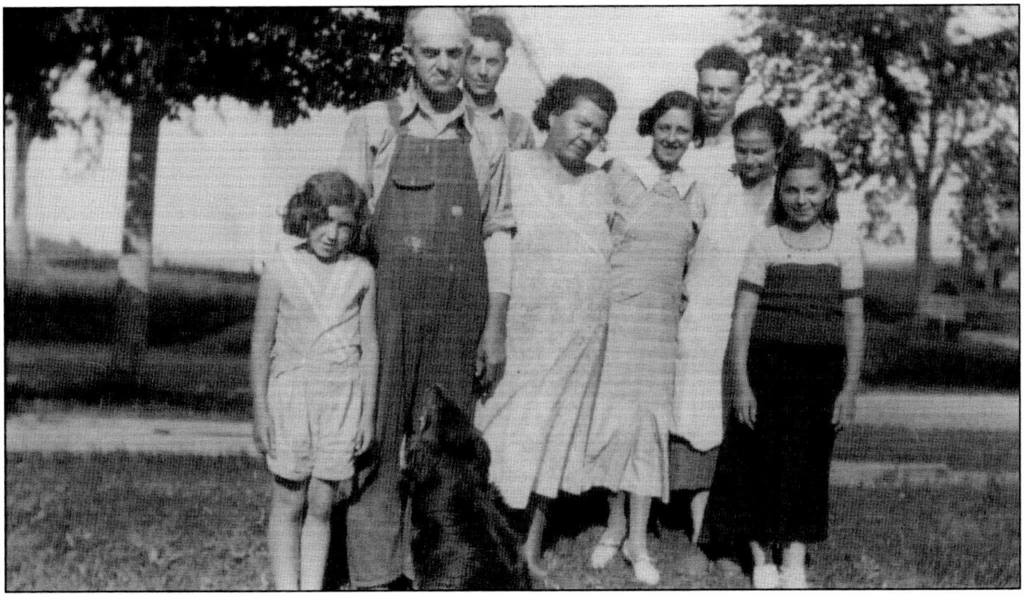

The Shackett family is seen here during the time they farmed at the blockhouse at Hand's Cove. From left to right, they are Barbra Shackett, Victor Shackett, Kenneth Shackett, Rose Shackett, Clarice Shackett, Quentin Shackett, Doris Norton, and Naomi Shackett. (Courtesy of Kirk LaDuke.)

Eight

SCHOOLS

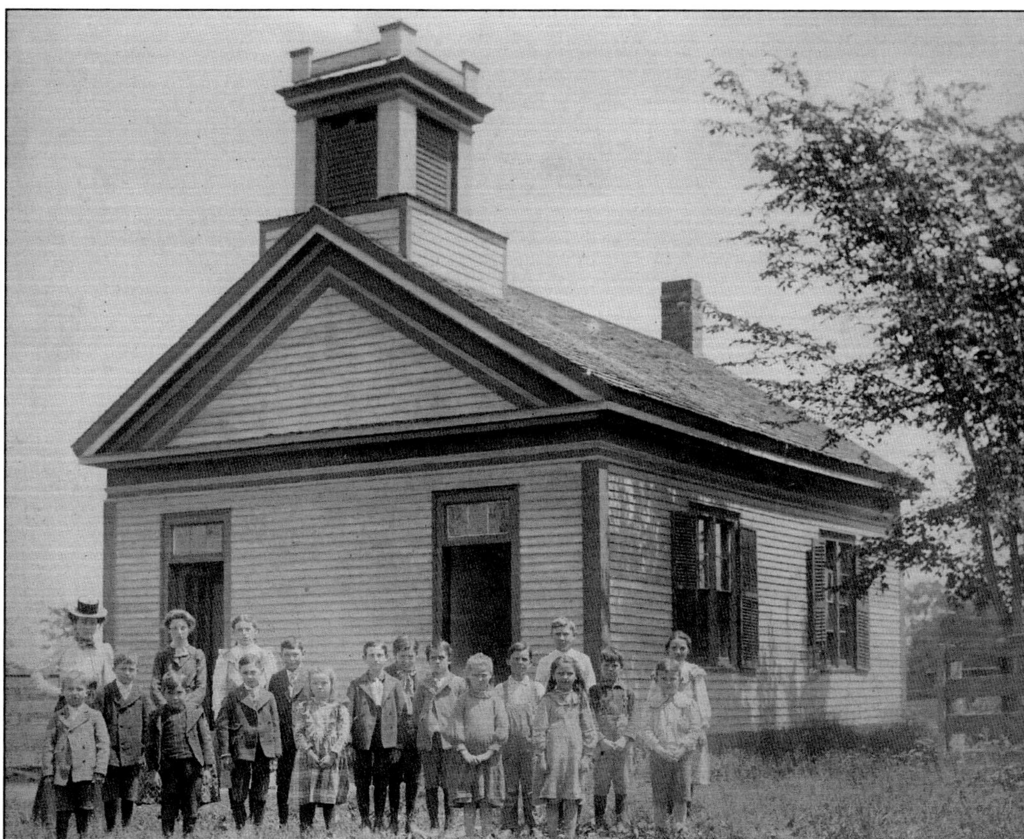

This photograph of the Cream Hill school (district one) was taken around 1900. It was the only one of the one-room schoolhouses in Shoreham that had separate entrance doors for boys and girls, which both opened into the same room.

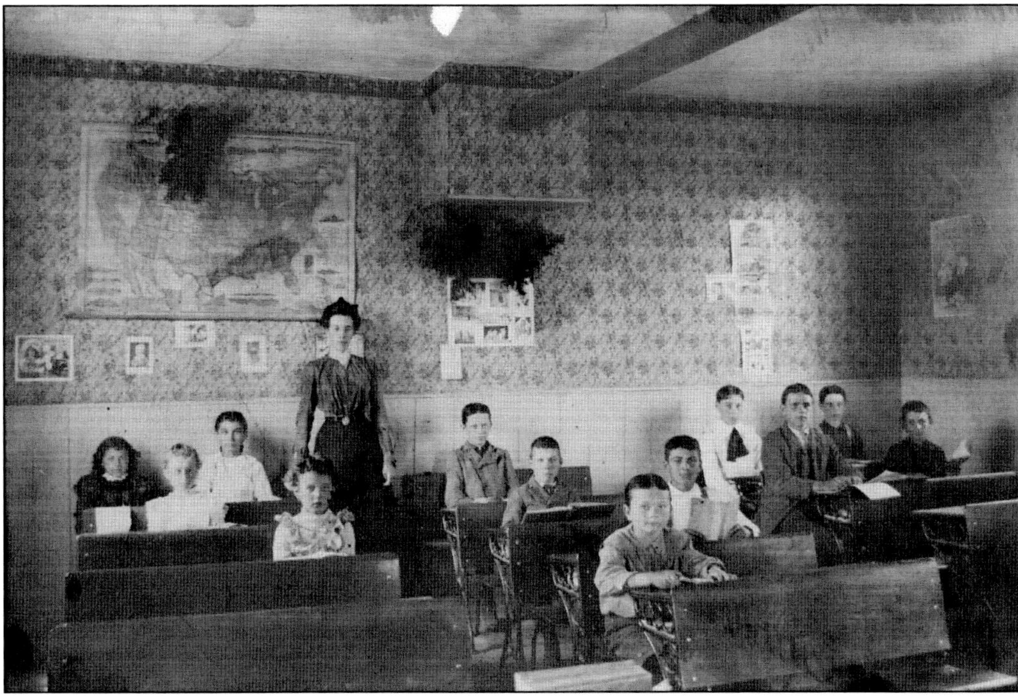

This photograph shows the interior of the Birchard school (district two). The teacher is Agnes Carty, and the students are, from left to right, Mabel Wimett, Katie Doner, Laura Doner, Ruth Delano, Raymond Birchard, Harry Delano, Rollin Birchard, Herman Wimett, Arthur Delano, Harry Birchard, Herbert Treadway, and Frank Doner.

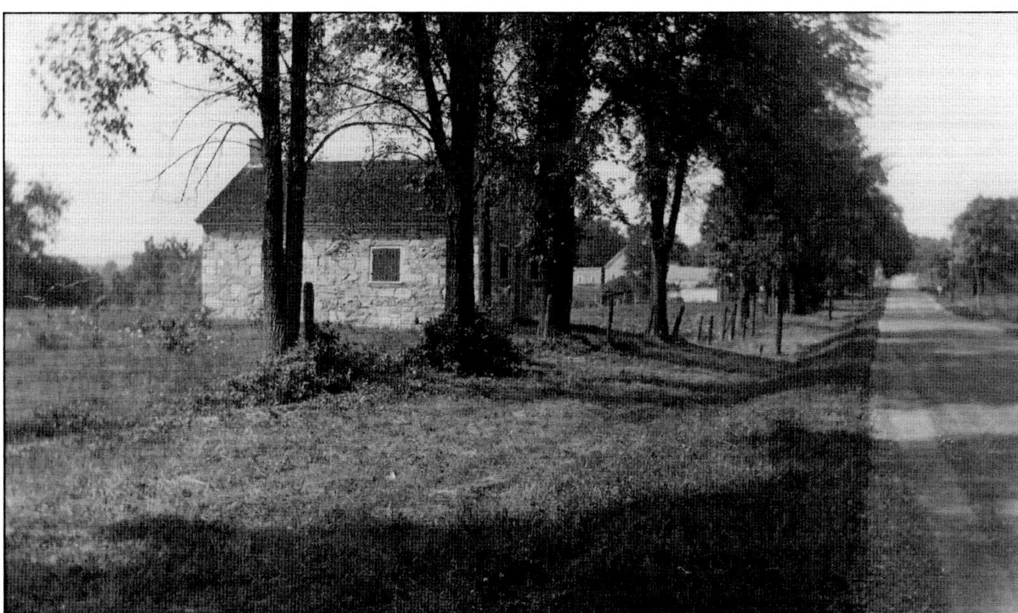

The district five village school is seen here. Tradition says that this school and the district six school, both built in the 1830s, were built of stone carried across the lake from the tumbling down old fort at Ticonderoga. This building is currently the home of the Shoreham Historical Society.

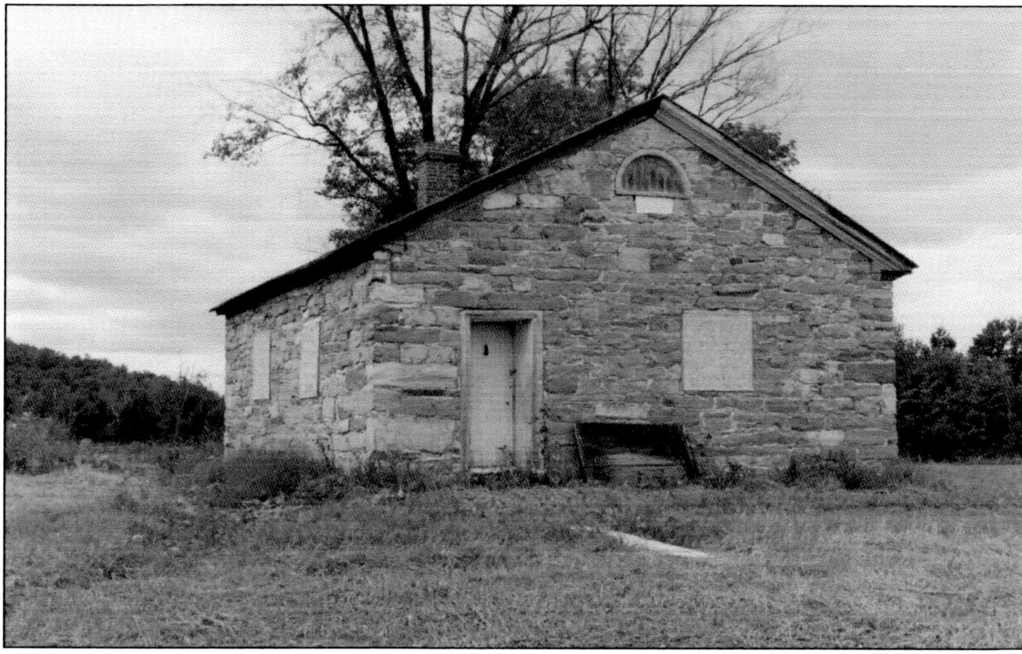

The Worcester Hill school (district six) is now a private residence.

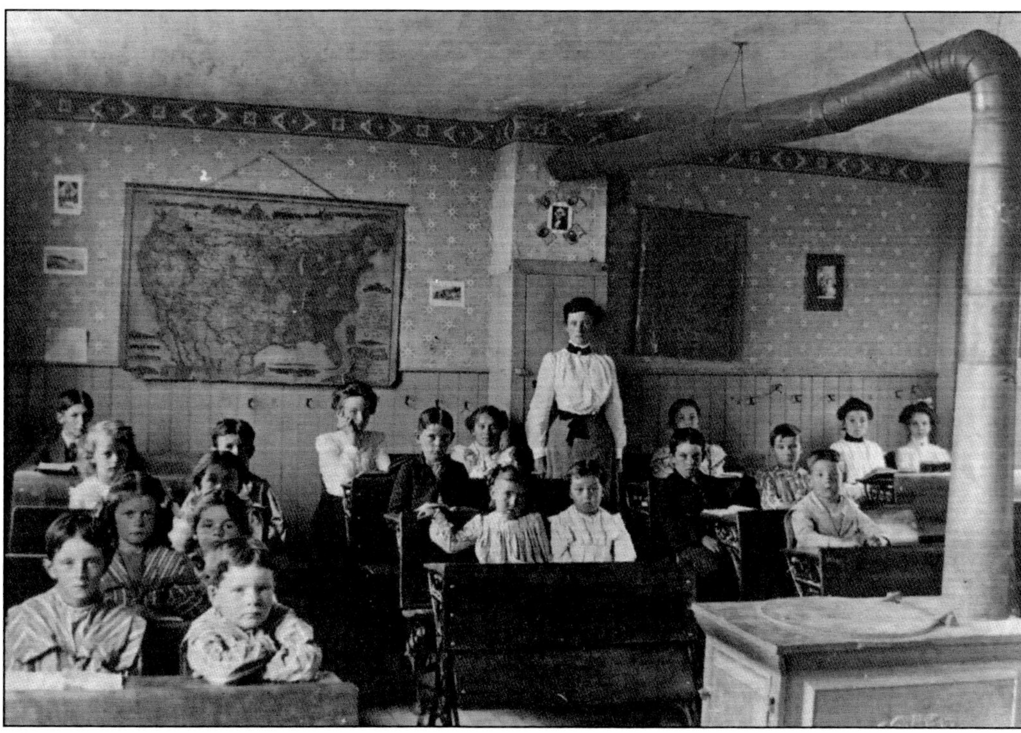

The Larrabee's Point school (district four) is seen here in 1902. The two boys on the far left of the first row are Ernest Larrabee and Alverton Baker, the two girls on the far left of the second row are Mabel E. Larrabee and Mary Macauley, and Rollin Baker is third from the left in the third row. The remainder of the students and the teacher are unidentified.

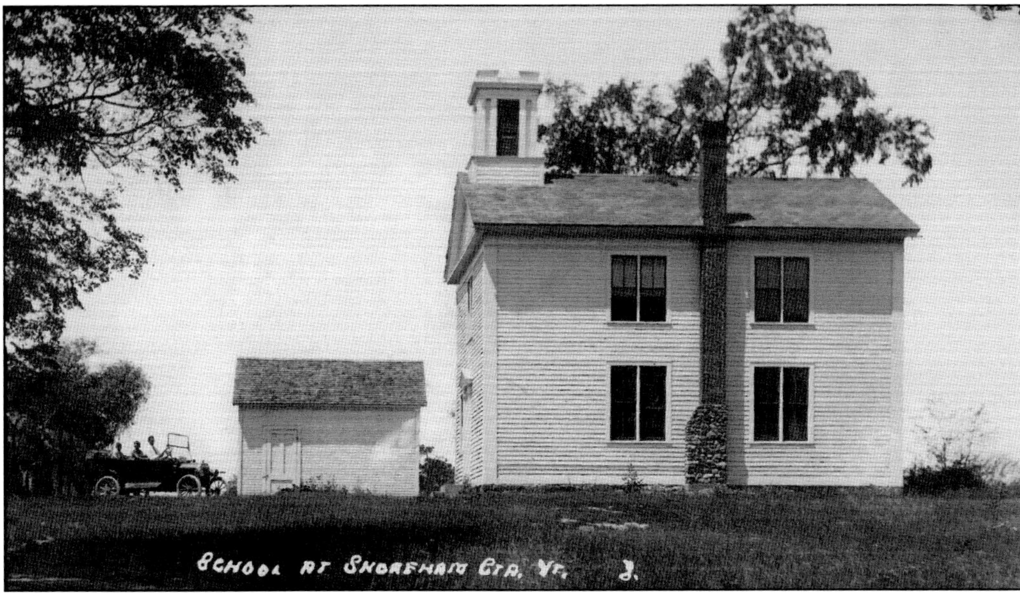

The Richville school (district eight) started out as a one-room schoolhouse. When the time came to expand, a second floor was added.

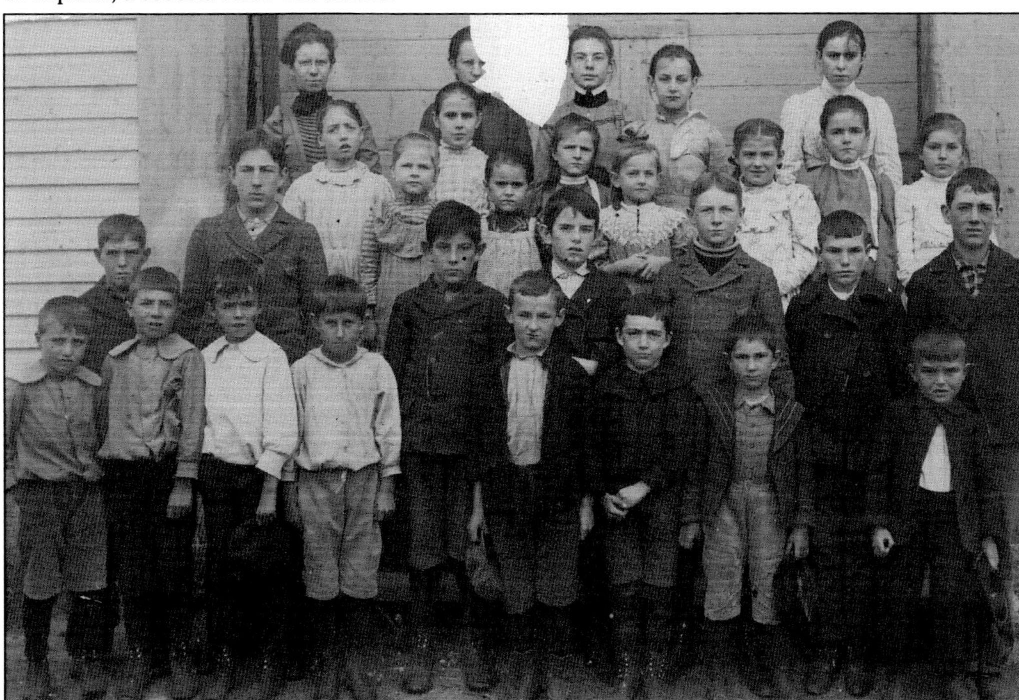

These students at the Richville School are, from left to right, (first row) George Dumas, Carl Lewis, Arthur Lewis, Theron Cook, Henry Dumas, Abraham Trombley, Ira Baldwin, Dayton Dumas, and William Hickory; (second row) Noble Dumas, Frank Dumas, Frank Lyman, Joseph Hickory, Arthur Delano, and John Ward; (third row) Alice Dumas, Elizabeth Dumas, Jo Brookins, Gladys Cook, Vera Lyman, Ida Trombley, Ada Hickory, Ruth Brookins, and Elizabeth Morris; (fourth row) teacher Jessie Baldwin, Rose Gokey, Inez Cook, Lena Trombley, and Joan Lyman.

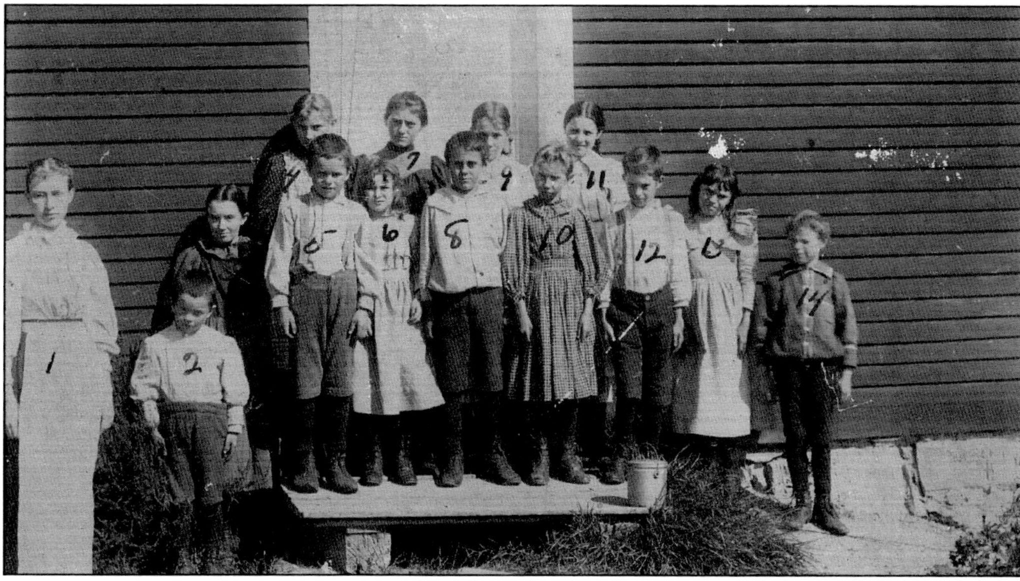

East Shoreham teacher Jennie Holmes stands with students (from left to right) Raymond Birchard, Georgia Parnell, Jessie Webster, Harry Birchard, Lilly Desjadon, Nellie Patenode, Arthur Patenode, Maude Bissell, Daisy Webster, Mable Delano, Herbert Treadway, Aurilla Desjadon, and Arthur Delano.

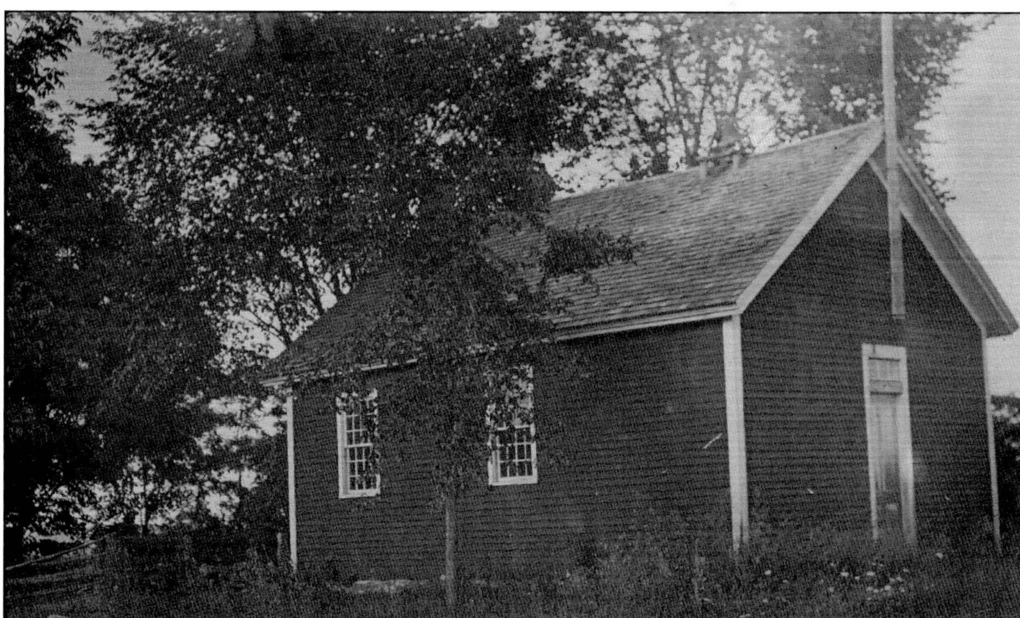

The East Shoreham school (district nine) still stands on Cutting Hill Road and is now a private residence.

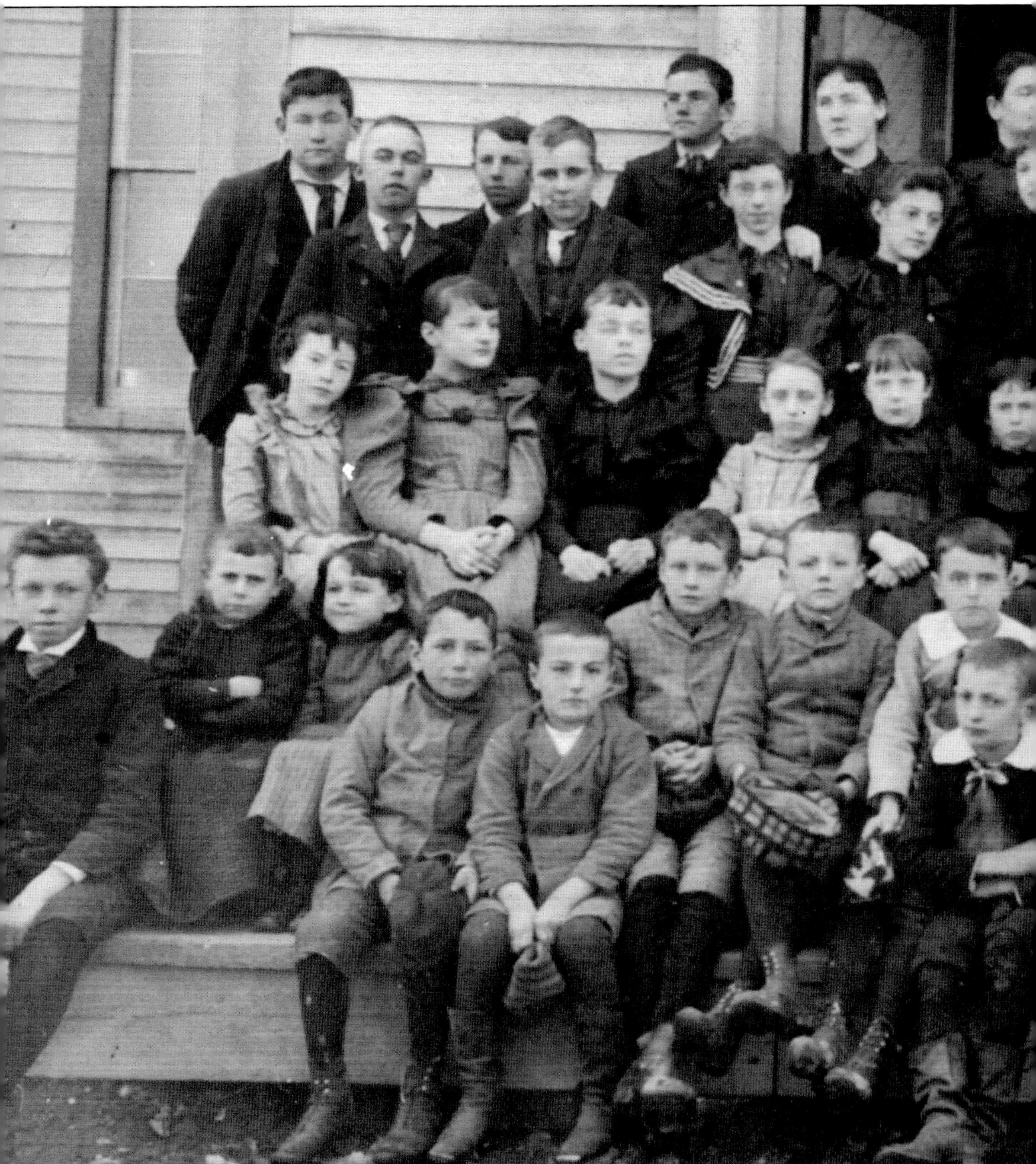

This photograph shows the entire school population at Newton Academy in 1894. The teachers are, in no particular order, Mr. Holbrook, Sadie Wood, and Mary O'Hearn. The students are, in no particular order, Charlotte Hull, William Brown, Charles Shaw, Irving Rich, Bowman Tottingham, Jessie Baldwin, Grace Bingham, Elizabeth North, Florence Howard, Nellie Sullivan, Stella Aunchman, Kit Waite, Lucy Brown, Harley Cook, Robert Holmes, Kate Mullaly, Jessica Kendall, Ella Wisell, Nellie King, Elizabeth Meehan, Mary Mullaly, Bernice Douglas, Delina

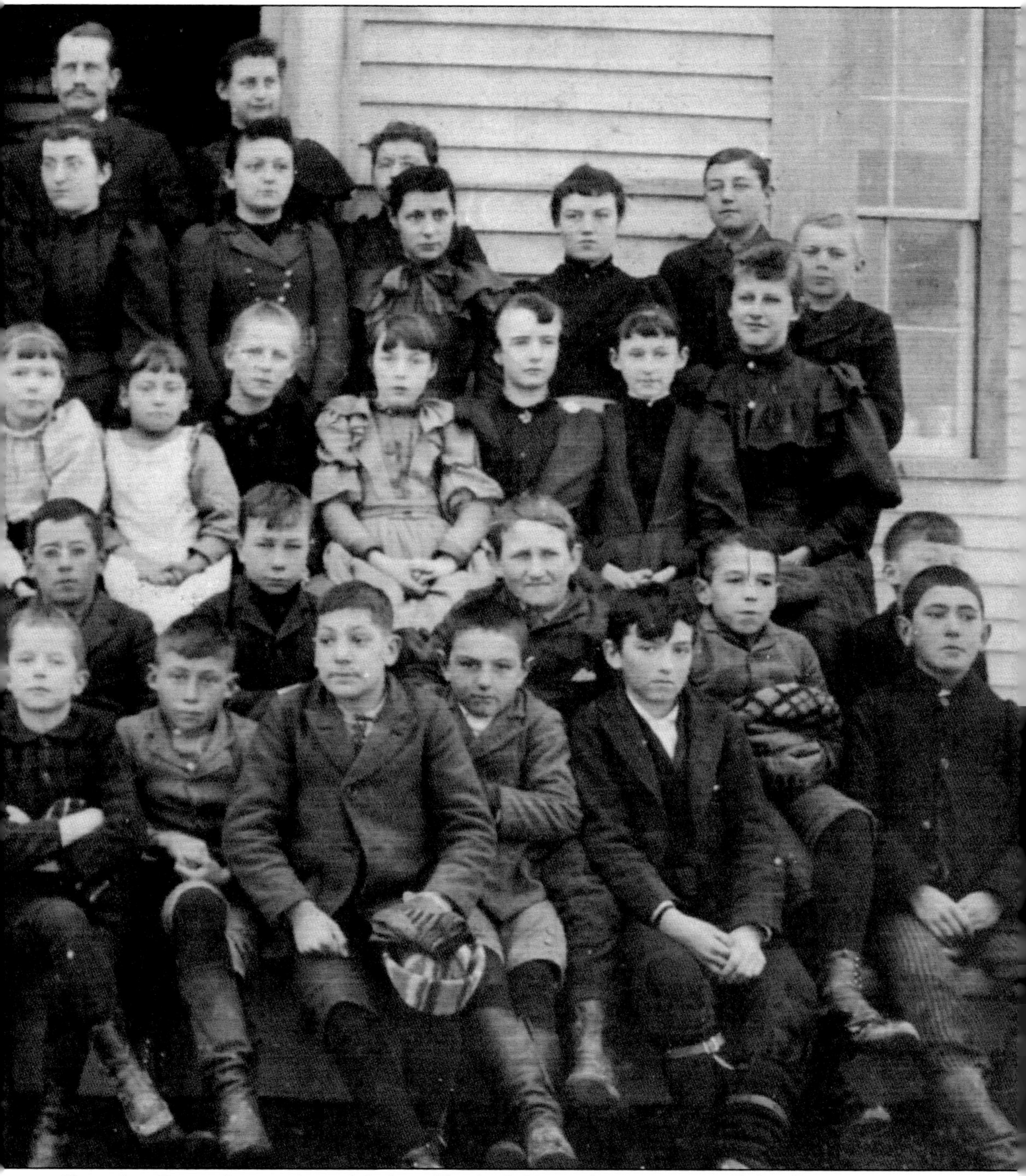

Desjadon, Bessie Austin, Anna Meehan, Elizabeth Tottingham, Anna Mullaly, Ella Meade, Lelida Harper, Elizabeth Wisell, Nathan Austin, Gustavius Wisell, Earl Sunderland, Jonas Hawthorn, Maurice Manley, Alvira Frost, Wilbur Wisell, Joseph Desjadon, Harold Baldwin, Solomon Todriff, William Prunier, Ralph Holmes, Napoleon Desjadon, Robert Collette, George Prunier, Henry Sharkey, Joseph Todriff, and Earl Hopkins.

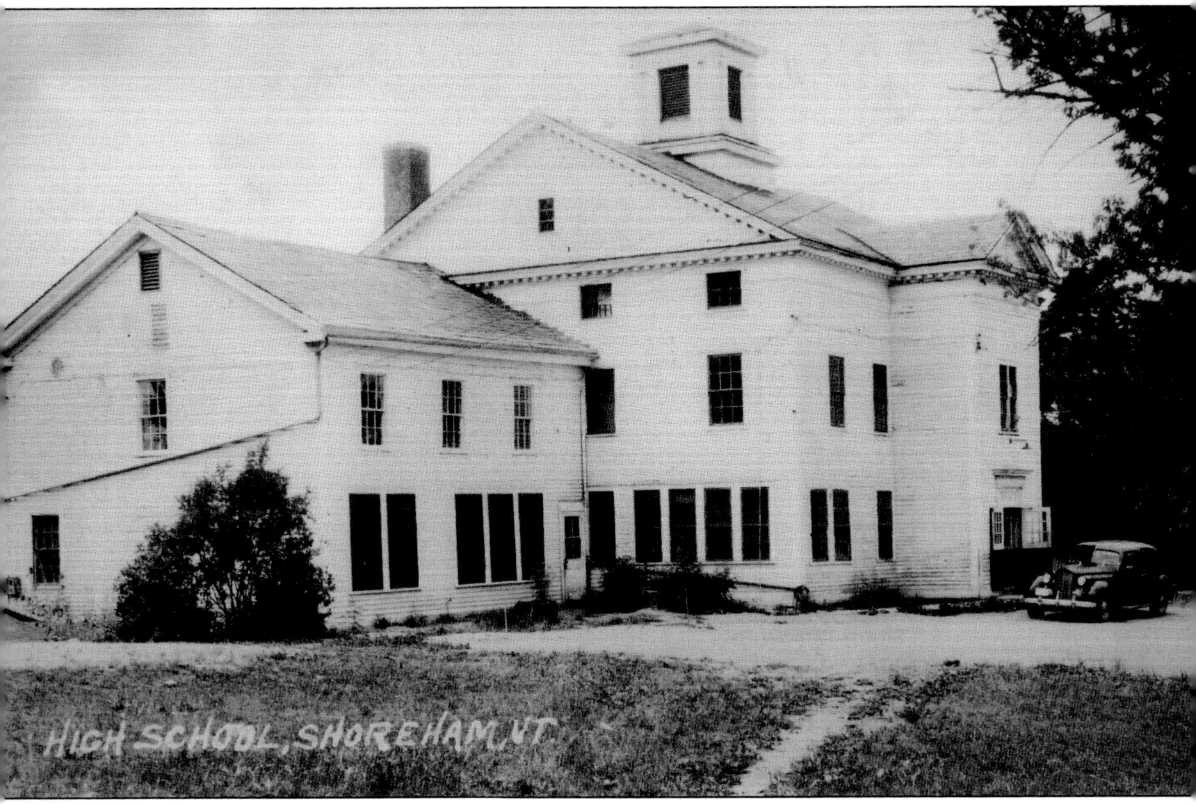

The 1810 Newton Academy building was taken over by the town in 1873, where it began housing all of the grades from one to eight. In 1910, a two-year high school was started in the building. In 1937, the town voted to make the school a three-year high school, and the following year, Shoreham High School became a four-year high school. The last class graduated from Shoreham High School in 1969. Beginning with the 1969–1970 school year, students were bused to Middlebury, where they attended the Middlebury Union High School.

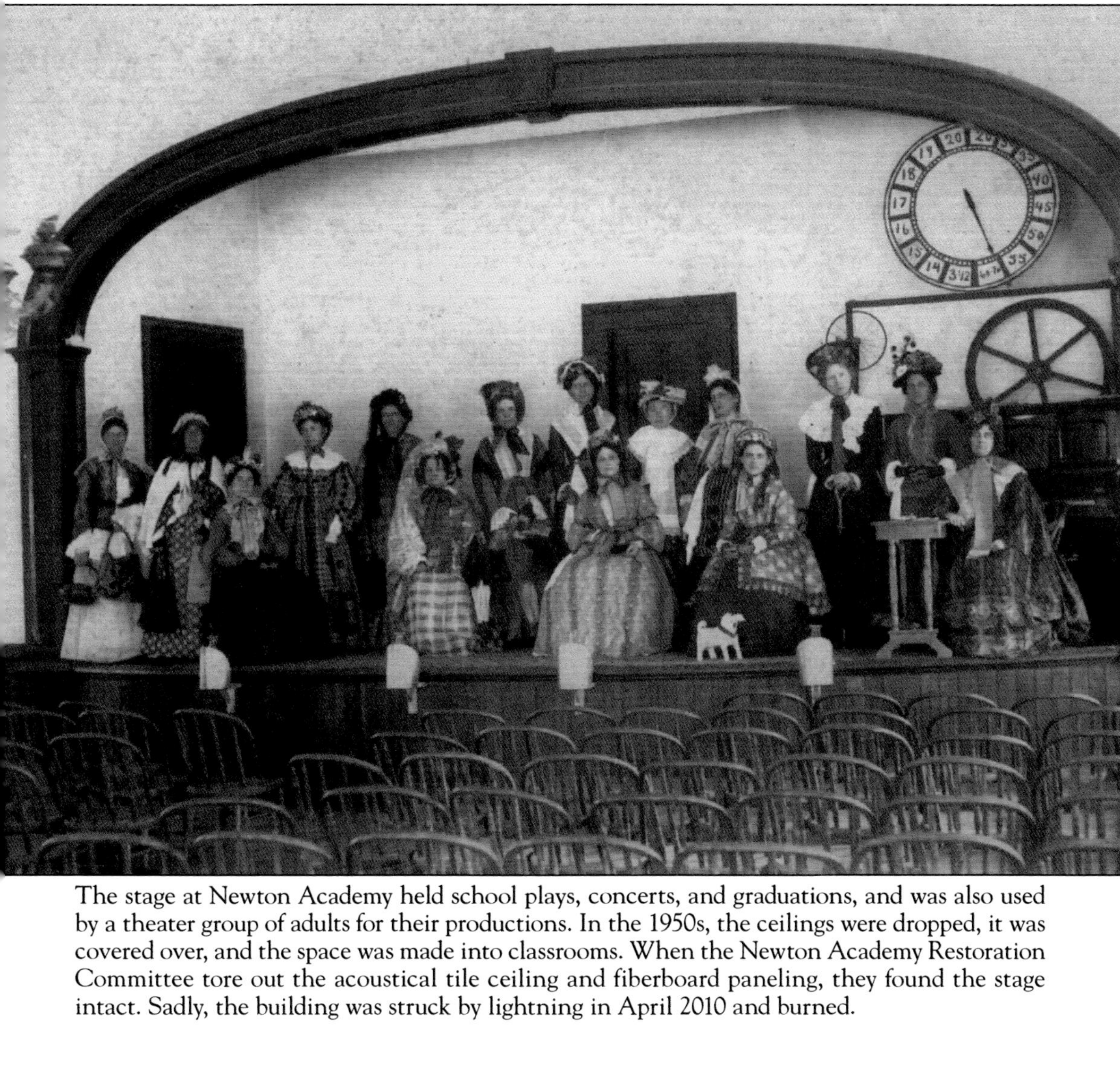

The stage at Newton Academy held school plays, concerts, and graduations, and was also used by a theater group of adults for their productions. In the 1950s, the ceilings were dropped, it was covered over, and the space was made into classrooms. When the Newton Academy Restoration Committee tore out the acoustical tile ceiling and fiberboard paneling, they found the stage intact. Sadly, the building was struck by lightning in April 2010 and burned.

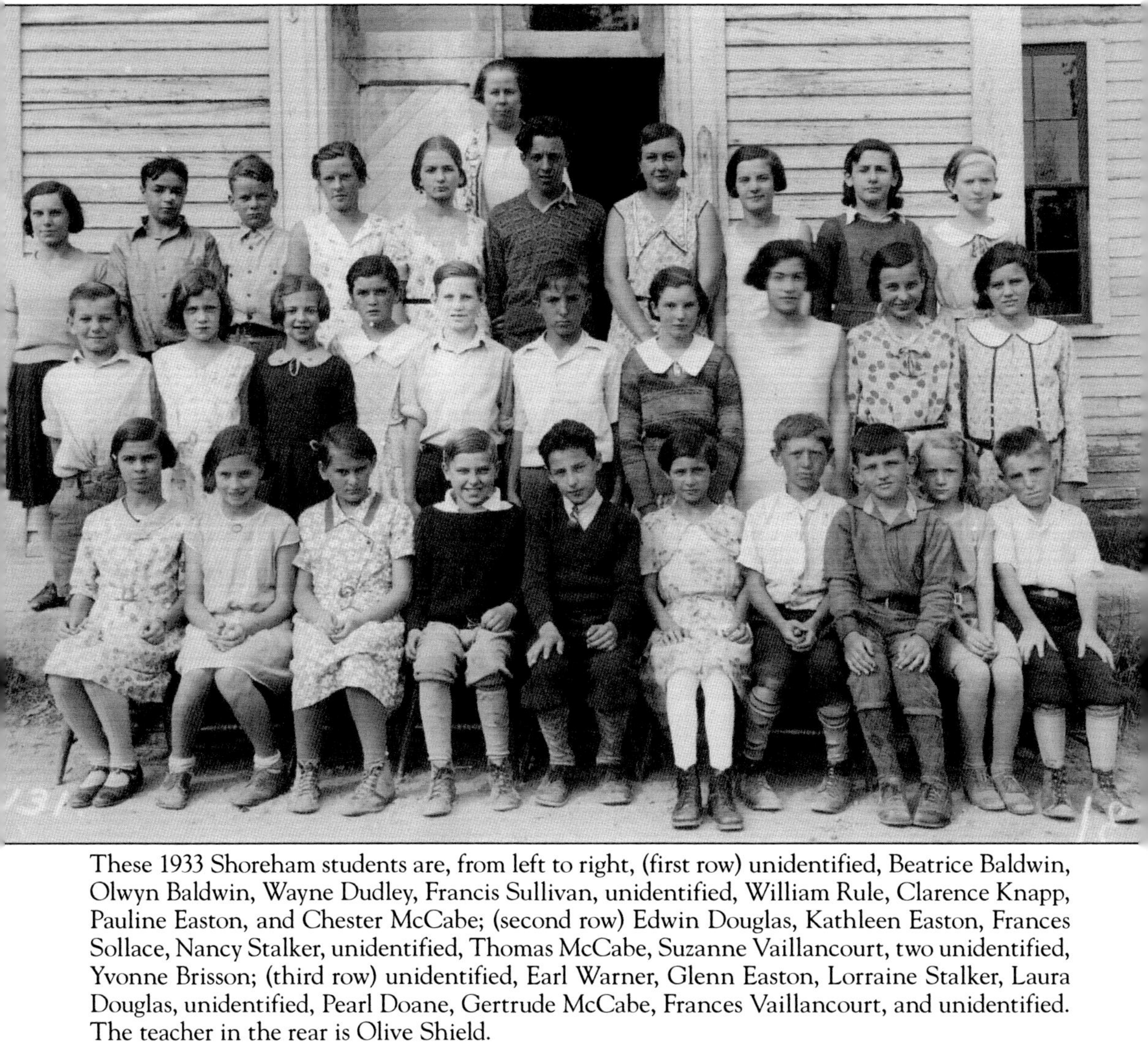

These 1933 Shoreham students are, from left to right, (first row) unidentified, Beatrice Baldwin, Olwyn Baldwin, Wayne Dudley, Francis Sullivan, unidentified, William Rule, Clarence Knapp, Pauline Easton, and Chester McCabe; (second row) Edwin Douglas, Kathleen Easton, Frances Sollace, Nancy Stalker, unidentified, Thomas McCabe, Suzanne Vaillancourt, two unidentified, Yvonne Brisson; (third row) unidentified, Earl Warner, Glenn Easton, Lorraine Stalker, Laura Douglas, unidentified, Pearl Doane, Gertrude McCabe, Frances Vaillancourt, and unidentified. The teacher in the rear is Olive Shield.

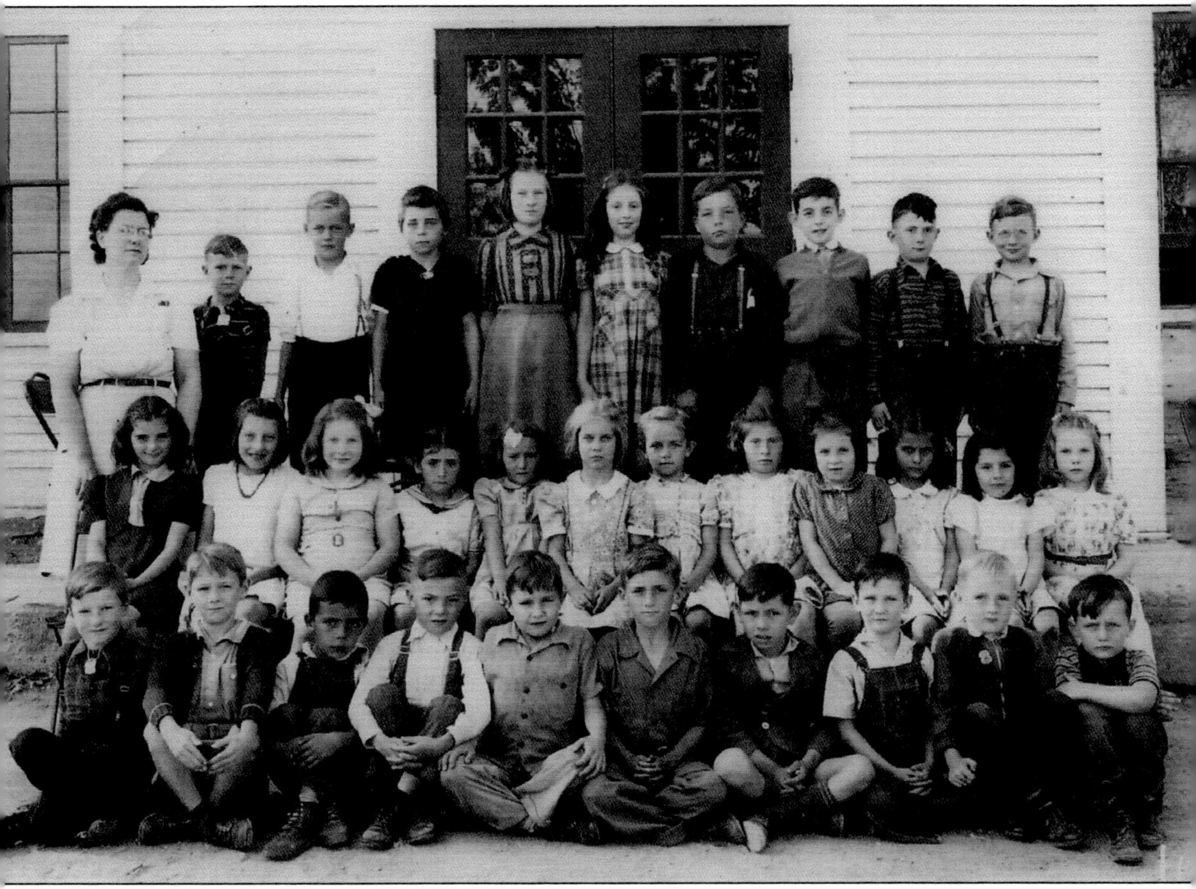

Shoreham grade school is seen here in 1942. From left to right are (first row) Edwin James, Garland Bashaw, unidentified, Normal Langlois, Paul Blair, Francis Farnsworth, ? Elithorpe, Lee Parsons, John Birchard, and Ross Sunderland; (second row) ? Brisson, unidentified, Louise Doane, Joyce Farnsworth, Viola Parsons, unidentified, Barb Fuller, two unidentified, Doris Kemp, Phyllis Blair, and Carol Doane; (third row) teacher Valna Bosworth, unidentified, Robert Brileya, two unidentified, Susan Pelkey, unidentified, Theodore Sanders, Gordon Murray, and ? Bingham. (Courtesy of Edwin C. James.)

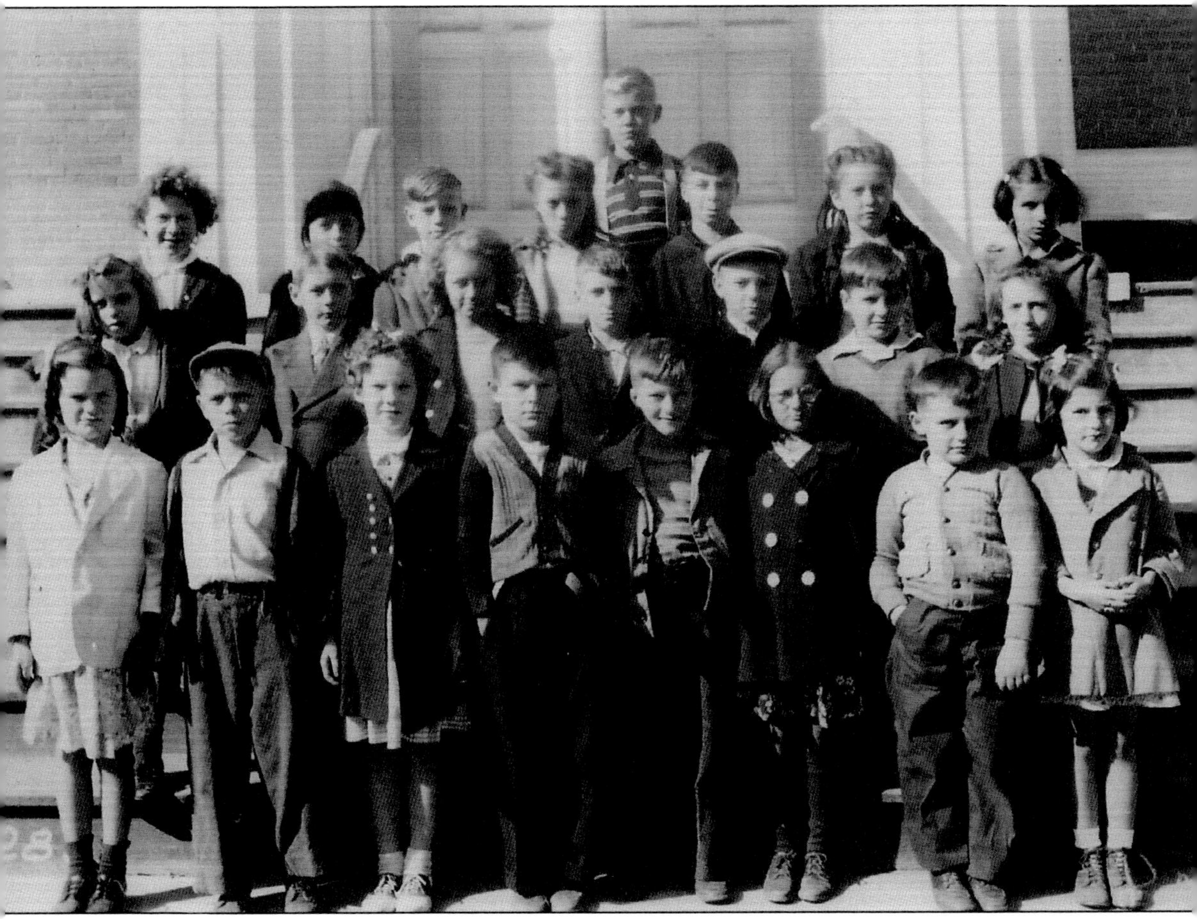

This 1944 grade school photograph was taken on the front steps of the Congregational church. From left to right are (first row) Mary Brileya, Robert Blaisdell, Carol Doane, Robert Shackett, Edwin James, Francis Farr, Ross Sunderland, and Phyllis Blair; (second row) unidentified, Willard Barnes, Theo Fuller, Francis Farnsworth, Norman Langlois, Paul Blair, and Joyce Farnsworth; (third row) Louis Doane, unidentified, Leslie Ramsdell, unidentified, Allen Shackett, unidentified, and Doris Kemp. Standing in the back by himself is Robert Brileya. (Courtesy of Edwin C. James.)

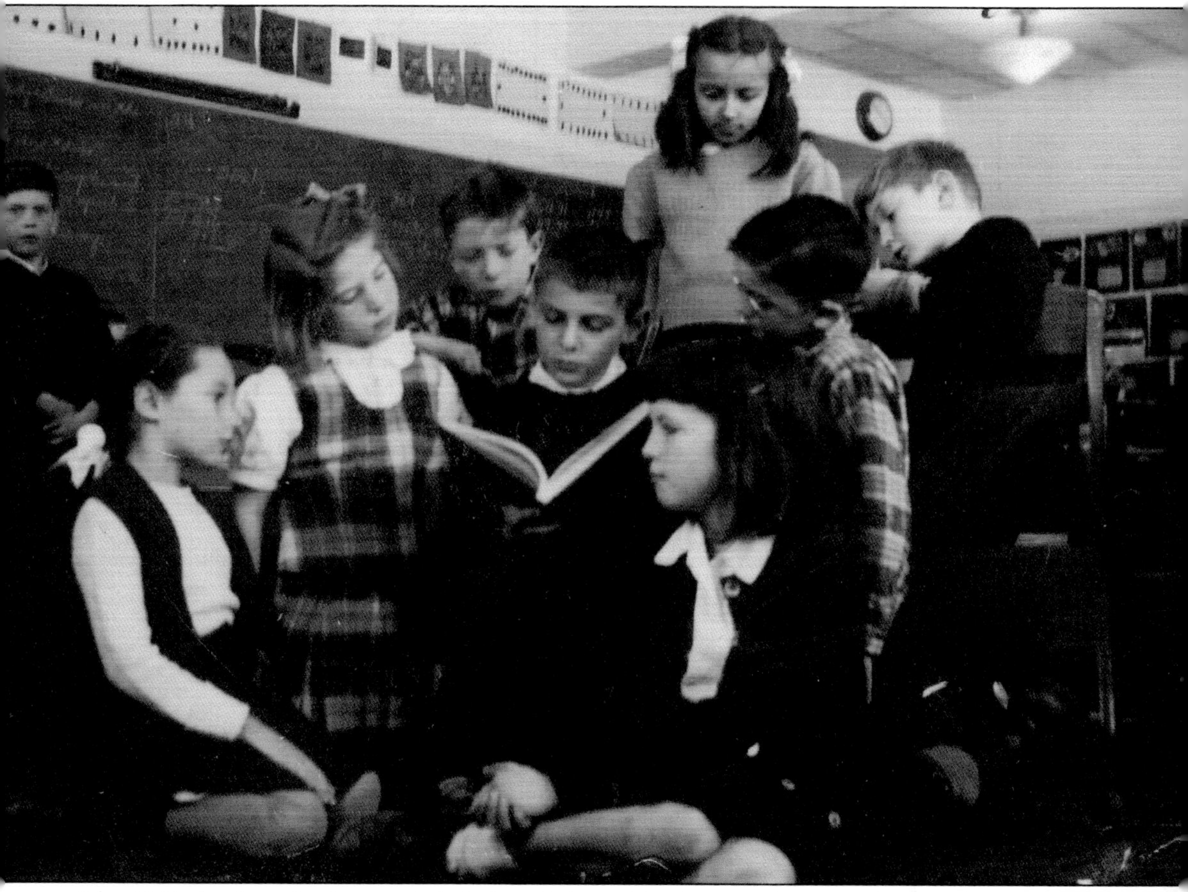

The 1948 third-grade class included, from left to right, Marcel Rochon, Jeanette Roy, Arlene Doane, Rodney Stagg, Sanford Witherell Jr., Janet Stalker, Thomas Blair, Harry Pelkey, and Elizabeth Kemp. (Courtesy of Mary Esther Macfarlane.)

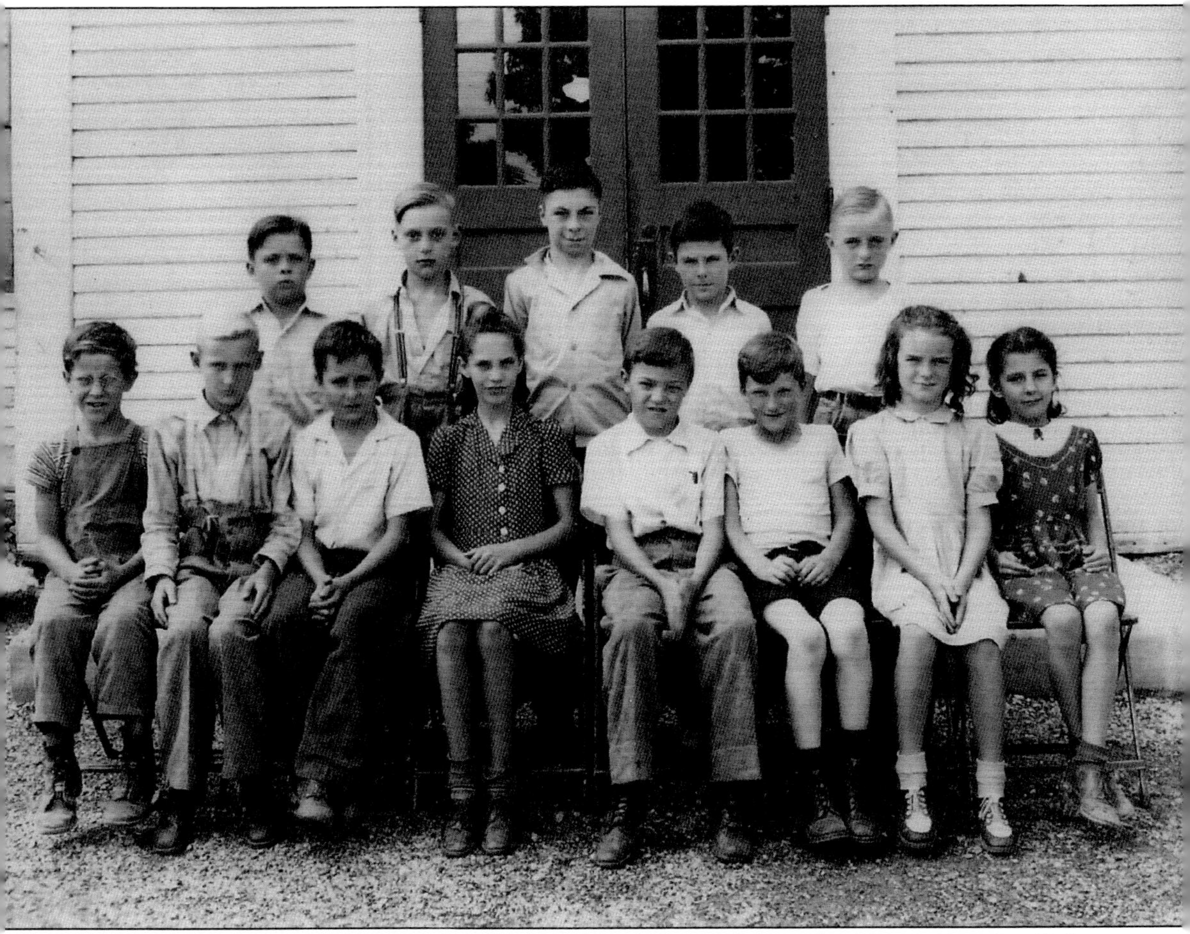

The 1945 fourth-grade class in Shoreham included, from left to right, (first row) either Bob or Ray Gebo, unidentified, Paul Blair, Elizabeth Barry, Norman Langlois, Edwin C. James, Mary Brileya, and Phyllis Blair; (second row) Robert Blaisdell, Charles Barry, Allen Shackett, Robert Shackett, and John Birchard. (Courtesy of Edwin C. James.)

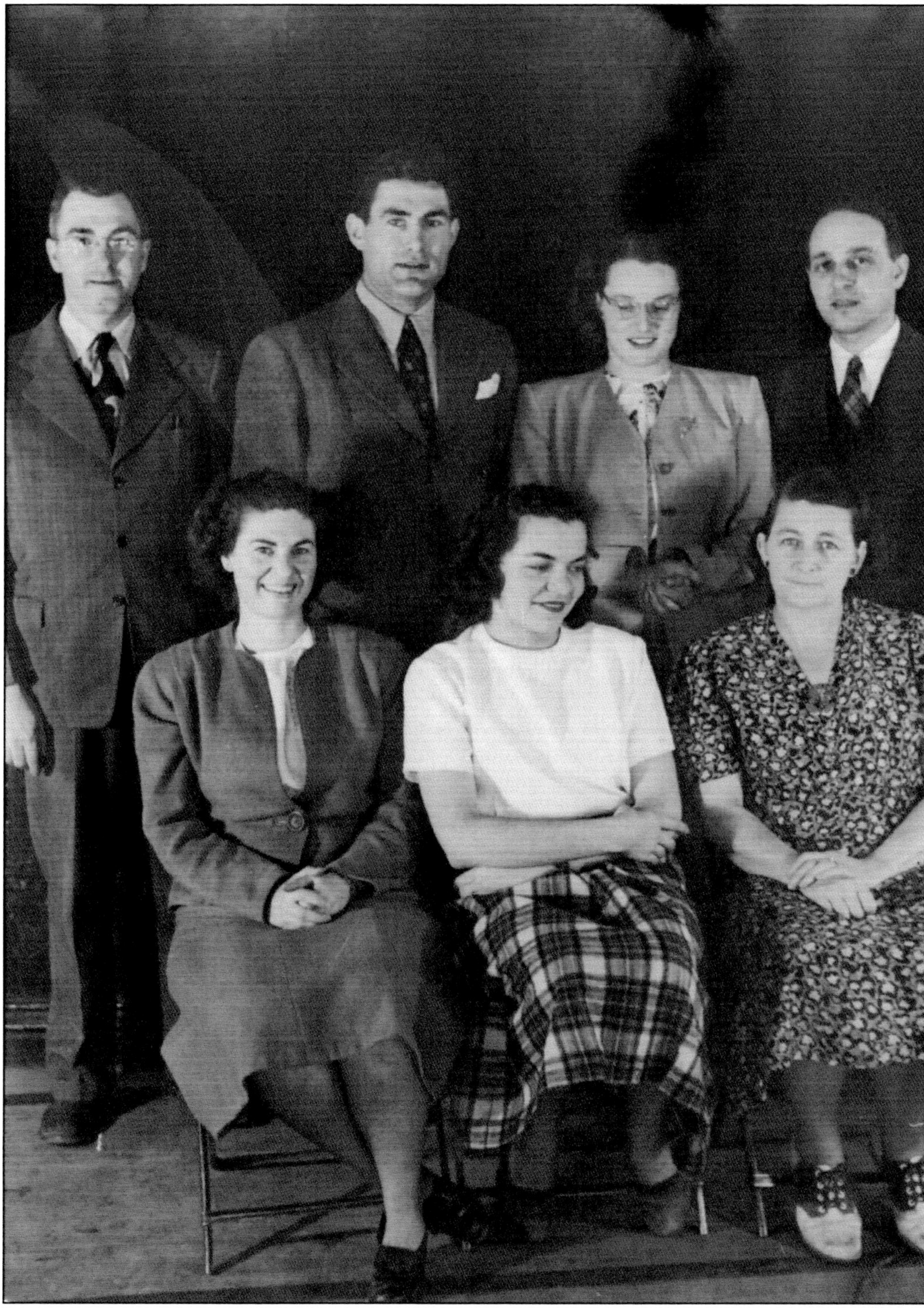

The 1948–1949 Shoreham High School staff included, from left to right, (seated) M.R. Farnham, Bettye Philips, and Helen Donovan; (standing) superintendent T.D. Sargent, principal D.F. Friedrichs, Margaret Rowell Arnold, and Irwin Lawn. (Courtesy of Kirk LaDuke.)

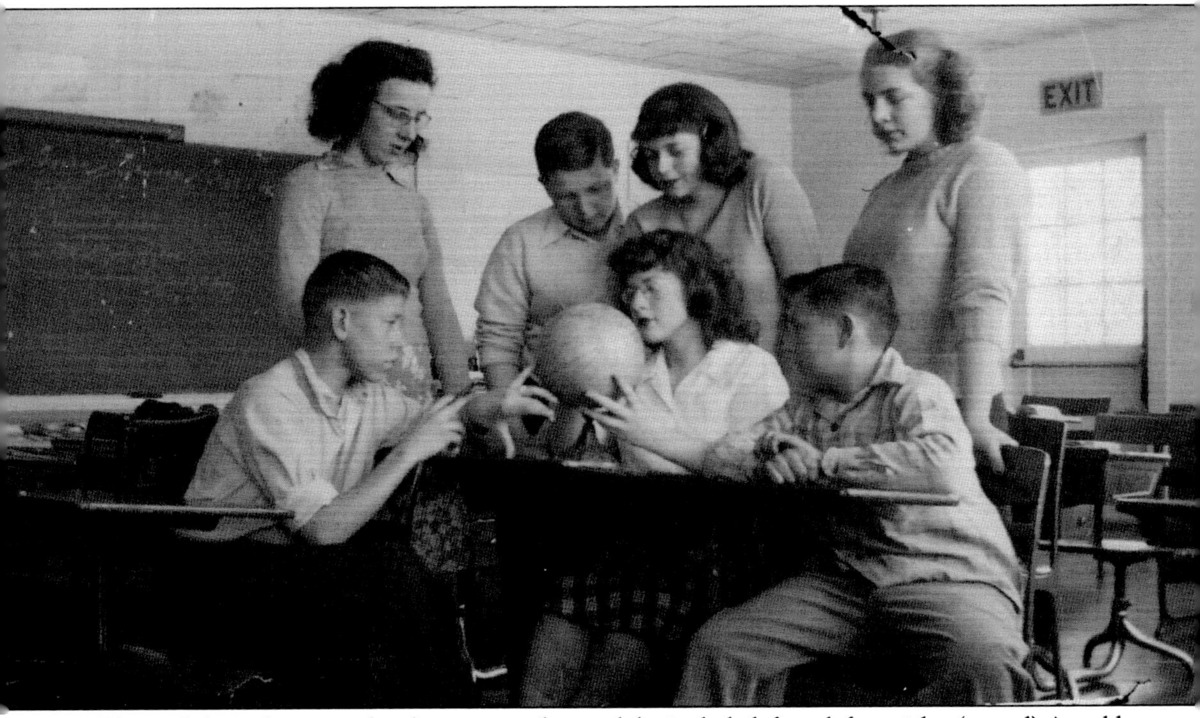

This eighth-grade geography class surrounding a globe included, from left to right, (seated) Arnold Elithorpe, Louise Doane, and Arnold Brileya; (standing) Phyllis Sheldon, Dennison Stanley, Eleanor Russ, and Mary Anne Fuller. (Courtesy of Kirk LaDuke.)

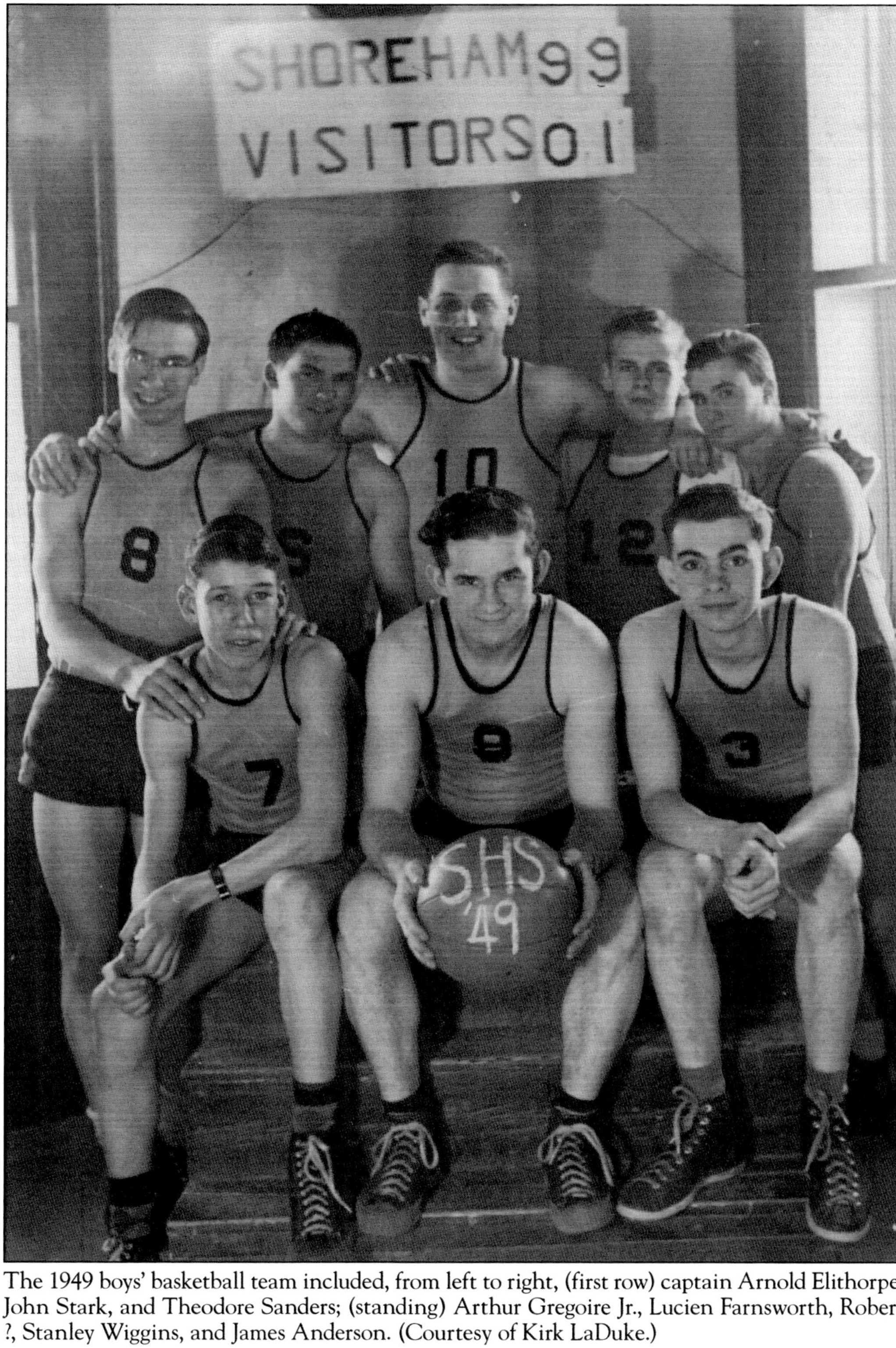

The 1949 boys' basketball team included, from left to right, (first row) captain Arnold Elithorpe, John Stark, and Theodore Sanders; (standing) Arthur Gregoire Jr., Lucien Farnsworth, Robert ?, Stanley Wiggins, and James Anderson. (Courtesy of Kirk LaDuke.)

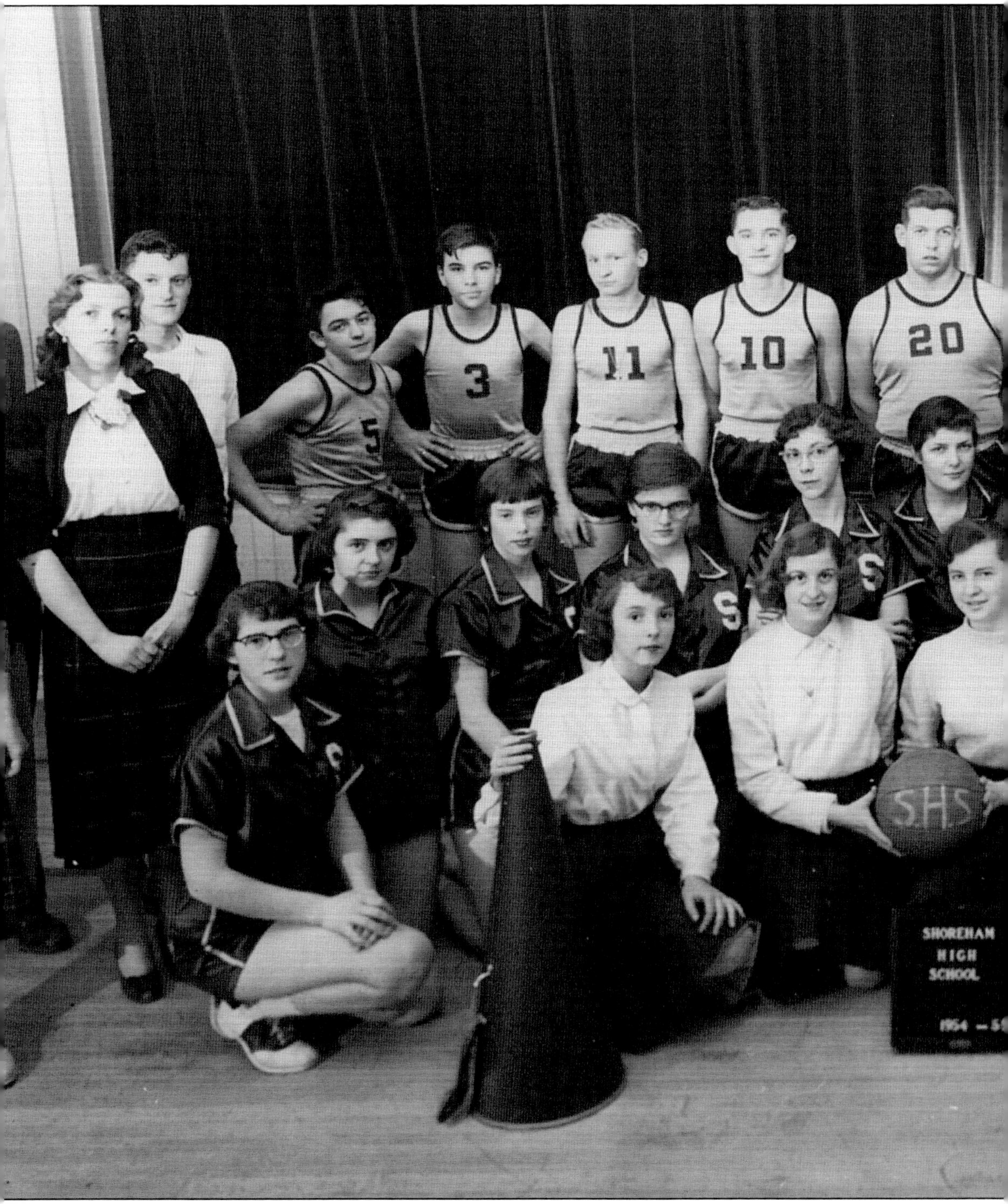

The girls' and boys' basketball teams for the 1954–1955 school year posed together for this yearbook photograph. They are, from left to right, (first row) Arlene Doane, Ann Cushman, Mina Stark, Kathleen Donovan, Elizabeth Cook, and Jean Doane; (second row) Arlene Drown (standing), Mina Dunsrer, Leona Martell, Joie Neven, Nancy Nevin, Brenda Shackett, Mary

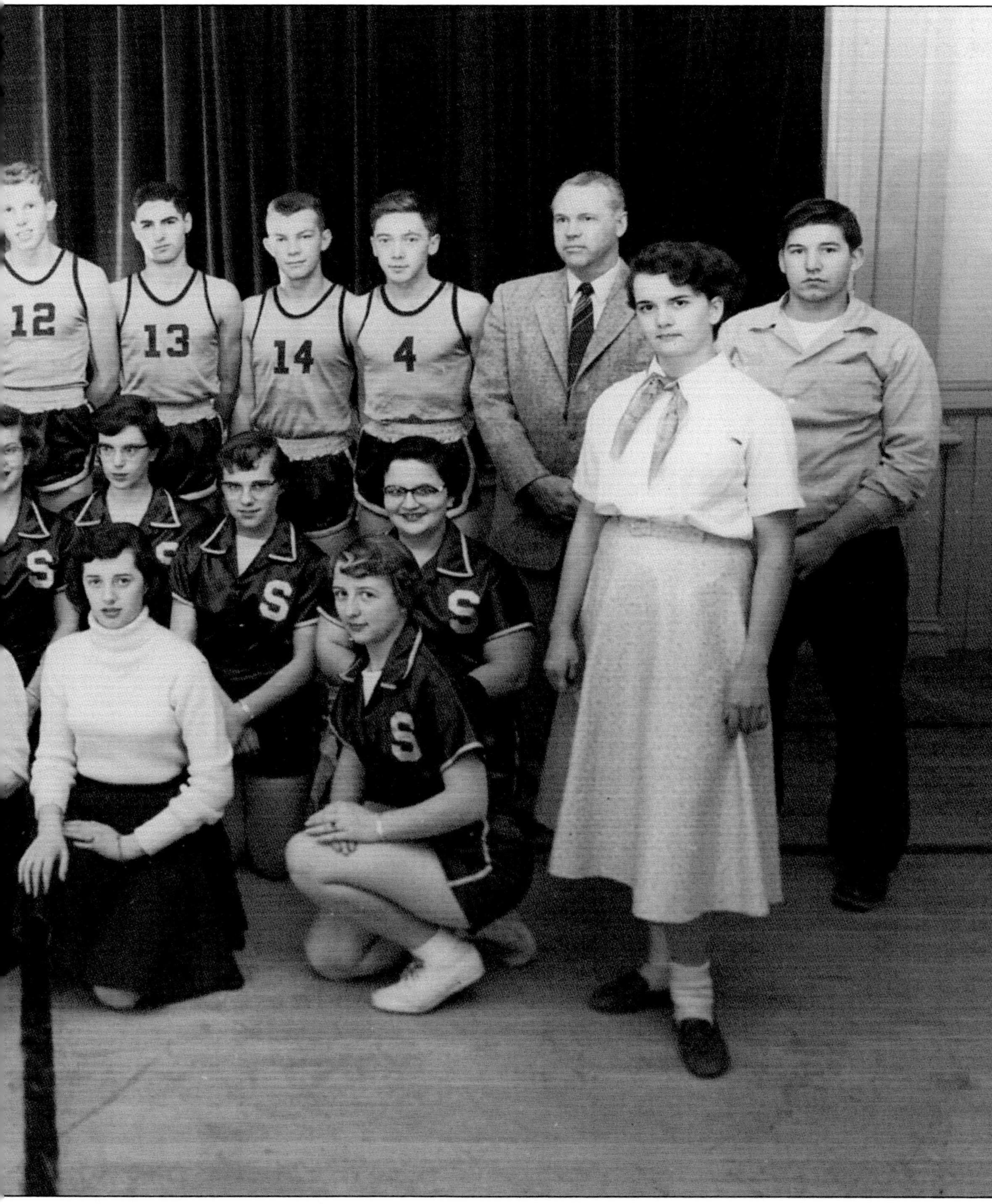

Esther Brisson, Nancy Bordeau, Anne Nevin, Martha Doane, Maureen Sullivan, and Marian Morse; (third row) Edwin James, Tom Blair, Dwight Menard, Dick Brown, Dan James, Kenneth Elithorpe, Brad Loomis, Robert Brandt, Tom Cronin, Dennison Stanley, Jerry Barker, and Fred Bishop. (Courtesy of Kirk LaDuke.)

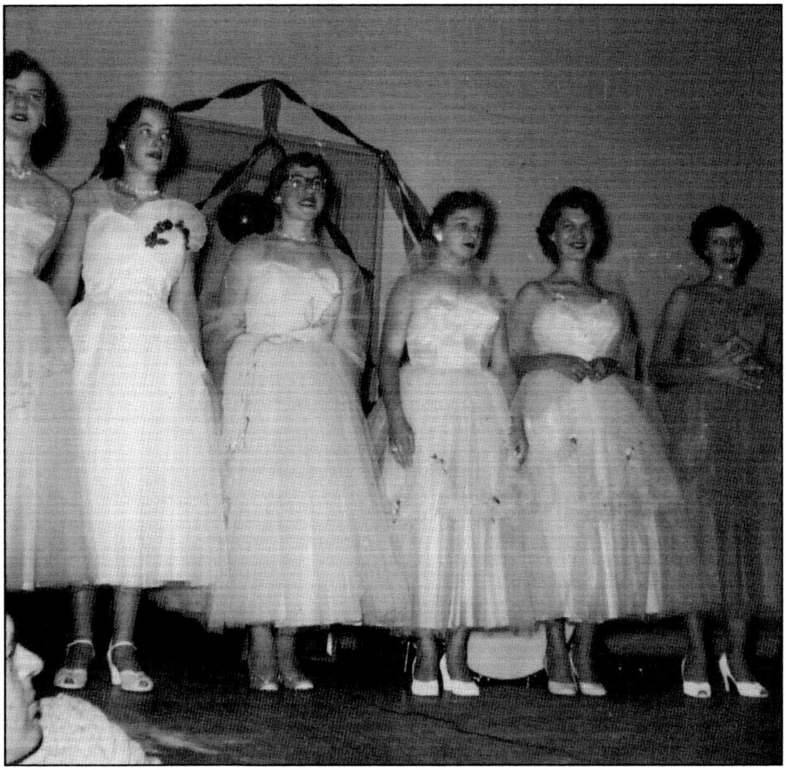

These excited girls are all dressed up for the prom in 1958. They are, from left to right, Kathy Donovan, Alde Plouffe's sister from Bridport, Arlene Doane, ? Manning from Middlebury, Claire Sabourin, and Theresa Carpentier. (Courtesy of Kirk LaDuke.)

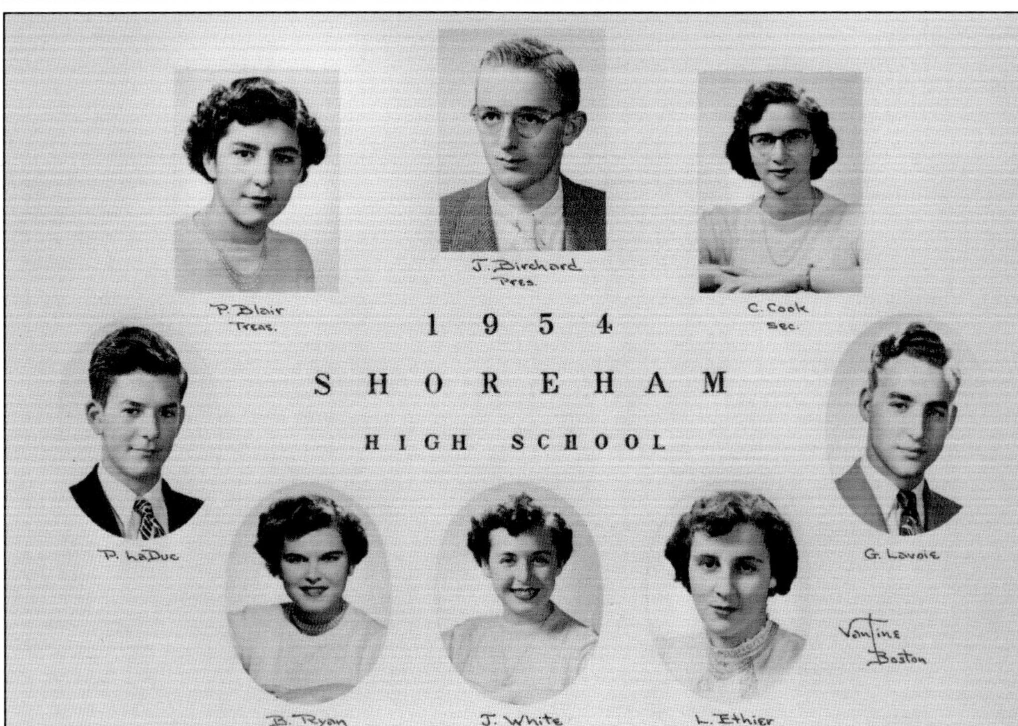

The members of Shoreham's senior class of 1954 are seen in this class photograph.

Bibliography

Beers, F.W. & Co., *Atlas of Addison County, Vermont*, 1871.

Child, Hamilton, *Gazetteer and Business Directory of Addison County*, 1881–1882. Compiled and published by Hamilton Child, Syracuse, NY.

Goodhue, Rev. Josiah F., *History of the Town of Shoreham, Vermont*. Middlebury, VT: A.H. Copeland, 1861.

Shoreham Historical Society, *Shoreham: The Town and Its People*. Rutland, VT: Academy Books, 1989.

Webster, Frank L., *The Addison Road*. Self-published, 1985.

Webster, Harold B., *The Old Addison Railroad*. Self-published, undated.